Gardening with Groundcovers and Vines

Gardening with Groundcovers and Vines

ALLEN LACY

Photography by Cynthia Woodyard

HarperCollins*Publishers*

HarperCollins books may be purchased for educational,
business, or sales promotional use. For information please
write: Special Markets Department, HarperCollins Publishers, Inc., 10 East 53rd Street, New York, NY 10022.

FIRST EDITION

Designed by Julie Duquet

Library of Congress Cataloging-in-Publication Data

Lacy, Allen, 1935–
   Gardening with groundcovers and vines / Allen
Lacy : photography by Cynthia Woodyard — 1st ed.
     p. cm.
  Includes bibliographical references.
  ISBN 0-06-016913-3
  1. Ground cover plants.   2. Ornamental climbing
plants. 3. Landscape gardening. I. Title.
SB432.L34   1993
635.9′64—dc20   92-56201

93 94 95 96 97 DT/RRD 10 9 8 7 6 5 4 3 2 1

For Glen and Virginia Johnson
Who gave me music . . .
and
Hannah Withers
Who gave me a treasured gardening friendship

Contents

Preface

Books come to be written in different ways. An editor at a publishing house may believe that a book is needed on a particular topic, and then seek out someone to write it. Usually writers choose a topic they fancy, and then look for a publisher. The happiest way a book comes into being, however, occurs when the topic, as it were, chooses the writer. I am richly fortunate that two books, first *The Garden in Autumn* and now *Gardening with Groundcovers and Vines*, have thus chosen me.

In 1991, I was working on what I thought would be my next book. Never mind the topic, for I may get back to it before long, but two of the subjects that obviously had to be covered were vines and groundcovers. Vines were appealing, considering the beauty of clematis, roses, morning glories, and wisteria—wisteria in all of its loveliness and wickedness. Groundcovers held scant appeal, for the word conveyed little more than the ubiquitous *Vinca minor*, *Pachysandra terminalis*, English ivy, and carpet junipers that predominate in American gardens designed to keep maintenance chores to a minimum.

I decided to write a brief chapter on groundcovers first, getting it out of the way so that I could go on to more congenial topics and more interesting plants. But it was a sabbatical year—a year not only to write at leisure, free of the duties of teaching, but also to travel and to visit gardens, both public and private, in New England, the Middle Atlantic States, and the South, as well as Arizona. Everywhere I started to notice how other gardeners were using as groundcovers plants I had never thought of as such, from cascading sheets of rosemary in Arizona to cheering tapestries of purple verbenas weaving through other perennials in North Carolina. My list of groundcover candidates began to grow, and my groundcover "chapter" had its own ambitions. It grew to 15,000 and then 25,000 words, with no end in sight. The material on vines was similarly insistent, and as expansive as a wisteria once it gets moving. Groundcovers and vines—these plants of low ambition or high aspiration—demanded to be a book. I surrendered to this demand, and here is the result.

But my topic is not primarily groundcovers and vines as individual plants, even though I necessarily discuss them that way at times. The topic is *gardening* with them. When judiciously chosen, low plants and ones that take to trellises and clamber up walls make magnificent contributions to the fullness and richness of gardens large and small, but they are insufficient in themselves to make a satisfying garden. They must consort with architecture—with pergolas and stone pathways, with fences and drywalls. They must keep company with handsome tall perennials like *Angelica gigas*. They are an essential part, but only a part, of a larger ensemble that includes bulbs, shrubs, and trees.

I make no claim that this book is complete or encyclopedic. It is instead selective, based on my experience and that of many friends in a network of gardeners that spans the country.

My debts are many, but this book owes the most to Cynthia Woodyard. All but a tiny few of the photographs are hers, and those few are used only because Cynthia could not be everywhere at once. Her eye and her camera enlarge the topic, giving it a geographical breadth a writer unaided cannot achieve. She has photographed specifically for this book in gardens both east and west, including her own lovely garden in Oregon. She has traveled to some of the finest contemporary gardens in Great Britain, France, Italy, and beyond. The final selection of photographs was no easy task, considering the richness of her offering—over 1,000 slides, only 145 of which could be used. She did far more than simply serve up an assortment of possible photographs for a writer's wish-list. She has been a true collaborator almost from the start. As her photographs arrived over many months, they contributed to the development of the text.

My other debts are heavy. Hella, my wife, accompanied me on much of the sabbatical travel. She sees things in gardens that I would otherwise miss; many echoes of our conversations are in this text. She is also a superb gardener who has worked heroically to turn my random collection of plants from a horticultural menagerie into a real garden. Helen Pratt, my agent, has been devoted and unstinting. I offer her abject apologies for once believing that writers don't need agents. As for my editor, Larry Ashmead, he has believed in this book and offered encouragement at every stage. I now count him as a friend, and look forward to future work together.

It would take pages simply to list the other gardening friends who have helped with information, insight, and criticism, but I must single out those who read much of the material in a primitive stage and offered suggestions: Allen Bush, Edith Eddleman, Nancy Goodwin, Dan Hinkley, Lynden B. Miller, J. C. Raulston, Jimmy and Becky Stewart, and Andre Viette. Douglas Ruhren and Barry Yinger went the second mile, returning pages so marked up with marginalia in red ink that I felt I was getting back a D − term paper in freshman English. They offered suggestions about plants that could not reasonably be omitted, even in a selective book, and they saved me from such errors as referring to the refreshing lemony fragrance of a plant that smells more like a polecat.

Besides Hella's garden and mine, two other places, both in North Carolina, are woven inextricably into this book. For almost a decade now I have drawn enormous inspiration from the Arboretum of North Carolina State University in Raleigh. Founded and directed by Professor J. C. Raulston, the Arboretum has a very large place in American horticulture in the late twentieth century. It is supported by a slender budget, the work of its dedicated volunteers, the efforts on its behalf of plantsmen throughout the United States, and, above all, the prodigious energy and enthusiasm of J. C. himself. The other place is Montrose, in Hillsborough. Montrose is many things: a historic house and lovely spacious grounds, with woodland, meadows, one of the oldest rock gardens in America, and magnificent trees of great age; a fine nursery that for its ten years of existence, ending in 1993, was dedicated to conservation and to testing and making handsome perennials available to gardeners everywhere including those in tough and nasty climates; and its ever-increasing, ever-more-beautiful gardens made by its owners, Nancy and Craufurd Goodwin, and by their associate, Douglas Ruhren. The gardens at Montrose rival even the best British gardens, which too many Americans believe impossible to match on our own continent.

The cultural information contained herein about plants—their height, spread, season of bloom, and so on—is based in large part on what I observe in my own small garden in the coastal plain of southern New Jersey; it is not meant to apply universally. Gardening advice, from whatever source, must always be regarded as suspicious at worst and suggestive at best. A perennial that grows twelve inches tall in one place may grow twice or half that size in a different soil or climate. It can't be helped. It's just the way plants are.

A word is in order about the botanical or scientific names used here. The feelings of gardeners about botanists, especially the taxonomists who occupy themselves with questions of plant classification and nomenclature, are often testy. When we trouble ourselves to learn that the proper name for sweet autumn clematis is *Clematis paniculata*, we grumble a bit on learning that it's really not that at all, but *C. maximowicziana*. But in time we accept the new name. Then it comes as a shock to learn that the question has been reconsidered (as it has been) and that this beautiful fall vine is now *C. terniflora*. These name changes do not take place because taxonomists are spiteful or nasty people. They just follow clear, though not always well-understood, rules, as, for example, when one genus is split into several genera, or several genera are lumped into one genus. *Hortus III*, until recently the most widely used reference for plant names, is so badly dated as to be obsolete. Where possible, I have standardized all plant names in accordance with the most up-to-date source, the four-volume *New Royal Horticultural Society Dictionary of Gardening*, which pays careful attention to the American gardening scene as well as the British one. Where a name has been changed, I use the new one, with the old one (which will still for a time be the name used in nursery catalogs) as a synonym: for example, *Tradescantia pallida* 'Purple Heart' (syn. *Setcreasea pallida* 'Purple Heart'). I have also standardized names of cultivars according to this dictionary's usage. For instance, in some catalogs, one liriope is listed as 'Munro's White', in others as 'Monroe's White'. I defer to the editors of the RHS dictionary and give it as 'Monroe White'.

August 1992

Prologue
Woodland and Train Tracks

In the Piedmont of North Carolina, a few miles from the busy railroad tracks that bisect the tiny hamlet of Efland, a rocky stream lies in a little valley between two ridges, in a place called Beech Creek. Leading off from the gravel county road, a pair of narrow dirt lanes runs along the top of the ridges. The roads were built in the late 1980s by a real estate developer in nearby Hillsborough, who had seventy acres of land to sell there, in seven plots of roughly ten acres each. All of the land has been sold, but only one house has been built. In 1989 my friends Martha and Garry Blake-Adams bought ten acres on the north side of the stream, which flows all year round, even in a summer drought, in its course down to the Eno River. Hella and I bought a similar piece of land, directly across from them, on the south side of the stream. The entire tract is covered in mature southern hardwood forest—mostly beech trees, with a scattering of oaks and black walnuts.

The four of us bought our part of this property with unclear intentions. The price was reasonable, since the land is just beyond the influence of the Raleigh-Durham-Chapel Hill Research Triangle that has caused property values to go sky-high for the past two decades. The taxes were low. It seemed like a good investment. Hella and I thought we might retire there one day and build a log cabin close enough to the stream that we could hear the water splashing past the boulders.

The most pleasant way of visiting this land of ours is to park the car on the main county road at the lowest point below the two ridges, where the stream enters in its rush toward the Eno. We have to push our way through the scrubby vegetation that forms a solid wall of green along the roadside, carefully avoiding the lush growth of alders, poison ivy, and prickly smilax and brambles that tear at our clothing. But once we are inside the woods, walking the narrow path that runs along the south bank of the stream, we are in a garden, although not a garden that anyone has made. There is virtually no understory in these woodlands, for the beeches and other hardwoods have reached their maturity. They form a solid canopy overhead, so dense that there is insufficient light to permit smaller trees to germinate and grow. The plants that grow within these woods are low and herbaceous. There are many mosses and ferns, including Christmas ferns and others that are evergreen. The ground is emerald in the faint light that filters down from the leaf cover above, which is so thick that in a sudden summer shower one can walk for several minutes without feeling a raindrop. In early spring, the earth is spangled with hepaticas, claytonias, bloodroot, tiarellas, wild gingers, mayapples, trilliums, and rattlesnake plantain and other little native terrestrial orchids, all blooming to catch the light from above. This fern and wildflower garden, the natural product of forest succession in the Piedmont—pine woodlands gradually moving toward the climax vegetation of a hardwood forest—is a garden that lies at my feet. I have to look down to see it, and to take a really close look at the dainty and delicate flowers that bloom here I must squat down, or even sit on the cool, damp forest duff. It is, in short, a garden of groundcovers, many of them in spreading colonies that claim particular patches of ground as their own. And it has its lessons to teach gardeners who have not already learned them in other ways. But I do not want to draw out these lessons too soon—not, at least, until another, very different American landscape has been given its due.

Whenever I must travel to New York City, which is as seldom as I can get away with, I take Amtrak from Atlantic City, changing trains in Philadelphia. I have my reasons. Like many persons of my vintage, I have a love affair with trains that goes back to earliest childhood. I miss the whistles that punctuated the day so predictably, and I envy the few people left in this country who live a couple of miles away from one of our remaining train tracks still in service. They can still hear those whistles and think to themselves, "That train is going somewhere. If I were on it, I'd be going, too."

I enjoy the comfort of a passenger train. I can spread out in my seat and work. I can walk to the club car for iced tea or beer. If the train is a Metroliner, I can make phone calls if I wish. I don't have to dread driving through the Lincoln Tunnel or worry about finding a place to park. And the ride is an easy one, since the train between Philadelphia and New York seldom stops anywhere in New Jersey, except sometimes at Iselin for a minute or two. Furthermore, a train ride carries with it a true sense of journey and of seeing details along the way. If I drive, I miss the details, as I am mostly watching what other drivers are up to, with constant wariness, if not anxiety. A plane ride is only a departure and an arrival, and unless there is turbulence en route, the time between taking off and landing is as featureless as limbo.

The view from the coach window is lovely in some places, beginning with the salt marshes between Absecon Island and the mainland, where the ripening plumes of tall phragmites reeds move in the breeze and under the weight of the flocks of small birds that use them as momentary perches. The train then passes through scrub forest on the fringes of the Pine Barrens and alongside huge peach orchards and fields of blueberries around Hammonton. The view approaching and leaving 30th Street Station in Philadelphia is beautiful, for the old waterworks disguised as Greek temples and the boathouses of the rowing clubs of the University of Pennsylvania make the Schuylkill River seem even still like a scene in a painting by Thomas Eakins. Trenton, seen from the bridge across the Delaware River, looks like a civilized and habitable city. The forests and farmlands south of Princeton remain so bucolic that real estate developers lusting to turn them into subdivisions seem, for now, as improbable as vampires.

But for the most part, this train ride is a journey into rot, rust, and ruin. Factories that once flourished along this Northeastern corridor —manufacturers of dyes, carpets, electric batteries, railroad freight cars, and thousands of other products for our forebears—now stand vacant, looking as wounded as a bombed-out city after a long war. Windows are broken or missing everywhere, brick walls are tumbling down, and graffiti are omnipresent. Junked cars litter the verges of the right-of-way. Rubber tires are heaped into huge mounds, catching water that breeds mosquitoes, as a reminder that the possibility of pestilence should never be discounted. It doesn't take a keen observer to note that rats are plentiful among the rusting and broken artifacts of an earlier time. Perhaps the most disturbing sight, however, is the shiny concertina barbed wire coiled for miles and miles along the tops of walls and fences, for the wire carries a message: Beware to all thieves who would break into this wasteland to plunder what little is left of value.

But on a crisp, clear day in early September, the journey to New York becomes almost beautiful at every point, because the wounds are partly concealed, if not healed, by luxuriant vegetation. Tall annual sunflowers, of some species that bears scores and scores of deep yellow blossoms on multi-branched plants, brighten the eye with their simple cheer. Thick stands of bamboo catch the light and fairly sparkle as their narrow leaves rustle in the wind. Japanese knotweed, a true thug that no sensible gardeners would ever invite onto their premises, is, here, a beauty for its soft and fresh green leaves, strong yet gracefully arching stems, and panicles of greenish cream flowers. Knotweed is an exotic plant, introduced to North America by some horrible accident, but another plant, a native, holds its own in the struggle for territory along the tracks. It is *Phytolacca americana*, or poke. Here it easily reaches six feet or taller, and in September it bears long and drooping clusters of small white flowers, together with deep purple, almost black clusters of fleshy fruit.

But it is pre-eminently the vines that grace this unloved and unlovely gash in the earth. Exuberant in their burst of growth from the beginning of the growing season toward its closing days a couple of months from now, they soften harsh and jagged edges with a cloak of green and with their aerial ambitions. Virginia creeper covers heavy metal fences, ascends tumble-down brick chimneys, and carpets patches of earth littered with broken bottles and old metal cans. Its leaves, already beginning to flame toward its incandescent season, tremble in the rushing air as the train speeds down the track. Their leaflets move in waves, as if applauding something just out of sight. And this native vine has more exotic company in vines from Asia that have made themselves thoroughly at home in America. Wisteria insinuates itself upward through a broken window in a paint factory, then bursts through the rusted metal roof in an explosion of green. Japanese honeysuckle, still showing the occasional white or dark cream flower, twines and trails wherever it can. Silver fleece vine, a vigorous species of *Polygonum*, in the same genus as knotweed, foams into huge sheets of tiny, pearly white flowers spilling like a waterfall from mounds of rusting drums that once held oil or chemicals. Another rampant plant is Oriental bittersweet (*Celastrus orbiculatus*), which seems intermediate between a vine and a shrub. It is much more common now and much pushier than its native North American counterpart, *C. scandens*. Oriental bittersweet also covers a lot of territory along these railroad tracks, bearing huge crops of orange-coated fruits, which open to show the yellow fleshy seeds within.

The king of all the vines at this time of year, however, is sweet autumn clematis. There is hardly a half mile along this track between Philadelphia and New York where it is absent. It climbs up guy wires forty or fifty feet, and then hangs in huge swags and garlands of sparkling, pristine white flowers. Wherever it grows, it smothers ugliness and dereliction with beauty that somehow seems to bespeak innocence, gentleness, and healing. I cannot catch its scent from the train, of course, but I know that it is there—a rare, delicate, and subtle honey that carries far on the wind.

By no stretch of the imagination could this busy railroad track through the broken and rusting remnants of the former industrial age in the northeastern United States be called a garden, even if many of its plants, the vines in particular, are escapees from gardens. I believe, however, that it also has its lessons to teach about gardening.

Comparison and contrast—sorting out the things that are alike and those that are dissimilar, and giving an account of what makes them similar to or different from one another—are considerably more than techniques of rhetoric. They are essential to thought itself, and to getting our bearings in the world. These thought processes are especially evident in very young children as they lose themselves almost entirely sorting out blocks, separating red ones from blue ones, or placing together those that are similar in size or shape. Much of the play of children is really thinking. (And I would add that I trust no grown-up whose thinking has lost all element of play.)

In my mind, that strip of railroad right-of-way through the industrial graveyard of the Northeastern megalopolis and those ten acres of North Carolina forest somehow pertain to one another. Their differences are many and patent. The beech woods are hardly undisturbed land, considering the new lanes and the house that has gone up already and the power lines already in place, but they are at least a metaphor for the American wilderness before European settlers came to what is now Orange County. Once I have fought my way through the tangled thicket at its edge and am inside the forest, whose farthest edge I cannot see, I can imagine that these woodlands go on from horizon to horizon and that the only human beings who ever pass this way hunt their meat with bows and arrows. Those railroad rights-of-way through Philadelphia and the other towns and cities on the way to New York City are the very essence of disturbed land. The former factories and warehouses, dilapidated and forlorn, testify to an earlier time, when they were busy manufacturing the goods of the industrial age. Nothing is left here of the natural landscape before the Europeans came.

Characteristic of disturbed land is a flora that is dominated in large part by non-native plants. The only exotic plants I have encountered in those woods in Carolina are at their fringes by the road, where there are European plants like dandelions, plantain weed, and crabgrass, and Oriental ones like Japanese honeysuckle. (There is, thank heaven, no kudzu, as there is just down the road!) These railroad tracks, on the other hand, abound in exotic plants. Many of them were brought to America by explorers and nurserymen who thought they would be delicate and difficult to grow. But honeysuckle, ailanthus, wisteria, sweet autumn clematis, and other woody plants proved to be tramps with hoydenish ways—able to take care of themselves under adverse conditions, and then some. They aspire to heaven, and in their ascent, they cover the festering wounds and scars of this abandoned industrial landscape. They do not turn it into a sweet dream—nothing could do that—but they make it less of a nightmare in this ripening season of the year.

If, in my mind, those woods and these tracks pertain to one another, they also pertain to gardens, and they teach two specific lessons: the great value of vines, and the equally great value of groundcovers. I have tried to creep up (please forgive!) on these twin topics, which are strongly related, because groundcovers and vines are often treated as the plebeians of the garden—utilitarian plants that merit faint praise, if any, with some notable exceptions like climbing roses, clematis, and hostas, all of which have their fervent partisans.

"Groundcover" is one of the dullest words in the gardener's vocabulary if used solely to denote those plants, other than turf grasses, that fill in spaces where otherwise weeds would grow or the sight of dirt would offend the eye. But groundcovers are much better appreciated when considered in combination with vines: *where they are well chosen and well grown, together they enlarge the garden, giving it an additional dimension.*

I confess to having come late to this appreciation. Like many people, I was for years an "eye-level gardener," which means that I was primarily interested in flowers, often those I first encountered in their tight mug shots in nursery catalogs. And when I planted them, my attention was focused straight ahead, into that space in the air that extends from about eighteen to seventy inches about the ground. Although some ornamental perennials and shrubs grow shorter and some taller than that, most fall within this range of altitude, where they can be looked in the eye, so to speak. Groundcovers, however, must be looked down on. I mean this literally, but it does have a figurative meaning, too—one of condescension. "Low" is strictly a neutral descriptive term where it refers only to height, but it also has negative connotations. Any dictionary will leap quickly from a definition meaning "not tall" to synonyms such as enfeebled, unadvanced, poor, and even vulgar, debased, and coarse. I planted groundcovers mostly to keep down weeds, of course, but with no special appreciation of their other merits.

Sometimes a chance remark can alter somebody's entire view of things. Thus it was one day when one of my gardening friends (I don't remember who it was exactly, although I suspect it was Edith Eddleman) said that she didn't think of groundcovers as groundcovers so much as "plants of the lowest tier." *Click.* Yes, exactly. And if they were the plants of the lowest tier, then there had to be a tier above that. And then a higher tier yet, and several others above it. Eye-level gardening was short-sighted gardening, blind to an obvious fact that I took my time in recognizing: *Tiers.* Any garden occupies a layered space, a series of horizontal planes in a successive vertical order. A better garden can result if one deliberately thinks about what to plant for interest in every tier. Then something else occurred to me. For years, if asked about the size of our garden, I would say well under 15,000 square feet—the part of our 100-by-150-foot lot that was left after subtracting the ground occupied by the sidewalks, the house, the shed, and the driveway. But recognizing that this was, after all, a three-dimensional space enlarged the size of the garden in my mind considerably indeed. I don't know how many cubic feet our garden fills, but it's a lot.

The line between vines and groundcovers is not absolute in every case. *Campsis radicans* is called both trumpet vine and trumpet creeper, for this woody American plant will run along the ground until it encounters an obstacle, whereupon it begins to ascend, clinging to its host by the stick-tight structures on its stems. The same is true of Virginia creeper and of English ivy.

But even allowing for a certain amount of overlap, the general distinction between the two types of plants lies in the different planes they occupy within a garden space.

Groundcovers grow in a horizontal plane, taking up a lot of space. But if they are low and well-mannered, that is, not excessively greedy in their demands for moisture and nutrients, much taller plants can grow with them in harmony. My favorite examples are hybrid lilies, which, when carefully chosen to provide over three months of bloom in summer, lend the excitement of color to an otherwise low-key spot planted in a solid sheet of *Vinca minor.*

Vines grow in a vertical plane, according to their habit. Even though they may spread out once aloft—after they have reached a roof, the top of a wall, or the limbs or canopy of a tree—they take up minimal space on the ground. Thus they enlarge the diversity and number of plants that a garden can be home to and increase the pleasures it offers to the senses.

Groundcovers and vines, in concert with other plants, combine to offer a fully dimensional garden where every square inch offers excitement and satisfaction.

Climbing rose 'Old Dawson's' covers an arching trellis that frames the view of a part of Cynthia Woodyard's garden in Portland, Oregon.

1 Groundcovers Reconsidered

"Groundcover" is a fairly recent word in the vocabulary of horticulture. I have found only scattered use of the term in American garden literature in the first quarter of the twentieth century, although many books devote whole chapters to vines. There is no entry for this word in the 1930 three-volume edition of L. H. Bailey's *The Standard Cyclopedia of Horticulture*. Six years later, *The Garden Encyclopedia*, published by the William H. Wise Company, gave one brief paragraph to the topic, naming as examples fewer than ten plants. In contrast to the old Wise encyclopedia, the second edition of *Wyman's Gardening Encyclopedia* (1986) lists well over eighty different genera of groundcover plants, whose species and cultivars are often discussed in some detail in the entries devoted to them.

The discussion of groundcovers didn't really get going in America until after World War II, and it was obviously tied to major changes in our nation's history, including new patterns of suburban development. The old nineteenth-century suburbs like Stamford, Connecticut, and Evanston, Illinois, linked by commuter rail lines to the business and financial districts of large metropolitan centers, continued to exist as convenient outlying Edens with well-established gardens and cool streets lined with mature shade trees. But in the late 1940s, the suburban ideal was democratized, as tracts of inexpensive housing seemed to spring up overnight in former potato fields on Long Island or cornfields in New Jersey.

In the beginning, in these raw suburbs, was the lawn—turf grasses planted by seed or by sod almost immediately, to keep mud from being tracked into ranch houses far from the nearest ranch and to give children a place to play. The lawn was more than a stretch of grass, however. It was also an idea—no, an ideal—that had been perfectly formulated and expressed by the American landscape architect Frank J. Scott in *The Art of Beautifying Suburban Home Grounds*, an influential book published in 1870, just as the posh railroad suburbs of the Northeast were burgeoning. *Suburban Home Grounds* was an etiquette book for members of the comfortable middle class, who were eager not to offend their neighbors by some lapse in taste. Scott didn't mind being a horticultural forerunner of Emily Post, and he was enamored of lawns. He devoted a key chapter to them, opening with this sentence: "A smooth, closely shaven surface of grass is by far the most essential element of beauty on the grounds of a suburban home." He rhapsodized about grass, described as "a close-fitting green robe thrown over the smooth form of the earth, through which every undulation is revealed, and over which the sunlight will play as upon velvet, and the shadows of environing objects be clearly outlined as upon a floor." He romanticized turf, making light of the work involved in tending it.

Hand machines for mowing are now so simplified and cheapened that they are coming into general use on small pleasure grounds, and proprietors may have the pleasure of doing their own mowing without the wearisome bending of the back, incident to the use of the scythe. Whoever spends the early hours of one summer, while the dew spangles the grass, in pushing these grass-cutters over a velvety lawn, breathing the fresh

Maintaining a large
expanse of unblemished lawn,
such as this one at the
Huntington Botanical Garden in
California, can be a lonely
chore, but too noisy to
encourage quiet meditation.

Frank J. Scott, historically
America's leading propagandist
for lawns, would have admired
this splendid turf in the garden
of Susan Ryley in Victoria,
British Columbia. But he would
have deplored its being
enclosed as uncivil and
undemocratic. Scott was wrong
on many a matter.

At Great Dixter in
England, Christopher Lloyd's
head gardener gives a patch of
lawn a tidy manicure where it
abuts a stone path.

sweetness of the morning air and the perfume of new mown hay, will never rest contented in the city.

Scott also understood that the ways people landscaped their properties conveyed messages about social status. He wrote of "that air of elegance which most persons desire to have their places express" to obtain "the admiration of cultivated people." It is easy to imagine Rhett Butler reading *Suburban Home Grounds* in Atlanta after the Civil War, looking for advice on how to landscape his imposing new house so that his daughter Bonnie could grow up in an atmosphere of respectability, despite her parents' record of cunning and roguery.

Scott's admiration for lawns, however, went far beyond aesthetic preferences and expressions of taste. He insisted not only on lawns, but on lawns that were open to the street, unimpeded from public view by fences, walls, hedges, or other enclosures. All of these he described as "unchristian," "unneighborly," and "surly" (a quality he discerned in English gardens, whose "uncivil" walls or hedges served "to wall and hedge a lovely garden against the longing eyes of the outside world"). His ideas have triumphed. If someone maintains a lawn that is full of weeds and that goes more than a week without being mowed, everybody knows about it. Scott proposed only one valid reason for enclosing private property against public scrutiny: "If a man believes himself and his family to be bad neighbors, certainly they ought to fence themselves in, thoroughly." This influential spokesman on behalf of shorn turf made it virtually a sacrament of religion, patriotism, morality, and personal decency—a visible sign of an invisible Grace.

I suspect that the number of homeowners in places like Stamford who actually cut their own lawns prior to World War II was small. "Breathing the sweet freshness of new mown hay" while pushing a hand mower may sound pleasant, but it is hard and sweaty work, and there were generally servants on hand to tend to such arduous and repetitive chores.

The end of the war changed everything. Suburban lots grew smaller. Power mowers were manufactured and sold by the millions. The new suburbanites could easily tend the lawns that would earn the admiration of their neighbors and of passersby. Municipal water systems made it possible to irrigate lawns and keep them green from spring until early winter. (Roger Swain, the science editor of *Horticulture* magazine, has recently pointed out that before the late 1940s, lawns went brown in summer, their natural course.) Chemical fertilizers kept lawns in vigorous growth. Insecticides like DDT and selective herbicides like 2-4 D could easily handle intrusions into lawn and garden by unwelcome visitors. Magazines like *Better Homes and Gardens* praised the coming miracle of a weed-free, insect-free America. Rachel Carson had not yet had her say. People didn't know about the food chain, understand the word "ecology," or stop to think that an insect-free America would have no honeybees or other food-plant pollinators, with disastrous results. (The fascination with chemicals was by no means restricted to the United States. In one of her essays, Vita Sackville-West writes of inviting guests to spray unwanted plants with 2-4 D, enjoying the prospect of weeds writhing in agony before shriveling up and dying.)

It is really not much fun to mow a lawn. Furthermore, grass does not grow successfully everywhere in the garden. It is difficult or impossible to grow in dense shade. A steep slope planted in grass is unpleasant to mow at best, dangerous at worst.

And so a new idea entered the consciousness of gardeners, the idea of groundcovers. I cannot pinpoint the exact time historically, but I do know that by the 1950s, when I was in my teens, my mother, my aunts, one of my grandmothers, and other gardeners in my family were talking about groundcovers with some enthusiasm. They weren't talking about very exotic groundcovers, but just the common ones—English ivy, periwinkle (*Vinca minor*), *Pachysandra terminalis*, and maybe carpet junipers. There were two themes in their talk: Groundcovers were a substitute for turf grass where it did poorly. And they involved less work than grass; they promised the chore-shedding joy of "low-maintenance gardening."

There is, unfortunately, not a great deal of glamour surrounding groundcovers. I intend to argue that groundcovers, far from being the plain-Jane, strictly utilitarian plants of low-maintenance gardens, are actually a diverse group of plants that have great individual beauty and that can be combined judiciously and imaginatively to create fully dimensional gardens in which every square foot offers pleasure to all the senses during most of the year. But I know there are obstacles to persuading others on this point. The rhetoric that has accompanied most of the writing encouraging people to plant groundcovers is generally as dull as kindergarten scissors. An example is "Ground Covers Can Cure Headaches Such as Problem Sites, Bare Spots," an article by Henry Marc Cathey in *Landscape for Living*, the 1972 yearbook of agriculture published by the United States Department of Agriculture. Dr. Cathey praised groundcovers for such problem spots as deep shade under trees or exposed soil left behind at new houses when the building crews departed. Groundcovers "can cover bare spots in the yard, prevent soil erosion," and "regulate foot traffic." They also "filter out dust particles from the air." My favorite item on Dr. Cathey's agenda for groundcovers (and one that I would never have thought of myself) is that they "hide litter that might blow into your yard."

It isn't very sexy to talk about groundcovers as a substitute for something else, but when that something else is a lawn, some important things need to be said. Considering the number of companies that manufacture machinery for tending lawns, that grow turf-grass seed, and that synthesize chemicals for keeping lawns green and free of weeds, fungi, grubs, and other enemies of unblemished velvet, it is obvious that lawns occupy an important place in the American economy. They loom even larger when garden centers, hardware stores, and lawn-care services are taken into consideration. If America's long infatuation with lawns were to end overnight, the economic costs would be almost incalculable.

But lawns have other costs of equal and possibly even greater importance. Power mowers, whether run on gasoline or on electricity, pollute the atmosphere with exhaust gases, and they are a drain on fossil fuels. According to a report released by the Environmental Protection Agency late in 1992, there are an estimated eighty-three million gasoline-powered lawn mowers in the United States, each capable of emitting the same amount of polluting gases in a single hour as the average automobile discharges into the atmosphere in

This lawn in Victoria, British Columbia, owes its attractiveness to many tools and much hard labor.

several days of ordinary use. Some electrical utility companies have not let this news pass unnoticed, urging the substitution of electric mowers for those with gasoline engines. This substitution merely changes the sites where pollution takes place. Battery-powered mowers have been hailed as better, but batteries must eventually be disposed of, and they are a source of toxic waste. Fertilizers and other chemicals pollute streams, lakes, and groundwater through run-off. Watering a lawn to keep it green throughout the growing season puts a strain on an increasingly precious natural resource.

I do not expect many people to ponder these things right now and to run out and get rid of their lawns. But I do hear tales of people who have deliberately reduced the size of their lawns. One is my friend Tony Avent, who tells of a summer day not long ago when he went outside, revved up his lawn mower, checked his watch, and mowed for one hour. Then he turned off the mower, surveyed the unmown section of his garden, and sprayed it with glyphosphate, a nonselective herbicide that dissipates quickly into harmless substances and leaves no residue in soil. "I wanted a lawn I could mow in just one hour a week," he explains. The parts of his former lawn that he killed he then planted in woody and herbaceous groundcovers and other plants he considers "1,000 percent more interesting than fescue." I agree (my own lawn is vestigial), and I consider anything that reduces the area of lawns to be environmentally desirable.

What's a Groundcover?

I am by primary profession a philosopher, not a gardener or a writer. Socrates ended up having to drink hemlock and die because of his habit of pestering people to define the words they used. He had a good point, though it finally was fatal to him: people who can't say what they are talking about usually don't know what they are talking about.

Vines are easier to define than groundcovers, because what makes a plant a vine is its physiology, something written in its genes. Vines are plants that climb. They seek support by twining around something else, clockwise or counterclockwise, according to their particular wont, and then, as their lower tissue hardens, they twine again and again, climbing higher and higher. Or they form tendrils, in the leaf axils of their new growth, that search the air for something to hold onto, then spiral around it, harden, and give the vine a solid

The tawny daylily (*Hemerocallis fulva*) is almost ubiquitous in roadside ditches in much of America, as here in Connecticut. For weed-suppression this lusty grower surpasses all other daylilies.

platform for additional aerial upward progress. Or they put out structures like adhesive disks or hairy rootlets on their stems, which grasp brick and mortar or tree bark and then hang on for dear life ever after. Or they simply hurl themselves upwards, eventually leaning on or draping over whatever support they find.

Some groundcovers are groundcovers because of their genetic characteristics. They colonize the ground they occupy by relentless stolons or underground rhizomes. A prime example, both beautiful and beautifully aggressive, is dwarf green-and-gold bamboo (*Pleioblastus viridistriatus*), with leaves that gleam like polished malachite. Once established, the least sprig of this handsome foliage plant will spread by runners toward the horizon in all directions, choking out any less forceful plant in its path. Most forms of English ivy (*Hedera helix*) are similarly aggressive. Ivy, however, spreads not by underground rhizomes but by ever-lengthening woody stems that put down shallow roots just below the surface of the soil, then much tougher roots that plunge three or more feet into the earth. When ivy encounters something—a tree, a wall—that it can climb, it changes from groundcover to vine, adhering to solid surfaces, as if glued, by means of rootlets. Once aloft, ivy changes character again, in time altering the shape of its leaves and producing flowers and seeds that sprout where they are excreted by birds, starting anew the inexorable progress of this mighty plant.

Common periwinkle (*Vinca minor*) also is a natural spreader, throwing out runners in all directions from its crown—runners that root at the surface of the soil to form new crowns that, in turn, put out their own runners. Lily-of-the-valley (*Convallaria majalis*) spreads by underground stems that form, at intervals of an inch or two, the pips from which new plants will grow, blooming beautifully and sweetly in spring. Another rhizomatous spreader is the tawny daylily (*Hemerocallis fulva*), so familiar growing in roadside ditches in much of the eastern United States, although it is a plant of Asian origin that cannot reproduce itself by seeds because it is sterile.

The success of tawny daylily, lily-of-the-valley, vinca, and English ivy is almost guaranteed by their genes. In second-growth woodlands in my part of southern New Jersey, old farmhouses that have long since tumbled into their foundations and virtually disappeared nevertheless have left behind their traces. Vast colonies of vinca and other tough plants that once grew in the dooryard gardens stretch deep into stands of pitch pines and the first stages of hardwood forest on land that once was farmed.

The white-splashed leaves of *Lamium maculatum* 'Album' echo those of *Hosta undulata* var. *univittata*. In mid-spring, the lamium's spikes of pure white flowers add sparkle to this winning combination.

But the vast majority of groundcovers fit the category not because of their genetic tendency to spread (and often to spread out of reasonable bounds) but because of the uses to which they are put. Pulmonarias, most ferns, wild gingers, hellebores, brunneras, heucheras, lavenders, daylilies other than *Hemerocallis fulva*, and all but a handful of hostas—these and many other plants that make beautiful groundcovers do not spread. They are clump-formers instead. They may be capable of standing on their own as specimens or accent plants in a border, but if planted closely together, they will fill in the space they occupy as effectively as, say, *Vinca minor*.

These plants become groundcovers because gardeners intend them to be such. This point suggests another: Clump-forming groundcovers are mannerly and well-behaved, whereas the ones with large territorial ambitions and the physiological means to realize them can mean big trouble.

Many of us learn a lesson in humility when we encourage plants like English ivy, lily-of-the-valley, and *Vinca minor* to grow, then wait eagerly for them to spread—only to discover a few years down the road that keeping them in check has become a pesky, time-consuming chore. That it is a chore of our own making does not elevate our self-esteem.

In my own garden, there is an excellent case in point. Some years ago, in a lightly shaded corner, I planted a number of cultivars of *Lamium maculatum*. 'Aureum' has beautiful cream-striped golden leaves and pink flowers. 'Beedham's White' has similarly marked chartreuse leaves and sparkling white flowers. 'White Nancy' is lovely for its white flowers and for its handsome, slightly pointed heart-shaped leaves with silvery white centers edged with a thin margin of green. 'Beacon Silver' and 'Pink Pewter' both bear attractive silver-tinted foliage and pleasant pink flowers. I also planted 'Hermann's Pride', a cultivar of *Lamiastrum galeobdolon* (syn. *Lamium galeobdolon*) with small, sharply pointed, silver-speckled green leaves and yellow flowers. So far, so good. These low perennials have slightly spreading habits, but they are manageable. Their handsome foliage is persistent, thus providing winter interest, and their flush of flower clusters from spring into early summer is a welcome bonus.

Had I stopped with these particular plants, there would be a happy story to tell. But I also planted yellow archangel, the common, unselected form of *Lamiastrum galeobdolon*. Its leaves much resemble those of 'Beacon Silver', and its rich golden flowers in May are

Still and placid water is the noblest groundcover of all. At Wave Hill in the Bronx in mid-summer, water lilies, pickerels, and lotuses make a fine display in a pool whose banks are planted in lush miscanthus grasses.

fetching. But it is ill-mannered in the extreme, sending out long stems that bend under their own weight, root, and form new plants. Within three years it had swamped 'Hermann's Pride' and all of the lamiums, leaving me with 100 square feet of nothing but yellow archangel that was looking for yet more *Lebensraum*. Ripping it out didn't work; it just grew back quickly from the least bits of rooted stem in the soil. My only choice was to extirpate it by dowsing it thoroughly with glyphosate. A few weeks later, I ordered new lamiums.

It is time, however, to get back to the definition of groundcovers. Most of us think that we know one when we see one, but this general term covers a very diverse group of plants that embraces annuals and perennials, deciduous and evergreen plants, woody plants and herbaceous ones, and clumpers and spreaders. As I mentioned earlier, English ivy, at different stages of its life, is a groundcover, a vine, and eventually an epiphytic shrub that dwells in trees or atop walls. Hostas can be treated as groundcovers or as handsome garden perennials. The book of nature is almost never as tidy as a dictionary. But it is still fairly clear what is and what is not a groundcover.

My own rules—ground rules, if you will forgive the pun—for determining what plants qualify as groundcovers are as follows.

First, they are low plants, generally not over eighteen to twenty inches tall, often shorter than that. Some, such as golden creeping jenny (*Lysimachia nummularia* 'Aurea'), grow only a couple of inches high; the related *L. japonica* 'Minutissima' is a mere dense mat of green film on the soil. A good reason for admiring groundcovers is that they are looked down on.

Second, they are of interest over a long season. Some are evergreen or have foliage that is persistent well into winter, but in any case, groundcovers are a major presence in the garden over much of the year.

Third, as already mentioned, they tend to be associated with low-maintenance gardening, or at least to make such slender demands that gardeners can give them minimal attention, meanwhile pursuing more arduous tasks like keeping their roses free of mildew and black spot. A good groundcover, when established, discourages weeds. It is also important, given the prevailing summer climates in the United States, that it is resistant to hot and humid weather, to prolonged periods of drought, and also, paradoxically, to soggy soil, the result of thunderstorms one after the other.

Fourth, it is commonly claimed that groundcovers are best planted

In the Delaware garden of William Frederick, a well-known landscape architect, a pool formed by a slow stream lined with English ivy reflects light into a shady spot.

In this front yard in Los Angeles, gravel becomes a groundcover that is an effective foil for agaves, yuccas, palms, and mounds of low ornamental grasses.

Gravel lends additional simplicity and quiet elegance to the formal facade of the Old Rectory, Burghfield in Berkshire.

Many Americans regard moss in a lawn as a sign of poor gardening, and possibly human depravity. But the truth is that a lawn of moss can be a thing of great beauty, as evidenced by this natural one in the Bloedel Nature Preserve, Bainbridge Island, Washington.

in masses or colonies of just one kind, as their effect is cumulative, not solitary. They lend a sense of unity to a garden, and they also may serve as a backdrop to an individual plant that is more dramatic. This metaphor of drama suggests that some plants play starring roles; if so, groundcovers are the chorus or, at most, minor members of a supporting cast. But a warning is in order here, especially for smaller gardens. It is easy to go overboard, planting too much of the same groundcover. Unity then becomes uniformity, with the same ajugas or vincas present everywhere. Truly inviting gardens are ones that achieve an exuberance of diversity, and this diversity should be thoughtfully extended as much to the choice of groundcovers as to any other plants.

It is a grave mistake to take the advice about planting groundcovers in masses as an absolute rule, such that here be vincas, there be dwarf creeping astilbes, and over yonder is something else, all in perfect blocks, with nothing else intruding. I prefer gardens where things weave in and out of one another—where, for example, the tender, gray-leafed wanderer *Helichrysum petiolare* (or its yellow-leafed cultivar, 'Limelight') may thread its way amongst small sedums. Other wanderers do terrific work by softening the boundaries between one part of the garden and another. *Verbena canadensis* seems almost to have been created to escape from its tidy bed and cover part of a pathway with its abundance of bloom, and the nasturtiums spilling into the paths of Monet's garden at Giverny are the stuff of legend. The entire garden, including its groundcover plantings, ought to be a tapestry.

In its literal sense, "groundcover" means anything that covers the ground, whether it be low herbaceous ornamental plants or woody ones, a lawn of fescue or bluegrass or chamomile or moss, or even weeds. (Crabgrass, viewed with an unprejudiced eye, is a champion at covering the ground impenetrably.) I use the term here in its stricter, horticultural sense to mean low and desirable vegetation. But paths of pine straw or gravel or flagstones, wooden decking, patios of brick or slate—all of these also serve as groundcovers, and they should be kept in mind as such. Good garden design almost demands that these materials be employed, with their hard lines softened by plants escaping their boundaries, cascading out of them in exuberance and profusion. Water, too, is a groundcover, and one of the most beautiful. A pool, with waterlilies blooming at its center and semi-aquatic plants guarding its margins, should not be dismissed lightly or left out of account when one is considering worthy things that cover the ground. What other "groundcover" on a bright summer day reflects the blue sky above and its stately procession of snowy white cumulus clouds moving from one horizon to the other?

Biting the Bullet on Pachysandra and Its Chums

A casual drive through almost any residential neighborhood in suburban America testifies that the four groundcovers in most common use are *Pachysandra terminalis*, English ivy, *Vinca minor*, and the numerous cultivars of carpet juniper. These are the four canonical groundcovers. They rule the roost in local garden centers. Television quiz show contestants, if asked to name the best groundcovers mentioned in a random poll of 100 shoppers in a mall, would win with these, but get small reward for coming up with *Sedum spathulifolium* or *Rubus calycinoides*. But these four are basically fairly dull plants. It is vulgar to look askance at plants simply because they are common. Dull is different.

The dullest of the lot, I think, is ordinary *Pachysandra terminalis*. In its behalf, the most that can be said is that it covers bare dirt with a carpet of green, it has fairly decent manners (it is stoloniferous, but not in a troublesome way), it keeps down weeds, and it requires fairly little care. It obviously has its partisans, but I am not among them. There are two cultivars with more to offer. 'Green Sheen' has glossy, almost varnished-looking foliage. 'Silver Edge', its name notwithstanding, has white, not silver, leaf margins. They are worth consideration by people who would feel naked without pachysandra around the trees in their front lawns. Far too overlooked as a groundcover is *Pachysandra procumbens*, our native North American Allegheny spurge. It is deciduous in harsh winters, but the rather gray-green foliage of this genetically variable plant may have handsome markings of light brown.

I have already tipped my hand on English ivy. It may be a fine plant for large parks, but it is a Trojan horse in a garden, and I can testify personally to this claim. It seems delicate at first, almost frail, but this belief in the innocence of ivy is a cruel delusion. It is entirely tenacious of life, once it gets up steam. Most gardeners I know who plant it eventually regret the decision as they spend weeks ripping it out, often suffering prolonged, painful tendonitis and neuralgia from trying to dislodge the roots from their subterranean havens.

I must mention, however, that some cultivars of *Hedera helix* are more manageable. 'Spetchley' not only has very tiny leaves, but

Pachysandra terminalis is probably America's most overplanted groundcover. It is too familiar to be especially interesting. But it is tough, and when it is combined with other plants of greater interest, as in this planting at a corporate headquarters in Oregon, it serves a purpose.

Appropriately named,
Hedera helix 'Glacier' brings a
cool look on even the most
torrid days of summer to the
garden of Robert Fletcher, a
landscape architect in Pacific
Palisades, California.

(*center*) At Hidcote Manor
in May, blue scillas beautifully
punctuate the fresh new growth
of a massed planting of *Vinca
minor* along a path.

spreads at less than glacial speed. 'Gold Heart' spreads at a moderate rate, and the creamy centers of its leaves are suffused with light purple in winter. It is more aggressive than 'Spetchley', but it can be kept under control reasonably well. 'Glacier', well named for its cool variegated leaves of silver and gray, is seldom much trouble, and it is the best of all ivies to plant at the base of trees to cloak their trunks in loveliness. Moreover, the world of ivies extends beyond *H. helix*. Persian ivy (*H. colchica*) is a splendid groundcover with enormous leaves, though rampant enough that it must be watched. The variegated form 'Dentata-Variegata' has stunning gold and green foliage that can bring considerable dazzle to dim corners of the garden.

Of the four most common groundcovers, *Vinca minor* has the most going for it. The plain species is attractive year round for its evergreen foliage and produces an abundance of blue-violet flowers in the spring. It spreads, but its roots do not go deep. There are several interesting cultivars. I have a form with small leaves and tiny white flowers, which may be 'Alba'. 'Miss Jekyll's White' has larger blossoms. From a neighbor I got a vinca with wine-red flowers, and from a nursery, one called 'Multiplex', whose double purple flowers are produced rather sparsely—no bloom at all in some years—but are interesting when they do appear. My favorite vinca, however, is 'Aureovariegata'. It has white flowers, but the variegated green and warm yellow leaves are the main event. The variegation is not at all uniform; in fact, it is difficult to find two leaves that are similarly

patterned. Some are all yellow, some are two shades of green with faint yellow margins or blotches, some are yellow on one side of the leaf vein and green on the other, and some are intricately worked combinations of both colors. The effect from a distance is a bright golden chartreuse, like an herb butter, and the plants look warm and cheery in winter.

Every plant has its story, and I know part of this one's. I got my start from a distribution of plants to members of the North Carolina State University Arboretum, specifically, from the arboretum's director, Professor J. C. Raulston, Raulston got it from Christopher Lloyd in England, who in turn got it from the Hillier nursery there. When Don Shadow, a nurseryman in Winchester, Tennessee, who is well known for his interest in unusual plants, heard that Raulston was propagating it, he asked for a few plants. It had been Shadow himself who originally gave it to Hillier, then lost his own stock. This tale well illustrates the horticultural importance of the Biblical dictum about casting your bread upon the waters, that it may in time be returned to you.

Carpet junipers and other low and spreading conifers do not exactly make the heart beat faster at first sight, but they are easy plants that serve useful purposes, especially the numerous cultivars of our native *Juniperus horizontalis*. Although they insist on full sun, they are otherwise extremely untemperamental. They tolerate drought, once established. They aren't choosy about soil; clay or sandy loam and anything in between suits them just fine. They will

At Montrose, Nancy and Craufurd Goodwin's garden in Hillsborough, North Carolina, black elephant ears (*Colocasia affinis*) and bears breeches (*Acanthus mollis*) rise up above a vivid carpet of *Vinca minor* 'Aureovariegata'. In the background at left is the somewhat scandent shrub *Eleagnus pungens* 'Maculata', whose flowers in fall have a gardenia scent that travels far. ALLEN LACY

grow on fairly steep slopes where little else will, and thus are useful for controlling erosion. They vary in growth habit from almost prostrate to upright. The color of the foliage varies from straightforward green to bluer tones, silvery ones, and even gold. Carpet junipers are in general exceptionally hardy, able to take both the wintry blasts and sub-zero temperatures of Zone 3 and the hot, humid and prolonged summers of Zones 8 and 9 in the South. Problems with blight and with spider-mite damage are not unknown in the species, but experts on woody plants can advise on selecting disease- and insect-resistant cultivars. (Anyone who wants to see as many of these juniper cultivars as can be imagined growing in one place should lose no time in getting to the superb Arboretum of the North Carolina State University in Raleigh, North Carolina. Its collection of these plants is huge—eighty different cultivars, maybe more.) I confess to no great passion for *Juniperus horizontalis*, although I do admire and grow one called 'Blue Chip', whose needles are indeed a fine steely blue. And I am quite fond of an East Asian species, the shore juniper (*J. conferta*). It has a soft-looking texture, although it's bristly to the touch. In my garden, it wanders interwoven with a low cotoneaster, spilling into a path and softening its edges.

What's wrong with planting pachysandra, vinca, carpet junipers, and English ivy? The answer is nothing, if the goal is simply to cover the ground with a lot of biomass that will make minimal demands to tend it. Fairly low maintenance is a reasonable ideal for people who want something like a garden, but one that will leave them free for other pursuits. But using groundcovers exclusively or primarily to cut down on work has its costs, and chief among these costs is the loss of plant diversity, which is the very essence of the joy of gardening. I will argue, in a later chapter on groundcovers and bulbs, that beautiful things can be done in a garden with a large sheet of common groundcovers like vinca or carpet junipers, treated as a stage set against which a procession of seasonal dramas is played out. But I remain convinced that such groundcovers, in sheets, without other plants combined with them, are dull. It is *using* groundcovers, not *gardening* with them. This style of landscaping is highly suitable for schools, banks, fast-food restaurants, and similar institutions or businesses, for which it has solid virtues. It keeps down weeds. It offers something living to look at, instead of asphalt or concrete. It cools the air somewhat, and it carries on photosynthesis, producing oxygen and removing carbon dioxide from the atmosphere. But it isn't gardening.

৶৶৶

"I Want an English *Garden"*

I have long been puzzled by this frequently made comment by Americans who tour England's notable gardens and return, dissatisfied with their own gardens and wanting something . . . well, something *more English somehow.* My first inclination is to reply, "Sorry, but you just can't have an English garden, not in the United States." An English garden is not possible except in a climate like England's, which is nothing like the torrid, humid summers and the often-fierce winters that prevail in North America. We can forget those towering stems of delphiniums on plants that are reliably perennial. I know just three persons in the Northeast who claim success in growing blue meconopsis or Himalayan poppies. Perennials that bloom over many weeks or even months in England bloom much more quickly here, where their metabolism is speeded up by blasting heat.

We cannot have an English climate, but then I am no longer sure that it is solely climate that defines the English garden. I now believe that it is a style of planting that characterizes such a garden, a style that is as possible to achieve in New Jersey or in North Carolina as in Kent. Also involved is an attitude toward plants—as Barry Yinger has put it, "a willingness to let plants be plants."

The English style of planting, as I have seen it at Sissinghurst, Great Dixter, Hidcote, and other gardens in the United Kingdom, can be summed up with three neatly alliterative and interrelated words—*density, depth,* and *diversity.*

Density means that plants are set on tight centers—that they grow on intimate terms with one another, one thing growing up through another or weaving through something else. Considered horizontally, dense planting means that a given space is packed tight with plants, in the greatest profusion possible to grow them really well. It implies, of course, a steady supply of nutrients for all plants (except those that prefer to live on skinny rations), so that one thing doesn't starve another and sap its vigor. Considered vertically, density means that the lowest tier in a flower border is as richly populated as the middle and highest tiers. Flowering groundcovers and ones that are primarily grown for their foliage play a vital role in attaining this end.

A British gardener visiting the United States once said to me in exasperation, "Oh, you Americans! Why are you always displaying your *mulch?*" I got her point immediately. There is often a primness, even a prissiness, in the way we plant things. It almost always manifests itself in our public rose gardens, where hybrid tea roses are planted in narrow rectangular or semicircular beds. The roses are spaced so far apart that they seem to be afraid of touching one another, and the earth below them is ankle-deep in pine straw, wood chips, cocoa hulls, shredded licorice root, or other mulch. The naked mulch serves its purpose, but one longs to see it covered by ladies mantle, lavender, or santolina—by anything that would undercarpet the roses and conceal the mulch with handsome flowers or foliage. Here, a plea made by Sir George Stitwell to his fellow Englishmen in *On the Making of Gardens* (1909) deserves a hearing: "So, if it is to be a rose-garden, do not . . . banish other flowers which may do homage to the beauty of a rose as courtiers to a queen." Rose gardens (and display gardens of hemerocallis or bearded irises) may be the extreme cases, but I have seen many an American garden where things are planted at such distances from one another that they seem separate, not part of the living throng that a garden ought to be.

Depth has to do with the dimensions of the space that is set aside for a garden or a flower border. Suburban America is full of stingy, shallow mini-beds (bed-ettes?) barely big enough for a row of impatiens, red salvias, orange or yellow marigolds, pelargoniums, periwinkles, caladiums, and so on fringing the foundation plantings, which are a long-standing national passion second only to the front lawn open to the street, à la Frank J. Scott. A flower border needs to be spacious. A bed that is only three feet deep from front to back

The small enclosed garden of Ann Armstrong in Charlotte, North Carolina, with a small shallow stream crossing a brick path, makes imaginative use of *Vinca minor, Ajuga reptans,* and *Juniperus conferta,* plus the pansies that in the South bloom all winter.

constricts both the imagination and the stunning beauty that perennials and other plants can provide, in succession, from early spring to late fall. Some perennials, such as *Gaura lindheimeri*, bloom for months and months, but others, such as peonies or oriental poppies, have a brief season of glory. Flowering plants are like lights that turn on, shine for a time, and then cease to hold the eye. In a narrow bed, there may be weeks when nothing of much interest is in bloom. The depth of a border is a spatial matter, but it has temporal implications.

My deepest bed is a curving border, eighteen feet deep at each end, tapering down to nine or ten feet in the middle. As one plant subsides, others come on. The hellebores, *Arum italicum pictum*, and Darleyensis heaths bring cheer in late winter, followed by the earliest spring bulbs and the woodland ephemerals, like Virginia bluebells and celandine poppies. Pulmonarias and late tulips bloom in May, roses in June. Daylilies in huge numbers dominate in July, as does *Salvia guaranitica*, with its cobalt blossoms that are irresistible to hummingbirds. In midsummer, tall golden anthemis consorts beautifully with huge, shrubby *Lavatera* 'Barnsley', covered with scores of pink flowers like small single hollyhocks. In August, Joe Pye weed signals the approach of autumn, a lingering season when many glorious species of *Salvia* put on their show. The garden year does not end until November, when the enormous golden columns of *Helianthus angustifolius* and the billowing, rich blue clumps of 'Fanny's Aster' have sung their finale.

The plants just mentioned are all perennials, and mostly tall ones, but in a deep bed they can be faced down with groundcovers. In sunny spots in my generously proportioned back border, I have white sweet alyssum interplanted with the little Texas scarlet sage, *Salvia coccinea*. Here also grow ladies mantle, lamb's ears, Japanese blood grass, and the steely blue dwarf ornamental fescue grass 'Elijah Blue'. In shadier spots there are small hostas, several species of *Asarum* or wild ginger, ferns in great number and variety, and the pulmonarias, which are as wonderful for their mounds of spotted foliage in summer as they are for their pink and blue flowers in spring.

The generosity of the space in my garden means that I can play with it. I do not follow the tidy rule that says little plants go in front, middle-sized ones in the middle, and tall ones at the rear. This apparently sensible advice would be sound only if we were rooted in one spot, at some distance from the border, and if our only means of experiencing it were with the eye. But we have bodies, and we

In Susan Ryley's garden in Victoria, this dense and diverse planting of *Houttuynia cordata* 'Chameleon', lamium 'Silver Beacon', gray-foliaged dianthus, and spiraea 'Goldflame' is as bright as Joseph's Technicolor dream coat.

can move around in gardens, enabling us to have ever-changing experiences of what is there. I am free to bring tall plants forward where they are pleasing, as I have done with *Angelica gigas*. This biennial, or short-lived perennial that reseeds itself sufficiently to return each year, would hold its own even near the back of the border, for it stands shoulder-high and bears huge, celerylike green leaves on twisted, hollow purple stems that bend at unexpected angles. But I have brought it close to the edge of the border, to rejoice in an intimate sight of the immense, domed, deep plum flower clusters in late July that glisten with nectar and dance under the weight of the crowd of bees that come to feast on it. I am also free to carry a mixed planting of low plants deep into the border here and there, to lighten the oppression that results from nothing but enormous plants toward the rear.

The meaning of diversity is almost self-evident. Although herbaceous perennial borders are very fashionable these days, and although I would not garden without relying heavily upon perennials, I believe in the catholic, not the sectarian, garden. Herbaceous perennials are not sufficient to make a garden. They can mingle beautifully with woody plants that are naturally of modest size or that can be kept in bounds by pruning. Bulbs and flowering annuals also make a significant contribution to a garden that is, in musical terms, both harmonious and contrapuntal. The notion of diversity, of course, embraces not only the kinds of plants—those that form permanent woody tissue, those that die back to the ground in the winter to return the following year, and those that are creatures of a single season—but also the size that plants ultimately become. The individual plants that make up my own garden range from that most minute Japanese *Lysimachia*, which is a mere green film on the ground, to an ancient Virginia juniper, eighty feet tall and canopied in summer by the beautiful apricot flowers of an especially fine form of trumpet vine.

Barry Yinger isn't quite sure that what makes English gardens English is simply density, depth, and diversity, which Americans can themselves achieve by deliberation and work. There's that matter of "letting plants be plants," of adopting a relaxed attitude toward the garden and of not seeking to control everything that happens there. A plant that doesn't stay neatly confined in its bed isn't a disaster. If it escapes its boundaries, he says, then so be it. If one plant grows up through another, and it looks okay or even better than okay, it is an unexpected gift, and what it calls for is grateful acceptance. I've never heard Barry use theological language, but I think he's saying that gardens are places of Salvation through Grace, not Works.

And there's a thoughtful man named Raydon Alexander, a Texan, who thinks the ultimate origins of the English garden are found in a surprising corner of the world. He wrote me:

The English garden is very much an (unconscious) imitation of a typical Texas roadside in the spring. What the Brits labor over, the gods provide us in profusion. At a depth of over 12′ and an "infinite" length, it is the English Garden gone bonkers. The irony is, it was the British who had to show us how to use these beauties in our gardens, which have tended toward dreadfully timid ribbon borders. But times are changing.

Here's a list of plants that thrive in Texas—and are the pride of many an Englishman's border: Abronia, Achillea, Allium stellatum, Amsonia, Aquilegia, Aster oblongifolia, Berlandiera, Callirhoë, Calochortus, Calylopha, Camassia, Cassia, Castilleja

At dawn in late summer, the garden of Charles Price and Glen Wythey in Seattle comes to life. A narrow path is flanked by a dense, exuberant planting of daylilies, white oriental lilies, sedums, a number of ornamental grasses, and the variegated phlox 'Norah Leigh'.

purpurea, Cichoria, Cooperia, Coreopsis, Cuphea, Delphinium (DD. carolinianum, angustifolium, virescens), Echinacea, Engelmannia, Eupatorium, Helenium, Hesperaloe, Liatris, Lobelia, Monarda, Oenothera, Penstemon, Physostegia pulchella, Ratibida, Ruellia, Sisyrinchium, Verbena, Zexmania—to name only a few.

The additional irony is that drought has encouraged people to shrink their lawns here in favor of larger mixed borders. Texans who have never seen Sissinghurst are aping it under the disguise of xeriscaping (ugly word!)—with the result of the depth, diversity, and density that you find in British gardens. It's as if

Americans have to have an ulterior motive to invite the splendors of our floriferous roadsides into their gardens. Not so the English, for whom gardening is a way of life, not a way to save water or sell a house.

I would add to Raydon Alexander's intriguing hypothesis that Gertrude Jekyll and Vita Sackville-West were crypto-Texans, another point about those Texas roadsides in spring and early summer. Seldom does one find solid sheets of any one plant there. Even where Texas bluebonnets stretch almost to the horizon—a carpet of blue so intense that it seems as if the sky has fallen to the earth—they are intermingled with other wildflowers in riotous profusion.

Let our gardens run riot, too! Let ice-blue *Allium coeruleum* lean into more upright gray ballotas or helichrysums. Let sprays of white *Aster cordifolius* romp with blue-toned hostas and lamb's ears. Let pots of blue agapanthus bloom with the yellow button-flowers of gray santolina. And above all, let us enlarge the roster of groundcovers beyond ivy, periwinkle, pachysandra, and carpet junipers.

Were these four plants the only true groundcovers, the topic would be dreary indeed. The possible combinations or permutations of only four plants are tiny. But when there are at least a couple hundred to consider, their possible combinations are enough to exhaust the minds of mathematicians.

The limits are set only by the powers of the imagination—and gardening is one of the grandest arenas where the human imagination can work and play.

Mixed sedums and echevarias and other succulents, blue fescue, and other plants chosen with a great sense of harmony are tucked into crannies in steps of weathered concrete in the hillside garden of Harland Hand in El Cerrito, California.

2 Herbaceous Groundcovers for Sunny Gardens

radescantia 'Purple Heart', *Ipomoea* 'Blackie', and *Verbena canadensis*—no inevitable logic connects these three plants, beyond their all being trailing groundcovers that love the sun and thrive on heat. The connection is found elsewhere.

Tradescantia pallida 'Purple Heart' (syn. *Setcreasea pallida* 'Purple Heart') is a form of wandering Jew, lax in habit and lusty, if not rampant, with long, slightly cupped, dark purple leaves and small pink flowers. Often grown as a houseplant, it is surprisingly winter-hardy in the warmer parts of Zone 7, dying back to its roots in late fall but making vigorous new growth in spring. (It has not proved root-hardy in my part of Zone 7, but it can be brought inside during the winter; cuttings taken in early March and set outside in late April quickly conquer territory.) It can occupy its own separate space quite fully, growing to around a foot tall, but it also weaves through other plants, insinuating itself where it can.

Ipomoea batatas 'Blackie' is an extremely tender trailing plant— an edible sweet potato, in fact. Except in frost-free regions, it needs to be propagated from cuttings taken in the spring from mother plants indoors. It roots with prodigious speed; tip cuttings in a glass of water on a windowsill show new white rootlets in a day or two, which then can be potted up for planting outside when the soil warms up. This sprawling sweet potato's large lobed leaves, borne on maroon stems, are a rich blackish purple. Once hot weather arrives, 'Blackie' wanders where it pleases, which is everywhere. It will even climb up into things, though not very high.

Verbena canadensis is a virtually bone-hardy North American native perennial that will get through the winter at least to Zone 6, and possibly to Zone 5. In the wild, its color ranges from white to violet-purple, but many vegetatively propagated cultivars are now available in several colors. A stunningly beautiful, intense red-violet form, as vibrant as can be imagined, is my favorite. It blooms profusely and unceasingly from late spring until mid-October. Its blossoms at dusk take on an almost unearthly incandescent glow, a benediction to behold. I almost imagine I can hear Gregorian chant at Vespers.

As I said, no particular logic connects these three plants. Their association was born in the imagination of Douglas Ruhren, a garden designer with a brilliant grasp of color and Nancy Goodwin's associate at Montrose Nursery. In 1990, he planned and installed a new garden at the nursery, a purple-and-orange border. Although the choice of plants is lush and romantic and informal, the design is symmetrical and formal. A wide central pathway of crushed bluestone, flanked by two mixed borders that are very deep at each end but slightly narrower in the middle, leads from the imposing gateway below the nursery's office building to a lath house whose wide arches reveal another garden beyond, dominated by a huge urn on a tall pedestal.

Doug Ruhren makes much use in this border of that sweet potato, that verbena, and that tradescantia, but this wonderful corner of Montrose does far more than testify that all three plants are fine groundcovers for a sunny spot. They are part of a garden—and what a garden! Groundcovers are, once again, but one element in a garden. They are an important element, contributing fullness in its lowest tier that it would otherwise lack. They are useful, in musical terms, as a ground bass that unifies the shifting harmonies or counterpoint above them, but they can never make a symphony by themselves—and this orange-and-purple border is a symphony (by Mahler, not Haydn).

By late June, the red-violet verbena has invaded the crushed stone path in several places. 'Purple Heart' has spread in bold masses, and 'Blackie' has wandered like a nomad. But there's much, much more. In the lowest tier, *Zinnia angustifolia* (syn. *Z. linearis*) sounds forth like clear, bright cornet fanfares. This species, "unimproved" by hybridizers, is the best of all zinnias. Its foliage does not get the unsightly mildew that usually afflicts zinnias. Its prodigious crop of single, glowing apricot-orange flowers doesn't flag until frost. Low

In the purple-and-orange border that Douglas Ruhren designed in Nancy Goodwin's garden at Montrose in Hillsborough, North Carolina, *Tradescantia pallida* 'Purple Heart' combines handsomely in both foliage and flowers with the silken blossoms of *Callirhoë involucrata*. ALLEN LACY

carpets of another champion bloomer, *Delosperma cooperi*, an increasingly popular hardy ice plant from Africa, are covered with pale rosy purple daisylike flowers, adding to the ensemble. There are several hardy geraniums, but the most striking is 'Ann Folkard', with its slightly chartreuse foliage. The color of its blossoms closely matches the red-violet of the verbenas here, although the geranium's flowers have a darker, black-red eye.

In the middle tier, several annual gomphrenas, including one called 'Strawberry Fields' with rosy orange everlasting flowers, grow in pleasing masses, scattered throughout the border, echoing one another. In the higher tiers of this garden, taller annuals and perennials sound their own strong notes. Cleome stands fast in several colors, including an especially handsome shade of deep violet. Bronze fennel offers a visual paradox—bold and massive in size and volume, yet very delicate in its finely textured foliage. The leaves seem as insubstantial as smoke. When morning or evening light plays through them, they almost move, as if caressed by a breeze. In a spot near the front of one of the two large beds, self-sown dill, tall and majestic, serves as a scrim plant: its cloudlike umbels of yellowish green flowers in late June do not entirely block the view of the plants growing behind them. Near the dill, several perennials hold sway, including *Lysimachia ciliata* 'Purpurea' (syn. *Steironema ciliatum*, purple-leafed form), a fetching plant for its small yellow starry flowers and its chocolate brownish-purple foliage.

Then, vaulting toward the highest tiers, come the cannas—and a lesson for all garden snobs who mock this plant.

Cannas call up pictures of round beds containing nothing else, dotted about lawns in a meaningless way. This kind of planting, omnipresent in Victorian times, still flourishes in some municipal parks. Cannas have other civic uses. They are widely used in the South planted in big blocks by the ramps of interstate highways. They are well suited to this purpose: their foliage is bold and tropical looking; their bloom is profuse from June until frost; they thrive without irrigation; they seem to be immune to automobile exhaust gases; and they don't require lifting for winter storage in the South. (In the North, however, they must be stored inside over the winter.)

Their public uses may cause some people to believe that cannas are too vulgar and coarse for private gardens, but Doug Ruhren's handling of them shows that intelligence and imagination make cannas almost miraculous. The cannas of Montrose are its "Hallelujah Chorus." (The first time I saw them, in October 1990, I would have

At Montrose, Nancy Goodwin's selected red-violet form of *Verbena canadensis* gets along spectacularly well with geranium 'Ann Folkard'. ALLEN LACY

At a corner of the urn garden at Montrose, tradescantia 'Purple Heart' consorts beautifully with the nodding blue flowers of *Clematis integrifolia*, a nonvining species, and with its silvery and shaggy seed heads. ALLEN LACY

A splendid antique washpot filled with echevarias of unknown identity sits in front of a portion of Montrose's orange and purple border, with gaunt *Verbena bonariensis* at left. In the background are *Tradescantia pallida* 'Purple Heart', kniphofia 'Primrose Beauty', purple-bronze leafed canna 'Wyoming', and the swirling variegated green and yellow leaves of canna 'Pretoria'. ALLEN LACY

risen to my feet, except that I was already standing.) Two cultivars dominate here. One, a fairly recent introduction from India, goes around under two names, *Canna* X *generalis* 'Striata', and *C.* X *generalis* 'Pretoria'. Under either name, it is flamboyance personified. Its flower trusses are a rich orange but play second fiddle to the foliage, which is striped pale green and butter yellow in a swirling pattern that is dizzying to behold. The second canna is 'Wyoming'. Like 'Pretoria' (or whatever), it bears orange flowers, but, again, the foliage—a somber shade of bronzy purple—is the chief attraction. Separately handsome, these two cannas combine in one of those plant marriages that make the gods smile.

I cannot say what this garden's best season might be. In late June, when the air is filled with the scent of dill, the verbenas are in the full cry they will sustain over many months. *Zinnia angustifolia* has started to have its say, and the cannas that snake through the border in a sensuous curve are already head-high. The garden seems to

The purple and orange border
reaches its climax in October, when
purple gomphrenas and huge masses of
Zinnia angustifolia swell like great waves
of bloom beneath the tall cannas.
ALLEN LACY

have reached perfection. But more comes as the year unfolds. Yet to arrive is that day in October, in early morning, after a rainstorm the day before. In the first rays of the sun, the wooden gate above the orange-and-purple border and the lath house below it steam at the touch of heat. An enormous planting of tall ginger lilies (*Hedychium coronarium*) fills the air with the delicious sweetness of their flowers, which look like lovely, large white moths. And everywhere, on fences or trellises nearby, are lablab or hyacinth beans (*Lablab purpureus*, syn. *Dolichos lablab*), one of the loveliest of all autumn-blooming annual vines for its swags of smoky purple-toned foliage and its long clusters of wisterialike white and pale purple flowers.

This patch of earth teaches the lesson that gardening, like philosophy, has its dialectic, its interplay of contrasting and of similar colors, forms, and textures. It exemplifies to the utmost degree the principles of generous and imaginative planting, of density and depth and diversity. It soars into the upper tier of the space it occupies with its tall cleomes and cannas, and with even taller specimens of woody plants like purple smoke-bush and an elder with brightly variegated gold and green leaves. But it can soar because it is tethered to the ground, because the low plants that have been chosen to work with one another lend fullness to its lowest reaches.

Silvery Treasures for Sun

There are two rules about plants with gray or silver leaves. The first is that they thrive on heat and a sunny location, as they are prone to mildew and the mugs if planted in shade. The second is that they are the great peacemakers of the garden, ideal for separating colors that otherwise would clash. Crimson bee balms and scarlet crocosmias get on amicably if there's something gray in between. I suppose that it's theoretically possible for a garden to go overboard on gray or silver, but I've never seen one. Some plants with gray foliage are truly monumental, such as the formidably prickled biennial Scotch thistle (*Onopordum acanthium*) or plume poppy (*Macleaya cordata*), a thuggish perennial with olive-gray leaves backed by a cottony shade of white that shows off very prettily in a breeze. But others—two genera in particular, *Artemisia* and *Stachys*—prove to be useful groundcovers.

The artemisias are a rich and varied genus, running strongly to gray or silver foliage, although some species have leaves that are blue-green or just plain green. Among those with gray foliage, some call for great caution or even exclusion from the garden. Many people —and I am one—have planted 'Silver King', 'Silver Queen', and other cultivars of *Artemisia ludociviana* to their regret. It doesn't take long to discover the mistake. This species is a relentless colonizer, spreading large distances by underground runners in no time flat. It is pretty, and I have 'Silver Queen' growing in a barrel, safely confined and entirely admirable. But years ago I let it get loose in a border. I fear that I will never get rid of it and its bad manners, smothering anything in its path.

Artemisia schmidtiana 'Silver Mound' stays in a clump, a beautiful low tussock of ferny, finely dissected silver-gray foliage, but it is as sickly as a doomed heroine in a nineteenth-century sentimental potboiler. In the hot and humid summer weather that prevails in much of America, it will rot or die out at the center if you look at it hard. If one year someone were to give me a penny for every plant of 'Silver Mound' that died between June and late August, I'd start wondering what to call my yacht.

There remain some artemisias that pass muster, neither taking over the world nor whimpering into oblivion at the least provocation. 'Powis Castle', possibly a hybrid between *Artemisia arborescens* and *A. absinthium*, is a rather shrubby, clump-forming plant that grows anywhere from twenty to forty inches tall and can spread several feet in diameter. It looks good almost all year, even in Zone 6. Like many somewhat woody perennials, it plays out after a few summers, but it is easy to replace with new plants from cuttings. I also like 'Huntington', which is probably a cultivar of *A. absinthium*, the slightly hallucinogenic plant used to flavor the absinthe that damaged so many brains in late nineteenth-century France. On the West Coast, it can grow to four feet tall, a height that disqualifies it as a groundcover, but in my garden it stays under two feet high. The pale silver leaves are deeply cut, filigreed, and velvety to the touch. This artemisia is something of an exception to the rule about full sun. In mid-afternoon, it wilts when the summer sun beats down on it. It's happiest where it gets morning sun but very light shade the rest of the day. *Artemisia stelleriana* 'Silver Brocade', a welcome newcomer, is a slow spreader and a low grower, to only six inches or less. Its silver-white foliage makes a fine foil for small bulbs, such as purplish pink *Allium oreophilum*. My favorite artemisia is a mystery. It came from a nursery as *A. versicolor*. The name is invalid botanically, but it's the only one I've got. It is by no reasonable definition a groundcover, for it is so delicate of habit that smothering even a tiny

At upper right, artemesia 'Powis Castle' in the Price-Wythey garden in Seattle adds its silvery grace note to a dense composition whose other elements of harmony are pink hardy geraniums, a pale yellow hemerocallis, comfrey, and *Clematis X durandii*.

Marrubium rotundifolium and other of the ornamental horehounds are neat and tailored-looking, make a thick cover, and hold up well in winter.

weed would be quite beyond it. It is a spidery, skinny plant that looks like it was dreamed up by Giacometti. It grows about a foot tall and makes a neat little accent against a background of *Vinca minor*.

No other common name quite matches lamb's ears (*Stachys byzantina*), in aptness. The woolly gray leaves of this fine, mildly spreading groundcover for hot and sunny spots are so soft to the touch that it's highly likely that all children who are given one to rub against their cheeks will grow up to be gardeners. Increasing age, I can testify, does nothing to dim the sensual, well-nigh erotic appeal of this plant. I like its turreted spikes of tiny magenta flowers. Some people don't, but they have options. The cultivar 'Sheila Macqueen' produces spikes, sans flowers, and 'Silver Carpet' doesn't even bother with spikes. The problem with lamb's ears, like many plants with a downy texture that traps moisture, is that it may suffer unsightly meltdown from rot during hot, humid weather. Unless the plant rots out irretrievably, it will generally rejuvenate and produce fresh new leaves as nights begin to cool down and a hint of autumn is in the air. A new cultivar from Europe named 'Countess Pauline von Stein-Zeppelin' (for the woman who, since the 1920s, has owned a splendid perennial nursery near Munich) has a fine future. It romps all summer long, unsullied by muggy weather. It produces flower spikes, but not in great abundance. (Expect the full name of this plant to be abbreviated in various ways in nursery catalogs.)

There's one perennial with gray foliage that I wish I'd never planted—snow-in-summer (*Cerastium tomentosum*). This low creeper bears a huge crop of pretty little white flowers in late May and early June, and the attractive gray leaves persist through winter. Like most other things with gray foliage, it isn't fazed by drought. Unlike lamb's ears, snow-in-summer isn't subject to summer rot. Would that it were: its spreading power knows no bounds.

The Helpful Herbs

Gardens devoted entirely to herbs for culinary and other purposes have their merits, but there's no reason to restrict herbs to herb gardens like nuns in a cloistered convent. Here are a few to grow and love.

One of the catmints, *Calamintha nepeta*, sometimes sold as *C. nepetoides*, I discovered only recently, which was far too late. Like most herbs, it insists on perfect drainage and full sun. Its rounded little fresh green leaves smell deliciously of spearmint, although it is

a clump-former, not an underground marauder like mint. The leaves can be steeped in boiling water to make a refreshing tea. The plant grows eighteen inches tall and a foot across. From midsummer to frost, it produces a multitude of spikes of tiny white-looking flowers that, on closer examination, prove to be spotted with lavender. Planted in a mass, it lends a cool and airy note to the garden in late summer as other things flag and look weary. Every garden can use this calamint, and lots of it. It can be propagated very easily by dividing the clumps in spring or or by taking cuttings in the growing season. This herb combines especially well with *Dianthus*, or garden pinks. The two genera share similar cultural needs, and the calamints start blooming soon after most dianthus have stopped, as summer's heat arrives. The many species and cultivars of dianthus that have blue-gray or gray foliage provide interest in winter as well as during their season of bloom.

If I were to call a meeting to found The American Marrubium Society, I probably could hold it in a motel room, maybe a phone booth. But I'm getting passionate about the genus. *Marrubium* is simply horehound, so dear to the Smith Brothers of cough drop renown. There are several species, all of which can take rough to terrible winters and terrible to God-awful summers. *M. cylleneum* grows to about twelve inches tall and as much across, with yellow-green, soft, furry foliage. *M. incanum* has gray, slightly corrugated leaves that say "Touch me." *M. rotundifolium* bears light green leaves with deckled edges and woolly white undersides, but it tops off at under six inches. The flowers of all of these horehounds are so insignificant that it's possible to forget them while looking right at them. But they are sturdy, stubborn beasts with leaves that more than hold their own, even in winter.

I may be in the avant-garde of horehound-lovers, but many have come before me, including trillions of bees, in the sure knowledge that *Lavandula* is one of the nobler works of evolution. Lavenders in June are as indispensable as roses or clematis. The two most common cultivars of *Lavandula angustifolia* honor celebrated British gardens. The flowers of 'Hidcote' veer decidedly toward purple, those of 'Munstead' more towards violet. Both have gray foliage and deliciously aromatic spikes of flowers that are tremulous with bees in early summer. The reassuring, solid-sounding ring of their cultivar names is a delusion. Neither plant has been kept true to type in the general nursery trade; plants from one nursery can differ markedly from plants from another. I suppose it doesn't matter: lavender is lavender, a delight to the eye and nose alike, and even to the ear when those bees are at work. *L. angustifolia* 'Nana' is a dwarf form that has a prolonged season of bloom and grows to just twelve inches tall and wide. The slightly larger plant, *L. stoechas* var. *pedunculosa*, bears stubby spikes of purple flowers tipped with little bracts like the ears on a Mouseketeer cap. It is much less prone than most other lavenders to rot out in hot and humid summers. I also hear good things about *L.* X *intermedia*, but have not grown it yet. Full sun and perfect drainage are musts for all lavenders. I attribute a good record with them—I have yet to lose one in winter—to the sandy soil of the coastal plain where I garden. I have my eye on a sunny patch about ten by fifteen feet in the front garden, which thus far I've not gotten around to cramming full of plants. It's in front of a vitex tree, but gets practically no shade. It might make a fine spot for a miniature version of one of those lavender "lawns" that grow in Provence, but which turn out, on closer look, to be fields of lavender. The blue-violet spikes of the vitex, the gray of its marijuanalike leaves, the aromatic spice of the flowers on a hot August day, and the buzz of bees would echo the pleasures of the lavender that blooms in June.

Lemon balm (*Melissa officinalis*) is frankly something of a pest for the vigorous way it seeds itself about. I used to think its leaves had a bracing and refreshing scent of lemon zest that made up for its pushiness. "Smell again," Douglas Ruhren advised, "and see if you don't come up with formic acid." I smelled again. The memory instantly returned of the big, stinging red ants I grew up with in Texas. I do like the cultivar 'All Gold' for its bright color. This herb is one of the few that doesn't mind partial shade, although it's also happy in full sun.

The oreganos interest me almost as much as the marrubiums, and there are many that I haven't gotten around to growing yet. Like the lavenders, they revel in heat, perfect drainage, and slightly alkaline soil. Here are some I like: *Origanum laevigatum* 'Hopley's Purple' is a low creeper with eighteen-inch spikes of reddish purple flowers in summer. *O. libanoticum* (syn. *pulchellum*) is notable for its arching spikes of hoplike green bracts, from which little pink flowers peep out in midsummer. *O. vulgare* 'Aureum' is much more valuable for its bright green-gold foliage most of the year than for its modest flowers. In a sunny spot near my bog garden, it moved into a thriving patch of English ivy, pulled up its socks, and proceeded to form a solid round clump over two feet across, suppressing the ivy in a splendid show of cheekiness.

One native American herb that grows in my garden is shrouded in mystery. It is one of the Appalachian mountain mints, *Pycnan-themum flexuosum* (syn. *P. tenuifolium*), a sprawling, slowly spreading plant with narrow glossy leaves and a lax habit that gives it more than a passing resemblance to asparagus fern. The leaves have a peppermint scent when crushed. It bears abundant clusters of tiny pink flowers in late summer that look white from a distance. It is difficult to understand why this sun-loving, drought-tolerant native plant has been so neglected. And I haven't the faintest idea how it turned up in my garden. I thought I got it from Allen Bush's Holbrook Farm and Nursery. Then one day Allen paid a visit and asked what it was, and where I got it. My best theory, now that Allen has ruled himself out, is that elves brought it, planted it, and stuck the proper label in the ground.

As for the thymes, I just throw up my hands and say, "Well, for heaven's sake, there's got to be a whole lot of thymes in any proper sunny garden." Like scented pelargoniums and the multitudinous species of salvias, members of the genus *Thymus* are among the greatest olfactory mimics of the plant kingdom. There are thymes that smell like lemon, like caraway, and for all I know like chocolate or mothballs. Some thymes, content with their lot in life, just smell like thyme, not aping something else. Some thymes creep with glacial speed, in mats of truly tiny leaves that press themselves to the

No one who has ever seen the lavender "lawn" with its banksia roses on trellis hoops at Baroness de Waldner's home in the south of France can easily forget its simple but ravishingly seductive beauty.

surface of the soil with only slightly more vertical dimension than adhesive tape. Others make more billowing, flowing clumps, or manage to stand upright. Leaves can be gray-green with silvery margins, golden yellow, or just plain green. Flowers are generally in that lilac-lavender range between red and blue on the spectrum, although some are pink. I am firmly of several opinions about thymes. They smell wonderful. They smell especially wonderful on a hot day when they are trod on. Their names, from one nursery catalog to another, are mixed up almost beyond hope. And the very best of them, whose correct name is also in nomenclatural no-man's-land, is woolly thyme. It comes up every spring in the hottest, driest spot in my garden, in the cracks between some flagstones near our kitchen door. It gathers force; it fills the cracks with its tiny, deep gray, hairy leaves; it raises my hopes of an almost solid mass of woolly thyme to tread on, once it has passed the delicate stage. I tread not. It keeps spreading, raising my hopes to a higher level. Then, usually the third week of July, it succumbs to filthy rot. Only a few sprigs are left—just enough to gather force once again in the spring, to come and make me hopeful of what is probably never to be.

To continue with the theme of disappointment, there's rosemary. In the kitchen, it is my most beloved herb. Just one sprig can make a humdrum dish sing aloud. (Try it with new potatoes sliced in their jackets, a coating of an olive oil you can trust, and a crushed clove of garlic, all baked together for an hour or so in a slow oven, and you may conclude that atheism is an untenable position.) Rosemary is also a beautiful plant, particularly the prostrate forms that spill over walls. Their beautiful, slightly blue-gray leaves are almost hidden by small, crinkled flowers of Cambridge blue. I have thus seen it, with unconcealed envy, in Arizona. It's a bust for me in New Jersey. Hella and I nurse along some potted plants during the summer, clip sprigs for cooking, and bring them inside for the winter. Then they die, sprig by sprig, leaf by leaf. By January it's *Requiem aeternam, Rosmarinus officinalis*. One of my sons keeps his rosemary alive through the winter. "No trouble, Dad," he says.

Let us go on to more pleasant matters.

The Amiable Succulents

A sunny site, particularly for those of us who garden in light soils instead of heavy clay, usually translates into one that will naturally be dry in the absence of regular rainfall or irrigation. Such a garden

For people who associate oregano only with pizza, the very existence of such highly ornamental species as *Origanum libanoticum* comes as a pleasant discovery.

The purplish-pink metal lawn chairs underplanted with hardy geraniums and a carpet of aromatic woolly thyme lend a fine note of whimsy to the garden of Dr. Geof Beasley and Dr. Jim Sampson in Sherwood, Oregon.

environment puts a premium on plants without highly thirsty natures. Many such plants are herbs, in the horticultural, not the botanical, sense of the term—plants that are rich in aromatic oils, are used in cooking or in traditional medicine, and generally are native to areas with sparse to moderate annual rainfall and with well-drained soils. Others are grasses, although some grasses require ample moisture and some grasslike plants are semi-aquatic. A third group of plants that in general thrive in sun and on lean rations of water are the succulents—the ones that have thick, fleshy leaves (sometimes actually modified stems or other parts) that store moisture. Succulents are foot soldiers that carry their own canteens. The term refers to plants with similar characteristics, not to ones that are closely related genetically, since succulents are found in many different plant families.

The most commonly grown succulents are in the genera *Sedum* (from the Latin word meaning to sit, referring to the wall- or rock-perching proclivities of some species) or *Sempervivum* (meaning to live forever, notwithstanding the fact that once a leaf rosette of one of these plants blooms, it dies soon after, in a *Liebestod*).

I must, however, amend the first part of this claim: many succulents *were* in the genus *Sedum*. They are still so listed under that name in virtually every nursery catalog, but taxonomists crept in recently while our backs were turned and wielded their axes. They left over 300 species in the genus, but some of the most familiar garden "sedums" are now something else. The lovely October daphne, extremely elegant for its arching stems of blue-gray leaves and its clusters of pink flowers in late fall, used to be *S. sieboldii*. It is now *Hylotelephium sieboldii*. As for *S. spectabile*, whose cultivars include such garden favorites as 'Autumn Joy', 'Brilliant', and 'Meteor', it has also joined the genus *Hylotelephium*. I can steer clear of both this Scylla (many of the old botanical names are now invalid) and this Charybdis (the old names will still be used for some time to come) quite handily. The sedums I want to single out as groundcovers are still in their old, familiar genus.

I have heard people curse *Sedum acre*, the gold moss sedum or wallpepper, as a damnable pest, but I think they have it confused with *S. sarmentosum*, which is a thug of the first order. *S. acre*, the genuine article, is a low evergreen creeper, which is a bright shade of light green and barely lifts itself above the ground, except for its two-inch spikes of starry yellow flowers in late spring. It wanders far in sunny places, and it will grow from the merest sprig thrown on

The distinctive and immediately-recognizable foliage of *Sedum spathulifolium* is impossible to mistake for anything else.

When in flower, semper-
vivums bear an uncanny
resemblance to sea anemones
"blooming" on a coral reef far
below the waves.

This large sempervivum
spangled with dew at dawn
grows beautifully in Cynthia
Woodyard's garden.

bare earth—which means that once it is established, it might be difficult to eradicate, but it really doesn't matter, for this plant's modest needs for moisture and nutrients make it companionable and neighborly. This sedum is by no stretch of the imagination one of the stars of the garden. It's strictly a background plant through whose solid carpet more interesting plants can rise and then shine. In my sandy soil I have found it exceptionally serviceable in keeping down weeds, which, after all, is one of the main tasks that groundcovers perform.

Other good low sedums in this extremely rich genus include *S. brevifolium, S. nevii,* and *S. ternatum.* But I have a confession to make. Some years ago, I visited Porterhowse Nursery in Sandy, Oregon, where one of the chief specialties is sedums. I picked out over thirty that I liked and that the owners of the nursery recommended as groundcovers, most of them rare ones that few other nurseries offered. The nursery shipped them on to New Jersey. I planted all of them in a small raised bed, where I could study them close at hand. Usually I stick the labels of new plants right at their feet, so I can scratch around later, find the label, and identify what something is when memory doesn't work. But the sedums were little plants when I got them, and I thought that my usual practice would make it look like I had a collection not of plants, but of plastic labels. So, I made a map instead—and then lost it. Furthermore, I had forgotten that almost all of these plants were convivial spreaders and minglers. They spread and they mingled. Some no doubt died. A varied lot remains. Some have gray foliage, some green, and others are tinged with pink. Some bloom white, others yellow, and still others in shades of rose to light purple. I can tell you the name of precisely one, the Pacific Northwest native *Sedum spathulifolium,* because it is absolutely distinctive for its densely arranged leaves tinged with tones of both red and silver.

In regard to sedums, a note is in order for gardeners who live in the South: A good many species are grateful for at least partial shade, especially in the afternoon.

I also have a lot of different species and cultivars of *Sempervivum,* and I don't know their names, either. I can live with a little ambiguity in the garden, but in this case, I don't take all the blame for the members of Sempervivums Anonymous on the premises. Before sedum-lust hit me at Porterhowse, I went through a sempervivum craze, ordering ten from one nursery, ten from another, and twenty from another, carefully making sure that no name duplicated an-

other. When the orders came, I found that in a remarkable number of cases I had the same plant under three different names. The conclusion was obvious. The cultivar names in this genus were hopelessly screwed up, so to forget the names and just enjoy the plants was the sanest counsel.

Enjoy them I have done, for they are wonderful. They are prime plants to give children to lure them into an interest in gardening, because of the perfect aptness of one of their many common names, hen-and-chicks. Plant just one rosette of leaves in a pot or in the earth, and soon there are other little rosettes peeking out from under the mother plant, just like scared baby chicks under a mother hen's wing. The chicks in their turn become hens, producing other chicks, and soon the flock is large enough to interest Mr. Purdue.

Sempervivums are also splendid because of their enormous diversity, all variations on a common theme. Some are smooth, others are cobwebby. Some have rosettes six inches or more across, others are the size of marbles. Some are open like a rose in its fullness of bloom, others are as tightly balled as a roly-poly. Colors can be green, russet, gray, or slightly bluish. And they bloom at different times during the growing season, depending on the kind. Sempervivums produce trailing to upright stems topped by clusters of star-shaped flowers that usually are a dusty shade of rose, although they can also be yellow, purple, or white. These plants are, moreover, tough. I have several planted in shallow clay bonsai dishes on our deck, exposed to the worst that winter can offer. Not one has ever died from cold.

Anyone who plants hens-and-chicks is also planting a hefty slice of ancient medical lore, mythology, and history, hidden in some of the alternative common names for the genus, such as healing blade, Jupiter's eye, and thunder plant. Juice extracted by crushing the fleshy leaves was once held in high regard for healing burns, warts, and insect bites. Greco-Roman and Teutonic mythology alike held that such sky-gods as Jupiter and Thor exercised restraint in hurling bolts of lighting to the earth, where these plants grew, and this belief was adopted in Christian lore as well. Charlemagne had his subjects plant one species, *Sempervivum tectorum* (*tectorum* means "of roofs"), on their houses as safeguards against lightning, which explains another common name, houseleek.

I haven't explored another rosette-forming succulent genus, *Echevaria*, although I have enjoyed seeing its plump clusters of leaves (in some species they are a pleasing shade of blue-gray) in the gardens of friends. But I have grown *Orostachys furusei* ever since I first admired it in 1984 in Fred Meyer's garden in Columbus, Ohio. It eventually spreads to form a solid carpet of gray foliage. More recent acquisitions are *O. aggregata*, with chartreuse foliage, and *O. erubescens*, whose leaf tips are touched with a russet that changes to a franker red in the autumn. All three species hail from fairly cold climates in Japan, China, or Korea, and they put up strange, pagodalike spikes of flowers late in the year. Once a rosette flowers, it dies, just like hens-and-chicks, but again, plenty of younger rosettes are left to keep the plant going.

Most of the succulent plants in several genera that commonly are lumped together under the name "ice plant" are best left to gardeners in southern California and other places where winter has little meaning. Exceptions are two species of *Delosperma* (a genus that is fairly new in the nursery trade), which are surprisingly hardy, considering their South African origin. *D. cooperi* is a summer bloomer, with purple flowers, as I have already mentioned; *D. nubigenum* has yellow flowers in late spring. Both will eventually spread, but not aggressively.

Unfussy Cranesbills

The many species and cultivars of hardy *Geranium*, or cranesbill, are increasingly popular among American gardeners, so much so that people are beginning to understand that the tender "geraniums" (pelargoniums) sold by the millions in spring are really imposters. Hardy geraniums are frustrating to tidy minds who want plants to fall into clear-cut categories. *Geranium incanum* insists on full sun, but this South African species is winter-hardy only in Zones 9 and 10. *G. phaeum* is unhappy except in moist shade. But other cranesbills aren't fussy and grow equally well in full sun or partial shade—except that in the South the balance tips toward shade. I put them all here, as sun-loving plants that make good groundcovers, only because I have to put them somewhere.

I have some favorites. *Geranium* X 'Biokova' bears pink-toed white flowers abundantly in early summer, above low mounds of pleasantly aromatic foliage that stays handsome after the blooms cease. *G.* X 'Claridge Druce', which sprawls sufficiently to deter most weeds in its vicinity, bears pink flowers with darker veins over a five-week period in early summer. 'Johnson's Blue' has violet-blue flowers that appear sporadically over a season that stretches a full ten weeks. *G. macrorrhizum* 'Ingwersen's Variety', sometimes sold as 'Walter Ingwersen', has foliage with a scent reminiscent of Pinesol, pink flowers in late spring, a happy tendency to rebloom in the summer, and gorgeous red-orange leaf color in the fall and early winter. It is a premier groundcover for rather dry, shady, steep slopes. If I could grow only one plant in this genus, it would be *G. sanguineum*, the bloody cranesbill, which bears white or rose-purple flowers, depending on the cultivar, all summer long. It has the added value of stunning scarlet foliage in the fall. And I must mention 'Ann Folkard' again for its intensity of color and its chartreuse foliage.

Hemerocallis as Groundcovers?

Any discussion of daylilies, or hemerocallis, as groundcovers must be posed as a question, not an assertion, for several reasons. One is that my friends in the American Hemerocallis Society would blanch at the suggestion that daylilies are groundcovers, regarding it as an insult to a genus very dear to their hearts. Another is that the height of most daylilies in flower—usually between two and three feet tall —clearly puts them in a different category than, say, *Vinca minor*. A third is that most of the daylilies that are grown primarily for the beauty of their flowers in midsummer are woeful sights once they have finished blooming, unless one takes certain stern measures (to be explained momentarily).

But one species of hemerocallis is indisputably a groundcover, and a powerful one at suppressing weeds or any other plants in its path —*Hemerocallis fulva*, the tawny daylily. This highly stoloniferous Asian perennial with evergreen tendencies will eventually spread from here to kingdom come. It will grow in full sun or in fairly dense shade. It will take possession of a slope or a bank, keeping down erosion. Its muddy, pale orange flowers are unattractive, although those of the double cultivar 'Kwanso' are passable, even if liable to clash with anything else blooming nearby. But the scapes can be removed when they first appear, leaving a serviceable groundcover through much of the year.

About the fancy modern cultivars, virtually all of which are clump-formers rather than spreaders, I'm not so sure. Their mounds of fresh green foliage are handsome when they appear in the spring, and the leaves grow vigorously enough to suppress weeds. The blooms are often wonderful. Professional and amateur hybridizers in America, especially since the end of World War II, have given us a new race of garden perennials. The color range is vast, excluding only a real white and anything that could honestly be called blue, or even in the vestibule of blue. Breeders have given us immense blossoms, tiny ones, and everything in between. The petal edges are often as flounced as a 1950s petticoat. But, once blooming has ceased, a daylily patch is a sorry sight. The spent scapes turn brown and ugly. The foliage, in the hot and often dry weather that comes in late July and August, looks like something discarded in the alley from the produce department of a supermarket. There is, however, a remedy: Rev up the power mower. Attack the clumps of tired-looking daylilies, and chop them almost to the ground. (The old foliage can be left where it is, as a mulch, or it can be hauled off to the compost bin.) Water deeply, and then apply a liquid fertilizer low in nitrogen and potassium, but high in phosphorus. (I use one with an NPK ratio of 8-58-9.)

Over 30,000 daylily cultivars have been registered by the American Hemerocallis Society, and hundreds are sold commercially. Daylilies fall roughly into two categories: those that go dormant in the winter, and those with persistent evergreen or semi-evergreen foliage. The former are best suited for the colder regions of the country, the latter for the Deep South, Florida, and southern California. My current preference is for cultivars with small flowers. 'Corky' is a fine tiny-flowered form with many yellow blossoms on fairly tall and wiry stems. 'Pardon Me' is a splendid little red with a tailored look. 'Peach Fairy', a well-branched pink with slightly ruffled petals, is extremely elegant. I like almost everything I've seen that was hybridized by Pauline Henry of Arkansas, each of which has 'Siloam' as the first word in its name.

Carpeting Perennials that Flower

The thymes, the marrubiums, the delospermas, and several other of the sun-loving plants discussed thus far form mats or have a spreading, carpeting habit. This habit of growth is also typical of several spring-blooming plants commonly found in rock gardens whose owners see no reason to reject a plant just because it's often grown, and not the latest rare and difficult alpine to arrive from Nepal. These spring bloomers with low and spreading ways have their uses, even if the danger in relying on them too heavily is that once spring departs they leave behind little of interest in the garden during the rest of the growing season.

Five of them—*Aethionema, Arabis, Aubrieta, Erysimum,* and *Iberis*—are crucifers, or members of the mustard family.

The first is the least familiar member of this quintet. *Aethionema grandiflorum,* whose common names are stone cress and Persian candytuft, goes unmentioned in several standard books on rock gardening, although Elizabeth Lawrence gives it somewhat iffy praise in *A Rock Garden in the South.* Its habit of growth is far from dense, and I would not rely on it to keep down weeds. But I grow it in a narrow patch next to the front sidewalk, in a spot where blue leadwort, the sleepyhead groundcover that doesn't show itself until well into May, can take over. The narrow, blue-green leaves of Persian candytuft are handsome all winter, and the clusters of soft rose flowers from late April into May are pretty and faintly fragrant. The plant grows less than six inches tall for me, but might be somewhat more muscular in the limy soil it prefers. It is short-lived, but self-seeds freely, and the beige and brown seed heads, larger than the flowers and more widely spread, are themselves quite lovely when backlit by early morning light.

Arabis, or rock cress, is a modest spreader, happy in full sun to partial shade, and resistant to drought. The range of color in various species and cultivars extends from white to purplish pink. The forms with somewhat downy foliage are susceptible to summer dieback and rot in hot, humid weather. Better bets are *A. procurrens,* which grows about two inches high and spreads to ten inches or so, and the slightly larger species *A. sturrii.* Both sport clusters of white flowers in early spring and bear glossy green leaves that take summer humidity well. These are two variegated forms, also with white flowers. *A. caucasica* 'Variegata' has green leaves edged in cream; *A. ferdinandi-coburgi* 'Variegata' bears cream-colored leaves with green centers. Both of these culivars may revert to plain green and are short-lived.

The number of cultivars and seed-grown strains of *Aubrieta* X *cultorum* is almost boundless, in a rainbow of colors embracing white, ivory, pink, carmine, mauve, violet, and brilliant purple. The abundant flowers of this early spring bloomer almost conceal the foliage. Easy and undemanding in its cultural requirements, it is marvelous planted above a retaining wall, where it can cascade down in a torrent of bright flowers and where it is assured the perfect drainage it needs to do its best.

The genus *Erysimum,* whose name goes back to the ancient Greeks and derives from a word denoting the blister-causing qualities of

some species, is far-flung throughout the Northern Hemisphere. In England, a wealth of cultivars and strains of complex hybrid origins is available. Many are fragrant, their growth habit varies from low and spreading to tall, and flower colors include cream, yellow, orange, red, and mauve. Only a few of the British cultivars have reached the United States thus far, but they are so exquisite that they whet the appetite for more. 'Wenlock Beauty' is primarily a spring bloomer that grows slightly over a foot high and will spread three feet. Drought-tolerant and sun-loving, it has yellow flowers that age to purple to create a beautiful two-toned effect. 'Jubilee Gold' reaches a height of under six inches, spreads to twelve, and bears very fragrant lemon-yellow flowers over a long season, starting in spring. 'E. A. Bowles', a much larger cultivar that in a couple of seasons will become a shrubby plant twenty inches tall and well over thirty inches across, is virtually indispensable. It grows thickly from its base, without even a hint of a bare ankle. The soft bluish gray leaves persist throughout the winter. I have seen this plant described in a couple of British gardening books as a winter and spring bloomer, but it blooms almost perpetually in my garden. It slackens off in the dead of winter, but a few moderate days during a January thaw bring it back into fragrant bloom. 'E. A. Bowles' is sterile and must be propagated by cuttings. To guard against occasional winter losses, it is wise to root a few small plants and keep them in a cold frame.

The blue-gray foliage of sea kale combines handsomely with the chartreuse leaves of geranium 'Ann Folkard' in the imaginative garden of Susan Ryley in Victoria, British Columbia.

The last of the spring crucifers is *Iberis sempervirens*, or perennial candytuft. An evergreen, somewhat shrubby, spreading plant, it grows to ten inches tall and covers itself in early spring with a multitude of dazzling white flower clusters. It blooms at the same time as grape hyacinths. A few of these bulbs tucked into a planting of candytuft make the winter-weary eye rejoice. The cultivars 'Autumn Snow' and 'Alexander's White' are worth looking for because they sometimes rebloom in the fall.

The native spring phlox from a woodland habitat are more logical to discuss as plants for shade, but the evergreen or semi-evergreen species—*Phlox subulata*, or thrift—is a real toughie for sunny spots. It is commonly planted in places where few other plants will survive, such as on roadside banks near farmhouses. The colors can sometimes be violent—hot pinks and electric magentas that pain the eye individually and look even worse when they consort with each other. But 'Blue Hill' (two tones of blue), 'Snowflake', and 'Scarlet Flame' are beautiful, not hurtful to delicate sensibilities. The noted American authority on rock gardening, H. Lincoln Foster, produced several hybrids of *P. subulata* with other species that are remarkable. 'Laura', a soft pink named for Foster's granddaughter, was pollinated by a bee, so the other parent isn't known. 'Millstream', a deep rose, was named for the home in Connecticut where Foster lived with his wife, Laura Louise Foster, in a gorgeous woodland garden dominated by a huge mountain stream rushing down its steep, boulder-strewn course.

Late spring sees for a week or so the abundant bloom of semi-evergreen *Saponaria ocymoides*, or rock soapwort, which covers itself in bright pink flowers. There is also a much less common white form. Both the Latin genus name and the common English name refer to a peculiar trait of its foliage. John Gerard described it in the 1633 edition of *The Herball:* "It is commonly called *Saponaria*, of the great scouring qualitie that the leaves have: for they yeeld out of themselves a certain iuyce when they are bruised, which scoureth almost as well as Sope." *S. officinalis*, or bouncing bet, is a European plant that escaped early from American gardens to roadsides, which is where it belongs. Its pale pink flowers are rather pretty, and the plant blooms for a very long period starting in midsummer. But it is invasive, and it seeds everywhere in a troublesome way. The sterile form 'Rosea Plena' is a sprawling plant that can cover a lot of territory by runners, but I haven't found it a menace. It blooms freely over a long period, and the rather tousled double pink flowers

In the garden of Janette Waltemath in Portland, Oregon, spring is bright with aubrietas, *Alyssum saxatile*, *Phlox subulata*, a rivulet of tiny sedums, and *Euphorbia polychroma*.

have a sweet and spicy scent of cloves that travels far on the warm afternoon air. A new cultivar of soapwort, 'Max Frei', blooms its head off in midsummer on a spreading mat of foliage that gets only six inches tall.

The low, herbaceous potentillas do not make quite the long-blooming splash in the garden that their woody cousins do, but they have a charming modesty and blend in nicely in a planting of mixed groundcovers characterized by no obvious plan of doing one another in. *Potentilla tabernaemontana* (syn. *P. verna*) is a slowly spreading species with bright yellow flowers in the spring. *P. tridentata* is evergreen in coastal New Jersey. It produces a flush of white, strawberrylike flowers in early summer, but blooms sporadically throughout the rest of the year. I have found a flower or two on it on Christmas Day.

The long season of veronicas, or speedwells, begins in my garden in mid-April with 'Waterperry Blue', a very low, somewhat weaving plant with bronzy leaves and purple-blue flowers. I would never have recognized it as a veronica unless a friend had not so identified it. Most veronicas bear their flowers in spikes; this one has nothing spiky about it, and the little blossoms look somewhat like forget-me-nots. It's not an especially lusty grower, and I wouldn't hold my breath waiting for it to suppress a weed. The spring veronicas continue with *Veronica prostrata* (syn. *rupestris*), which bears tiny, deep blue flowers on low, spreading mats of small leaves. *V. prostrata* 'Trehane' offers bright chartreuse leaves in addition to blue flowers. Summer belongs to the much taller veronicas, stalwarts of the herbaceous border for their marathon season of bloom right up through frost. But there's a fine new one that grows under a foot tall and works well as a groundcover if several plants are set together on tight centers. It is a champion bloomer from early summer well into autumn, producing spikes of dark blue flowers. It's called 'Goodness Grows', after the nursery in Georgia that introduced it.

Too often neglected is a little Siberian and East Asian spring perennial with strawberrylike leaves, *Waldsteinia ternata*, whose yellow flowers are like those of potentillas in the spring. This is a fine carpeter, making a thick, evergreen mat that is effective in suppressing weeds. It is so untemperamental that it's almost a Pollyanna. Dry sun suits it fine, but so does shade, as long as the ground isn't soggy. Speaking of strawberries, an import from England to America in the early 1990s was *Fragaria* X *frel* 'Pink Panda', reputedly a bigeneric cross between a strawberry and a potentilla. It yields dark pink inch-wide flowers sporadically all summer, and spreads by plantlets on runners. Its fruits are edible, but insipid. It has the somewhat untidy spreading habit of most strawberries, and I find that its best use is in a large strawberry jar, where only a few of its plantlets are allowed to gain a toehold in the earth beneath. One true strawberry, with no mixed genes from another genus, is *Fragaria vesca* 'Variegata', which makes a beautiful and well-behaved groundcover. Its lovely green leaves are splashed with white, in a feathery pattern that calls to mind the frost flowers on windowpanes on frigid winter days. It, however, will burn in full sun and needs at least partial shade.

A warning is in order about *Duchesnea indica*, the false strawberry. It is a strawberry stand-in in almost every respect, save that its little flowers are yellow and its berries are inedible. It will grow in either sun or partial shade, and like its namesake, it spreads by plantlets on runners. Barry Yinger calls it "a horrible, vicious weed that I've been trying to kill for years." Douglas Ruhren says he's spent most of his life weeding it out, and that given a choice, he'd rather plant chickweed.

The Mossy Look

Unlike many people who regard finding moss in their gardens the same way teenagers regard finding a new zit on their complexions, I love moss. I would like to have a lawn of moss. I would love to live in a stucco house with a roof of terra cotta tiles laden with moss. It follows naturally that I also like some perennial groundcovers that have a mossy visual texture. They look wonderful growing around a half-submerged boulder in a sunny garden or filling in the cracks between flagstones in a path. Three of the best of these mossy plants are all "worts" (and don't ask me why some plants do and some do not fall into this category, as I've never figured it out). Sandwort (*Arenaria balearica*) gets no higher than one inch and has abundant white flowers in June. *A. verna* 'Aurea' also blooms white, but its foliage is chartreuse. Rupturewort or burstwort (*Herniaria glabra*) is evergreen, and a good spreader. It forms a dense mat only an inch tall, if that. Its spread is glacial—only a few inches each year—so a good many plants need to be planted together for effective use as a groundcover. Pearlwort (*Sagina subulata*), an evergreen creeper with many white flowers in midsummer, is especially fine between flagstones. *S. subulata* 'Aurea' shows off soft golden yellow foliage.

The bad news about all of these delicate-looking plants is that they *are* delicate, and subject to fungal disease and die-out in hot, humid weather.

Grasses and Sedges

From Victorian times well into the twentieth century, ornamental grasses enjoyed an enormous vogue in the United States, particularly in gardens on large estates of the wealthy. Their popularity faded right after World War I, but in the 1980s they again held great appeal, even for homeowners with small gardens. Ornamental grasses lend a sense of movement to the garden, and many of them are of interest even during the winter if they are left standing instead of being chopped back during fall cleanup. By no stretch of the imagination could the giant reed, *Arundo donax*, or other very tall grasses, such as most forms of *Miscanthus*, qualify as groundcovers, but some genera and species are useful for the purpose—or, even better, as accents punctuating other groundcovers.

As with ferns for the shady garden, so with grasses for the sunny one. That is, ferns in general like shade, but a few species prefer sun. Grasses in general prefer open, sunny spots, but some like the protection of partial shade. The beautiful *Carex elata* 'Aurea' or Bowles' golden sedge lights up the partially shady, moist corners where it is happiest. The equally lovely *Hakonechloa macra* 'Aureola' also wants partial shade and a bit of moisture. Its golden variegated leaves, all pointing in the same direction as if they were being raked by a strong and steady wind, stand out from afar.

For accents amidst other plants in sunny spots, here are a few good ones:

Among the carexes, I like several. *Carex morrowii* 'Aureovariegata' is indispensable. It stays in a neat clump about twelve by twelve inches, and it looks good all year round for its green and yellow foliage. *C. buchananii* takes some getting used to, as its bronzed foliage gives the impression that it is dead. But I have killed it a couple of times by accident, so I know that this plant looks entirely different when it is quick than when it is dead. It combines well with black elephant ears and gold variegated *Vinca minor*. And there's another sedge I'm eager to try—*C. texensis*, the Catlin sedge. It is still difficult to obtain, but it may be a plant with a bright future. John Greenlee points out in *The Encyclopedia of Ornamental Grasses* (1992) that this low evergreen tolerates sun or shade and very moist

Clematis montana, erysimum 'Bowles Mauve', and ophiopogon together hide a stump left by Hurricane Hugo in Genie White's garden in Charlotte, North Carolina.

to fairly dry soils, and is tough. It takes foot traffic sufficiently well to make a fine substitute for turf grasses between flagstones or even in paths. Since it grows only to four inches, it needs no mowing.

Arrhenatherum elatius bulbosum 'Variegatum', or bulbous oat grass, is quite a mouthful, but this soft green-and-white variegated grass under ten inches tall is a beauty. It tends to go dormant in summer, when it should be sheared back, but it returns with fresh new growth in the fall. The foliage partly hides the fantastic little twisted towers, which bear tubers that can be planted to get new plants.

I was never really happy with any of the cultivars of blue fescue, or *Festuca glauca*, until I saw one called 'Elijah Blue', a name that puzzled me. Cher, I believe, may have a son burdened with that name, but it seemed unlikely that he might have been immortalized by having a fescue named for him. Lois Woodhull provided the answer. This splendid grass originated at The Plantage, her admirable nursery near Cutchogue, Long Island. The nursery is on Elijah Road. 'Elijah Blue' is a fine steely color. It likes dry soil and full sun (partial shade in the South), and it combines beautifully with lamb's

At Dumbarton Oaks in the District of Columbia, concrete, pebbles, a shallow sheet of water, and thyme combine most handsomely.

ears. Another good blue one is *Helictotrichon sempervirens*, or blue oat grass. At twenty inches, it's twice the size of 'Elijah Blue'. Tufts of blue-green leaves with evergreen leanings make this clumping grass a steady performer most of the year, but it performs weakly where summers are long, hot, and humid.

Despite its comparatively small stature of under twenty inches, *Imperata cyclindrica* 'Rubna', or Japanese blood grass, is one of the most dramatic of all ornamental grasses. It starts off in the spring with green blades tipped in sienna red, but as the growing season progresses, the red travels down the foliage and intensifies to a glowering shade of cranberry. Planted where the late afternoon sun can shine through it, it is as vivid as stained glass. Japanese blood grass likes sun and a fairly moist soil.

Dwarf fountain grass, *Pennisetum alopecuroides* 'Hameln', forms a low mounded clump about eighteen by eighteen inches that remains quite striking in winter. Its blooms in midsummer are followed by graceful plumes of seeds. It thrives on sun, and takes dry, poor soil in its stride. I have seen this grass used brilliantly at Wave Hill in the monocot border, where it ties to the earth a splendid combination of tall cannas, miscanthus grass, elephant ears, and garden asparagus.

For Annual Groundcovers, A Place in the Sun

It's easy, as we gardeners begin to get a little experience under our belts, to feel contemptuous of annual herbaceous plants—those that are sold every spring by the billions in garden centers and even on sidewalks in front of grocery stores. There is surely a surfeit of blazing red salvias and hot-looking marigolds in the land. These often end up planted together in what might be called the gas station school of landscape design, except that this artless style also shows itself in many suburban front yards. I used to like petunias, but now I am bored by their ubiquity. The neighborhood bar down the street has planted the same red petunias—'Comanche', I think—in its planter boxes out front for twenty years in a row.

Having said this, I must say that any garden in which flowering plants are a primary focus is impoverished if annuals are excluded for pure snootiness. I have already pointed out the good uses of gomphrenas and *Zinnia angustifolia* in a carefully wrought garden that mixes these and other annuals with perennials, bulbs, and some woody plants. The great value of many flowering annuals is that they flower unstintingly throughout the growing season. Together with those plants whose major contribution lies in their foliage, they provide a continuity that some very popular perennials cannot give. Iris quickly come and go. Most daylily cultivars bloom for two, maybe three weeks at best. The blossoming of *Angelica gigas*, with its globes of deep plum flowers on immense bold plants, is something to look forward to and then to remember, but it is strictly a brief feast in early August. But the bloom of marigolds and red bedding salvias that begins in spring, when they are still in their market packs at a garden center, will still be abundant in late September, right up to the first serious frost.

It is a mistake to scorn what is common merely because it is common. I have no statistics to back me up, but my hunch is that the hybrid forms of *Impatiens wallerana* that have been around only since the early 1950s help pay the bills at many a garden center. These are shade-loving plants, not really suitable for the sunny garden, but they make a point. They bring a continuous flood of color to shady spots from the last frost in the spring to the first frost in the fall, enlivening the place they occupy. Bred to stay low, in mounds that seldom exceed fifteen inches in height, they do not know how to stop blooming. Planted about twelve inches apart in a solid group, they quickly fill in to become an effective groundcover that does a good job of suppressing weeds.

For sunny places, annual periwinkles, or vincas (no longer *Vinca rosea* but now *Catharanthus roseus*), are the equivalents of impatiens. These annuals, which in recent breeding programs actually involve more than one species of a tender tropical perennial native to Madagascar, are workhorses. Their glossy foliage is extremely handsome. They tolerate drought and blazing temperatures without wilting. They are strangers to disease. No insects will nibble on them; even deer won't touch them. (For good reason: the plants are loaded with toxic alkaloids used in two drugs employed in certain programs of chemotherapy.) Their white, pink, or lilac flowers, with red eyes in some strains, keep coming and coming once the days get hot. They don't have to be deadheaded, either to encourage continuous bloom or to remove ugly spent flowers; unlike petunias, periwinkles are tidy plants. In the late 1980s, new strains began to appear, offering even more abundant bloom and larger blossoms. The appearance of the Tropicana series, introduced by Park Seeds, foretells further improvements, including colors not previously seen in periwinkles. (I have a hunch that a true red is in the offing.)

California poppies and violas, Napa, California.

Impressive changes have also been made to an old-fashioned annual, portulaca, which my people in Texas when I was growing up called moss rose. In my childhood, it was available only in mixed colors—a dazzling assortment excluding only blue. The flowers were single. By noon, those that had opened at dawn had closed shop and turned to mush. Now the flowers are usually double, they come in an array of individual colors, and they hold up until four o'clock on a hot, sunny day, and even later if it is cool or overcast. This succulent annual is as tough and as drought resistant as its close kin, the purslane, which is a vicious summer weed.

Nothing much seems to have happened to sweet alyssum (*Lobularia maritima*) during my lifetime, and that's okay, for it's fine just as it is. There are strains with pinkish purple or violet-purple flowers, but I prefer the plain white form. It grows no taller than six inches, if that, and a tiny seedling quickly spreads to make a mat a foot across. Its bloom period continues well past the first black freeze. It is an extremely generous bloomer, producing so many clusters of pure white flowers at a time that from a distance it looks like a little snowdrift. It makes a trim edging for flower beds, and it is stunning with dark blue annual lobelias. I love to combine it with *Salvia coccinea*, a red sage from Texas whose small blossoms have all the grace that is so conspicuously absent in the clunky annual bedding salvias. This native annual salvia rises about eighteen inches above the froth of white alyssum at its feet, with winsome results.

Nasturtiums are another old-fashioned annual that serves well as a groundcover. They are too much neglected nowadays, I fear, because they won't bloom in a market pack and because they are resentful of transplanting. For anyone who has ever visited Claude Monet's garden at Giverny, or even seen photographs, these agreeably spicy and quite edible annuals summon up a vision of them spilling in a riot of leaves and bright red, orange, or yellow flowers onto a wide gravel path. I have no hesitation in proclaiming one strain of nasturtium to be the best. It is 'Empress of India', sold by Shepherd's Seeds. The flowers are brilliant vermillion, set off by blue-green leaves of surpassing beauty.

There are many splendid annuals—cosmos, four o'clocks, nicotianas, calliopsis, nigellas, and so on down a long list. But for shade, impatiens seems the annual best suited to serve as a groundcover in shade, and periwinkles, portulacas, and nasturtiums, in full sun.

Cactus and other succulents, Huntington Botanical Garden.

Japanese blood grass (*Imperata cylindrica* 'Rubra') at Greenlee Nursery, Pomona, California.

Like a scene from "Madame Butterfly," new-fallen cherry-blossom petals strew a walkway lined with ferns, hostas, and *Helleborus orientalis*, the Lenten rose, in the garden of Hannah Withers in Charlotte, North Carolina.

3 Herbaceous Groundcovers for Shady Gardens

If there's a problem with gardening in shade, it lies not in shade itself, but in the attitude of people who regard it as an obstacle, a handicap—a problem, in short. Shade becomes something negative that must somehow be overcome, because we make mental lists of all the plants that require full sun or almost full sun to thrive, and then we concentrate on the fact that we cannot grow them in the shady parts of our gardens, or grow them at all if our gardens are entirely shady. We have shade, so there go the evening primroses, the portulacas, the roses, the rudbeckias, and many other beautiful flowering plants. We feel deprived. I've never been a disciple of Dr. Norman Vincent Peale, being more inclined since my twenties to Miguel de Unamuno's "tragic sense of life" than to the confectionary optimism of the prophets of cheer. But we gardeners often let negativity get the best of us. If we live in New Orleans, we sigh for the peonies that geography and climate deny us. If we live in Massachusetts, we curse our fate in not being able to grow hedges of oleander or gardenias. We forget that the first rule of gardening is that all of us must garden where we are, not in some other place, whether that be on the Gulf Coast, in New England—or in the shade.

The most unpalatable fact about gardening in shade is simple. Flowering plants in shady sites, where the shade comes from deciduous trees, are largely spring bloomers. The life cycle of these plants demands that they finish their flowering season before the canopy of foliage overhead has become dense enough to reduce severely the amount of sunlight reaching the forest floor. Hence, most plants for shady locations are woodland plants—violets, hepaticas, tiarellas, and all the rest—that flower in the spring.

There are a few exceptions, of course. Some plants thrive in partial shade but bloom in the summer or the fall, including *Kirengeshoma palmata*, *Salvia koyamae*, *Tricyrtis hirta*, *Cyclamen hederifolium*, *Adenophora liliafolia*, and the myriad species and cultivars of the genus *Hosta*. People who garden in shade will seize on them and anything like them, for flowers after spring has passed.

But the case of hostas is instructive. Except for *Hosta plantaginea*, whose spikes of fragrant white flowers in late summer are beautiful enough to give it the common name August lily, the flowers of hosta are at best a bonus. Some people dislike them, removing the scapes as soon as they appear. It is their foliage, whether plain green or richly variegated, that gives hostas enormous value in shade. The lesson is that gardening in shade places a premium on foliage—its colors, forms, and textures. We must look to the wild gingers, arums, elephant ears, fancy-leafed caladiums, ferns, and similar herbaceous plants as indispensable elements in the shaded garden. We may even take into our hearts the mosses, which we once cursed when they began to invade our lawns as trees grew larger each year, casting more shade and sucking more nutrients from the soil. (Certainly, once we've seen it, we will make every effort to acquire the miraculous peacock club moss, *Selaginella unciata*, which grows in dense shade in a solid sheet on the ground, with turquoise, iridescent foliage. It isn't, however, a plant for the north.)

Shade is not an absolute, not just one kind of thing. It is a continuum that starts with places in a garden that get a couple of hours of sunlight in the early morning or in late afternoon but are shaded the rest of the day. It goes on to include spots that are in dappled shade all day long during most of the growing season. It ends with the heavy gloom beneath mature spruces or other large conifers, with the Stygian darkness below a ninety-foot southern magnolia, and with other deep-dim places where little will grow except fungi. Furthermore, shade and the plants that will grow in it are both qualified by geography. I can grow, in full sun in coastal New Jersey, plants that in the Piedmont of North Carolina would require summer protection in a lath house to thrive, perhaps even to survive.

Shade is not a problem. It is an opportunity—an opportunity to explore a wide variety of plants we might otherwise not have known or grown: Asian wild gingers, painted ferns, Japanese toad lilies, and that peacock club moss, to name a few. It is also an opportunity to enjoy our gardens. You can *work* with pleasure in a shady garden on blast-furnace days in July when working in a sunny one would be torture, like vacationing on Devil's Island.

I write as a Southerner, albeit one who by now has spent almost half his life in the Northeast. I know about heat, about screen porches, electric fans, enormous pitchers of iced tea. I know about canvas window awnings that went up in early May, just as the wool rugs were hauled up to the attic. I know the joys of seeking out the shade of pecan trees in July while listening to the katydids rasping in the distance and watching the heat shimmering in a watery mirage above paved roads where the tar melted by ten o'clock in the morning. I know that shade is a benediction, not a curse. I also know that in August it can get hotter than Satan's pitchfork, even in New Jersey, and that on a day like that, there is relief among ferns and hostas in a garden protected from the direct rays of the sun.

Shade is increasingly part of the conditions under which Americans gardens, for two reasons.

First, although agricultural land is still being cleared—as former potato fields become subdivisions with new crops of mansionettes and faux chateaux, all in the blazing summer sun for years to come —there are new patterns of suburban development. Real estate developers with woodland properties are resorting less to wholesale clearing with bulldozers, instead leaving as many trees as possible. The purchasers of new homes on such land move in to ready-made shade. If they have ambitions of gardening, they will quickly learn what will grow well on their shaded plots and what will not.

Second, as a garden matures, it grows shadier, even if it started out with the sun beating down on every part of it. As saplings that didn't look like much when they were first planted mature, they will bring shade. My own garden is a fine example of how gardens change with time, even if the changes accumulated gradually, almost imperceptibly.

Late in 1992, cleaning out a filing cabinet long overdue for purging, I ran across some faded color snapshots taken in 1973, the first spring after we bought the old house we still live in. The mood that instantly seized me was one of sic transit, the kind of sense of the transitoriness of life that the British Romantic poets loved to wallow in. I found a snapshot of myself, and the evidence is plain: I am not getting younger—less gray of beard, slimmer—nor will I.

But the most startling photograph was of our house. Taken in March from the front sidewalk, the only sign of a garden in the making, perhaps, was a small patch of yellow daffodils by a front porch long since replaced. We had only six trees—two tall Virginia junipers and two black cherries, all along the property line; a cute little Colorado blue spruce the previous owner had planted by the walk up to the front door; and a single large swamp maple smack in the middle of the back yard. I had forgotten that there was a time when I could stand on the sidewalk, look through the front yard and a side yard into the back yard, and then, beyond the end of our property, see seven neighboring houses and an elementary school.

We had almost no shade and even less privacy, in a corner lot on two quite busy streets. Much has happened in the intervening years, all of it good. Only the roof of our house is now visible from the street, and one day even it will not be seen. We have hemmed ourselves in by dense, high hedgerows on all sides—bayberries, bamboo, vitex, abelias, tall grasses, lilacs, pines, purple barberries, leyland cypress, and other trees and shrubs. Inside the confines of this thicket, we laid out many herbaceous borders. We planted trees: a dawn redwood, a paulownia, several hybrid witch hazels, a quince, crab apples, hollies, a Russian olive, a specimen of *Cornus kousa*, another of *Lagerstroemia faurei*—these are only a partial catalog of the woody plants, some now reaching maturity, we planted. Some trees arrived on their own, including a catalpa and a black walnut I should have removed, but didn't. I foolishly allowed the cute little spruce to remain, and it grew immense. We removed a ratty, crumbling concrete stoop by the back door and replaced it with a huge, handsome low wooden deck our elder son, Paul, built when he was in college. In time, half of it was roofed over with a sturdy pergola, now covered in hardy kiwi vines of stupendous vigor. Other things happened in the evolution of our garden. Most of the lawns that had originally surrounded the house have vanished, leaving only a tiny vestigial one out back. Where lawns once were, there is now a series of herbaceous borders.

The trees and the tall shrubs grew and grew, and as they did, the shade steadily increased. Part of our garden still lies almost in full sun during the summer, but its size is diminishing. In the late 1980s, I wondered why the plants in the sunny back border were looking peaked—why the heleniums were lanky and sparse in bloom, why some roses were wan and consumptive, and why the tall artemisias were prey to a horrible fungal disease. It sometimes is slow work to see the obvious: the sunny border had become a shady one. New planting strategies were called for. I had to move or discard most of the old, sun-loving perennials and replace them with ones that love shade. Many of the new perennials were groundcovers. I had already begun to see the uses of these plants and to borrow from other gardens the idea of a groundcover tapestry—a mingling of hostas, ferns, pulmonarias, lysimachias, and other companionable plants—rather than a mere sheet of ivy or periwinkle.

In what follows, I will introduce individually some of the cast of characters among shade-loving groundcovers, then return to some larger considerations about their use in combination.

Ajuga

Ajuga reptans, in its most common form, bears blue flower spikes about ten inches tall in late spring above a carpet of purple or deep green leaves that persist in winter. It is not to be despised simply because it is common. It multiplies rapidly by runners, providing quick cover in partial to deeper shade. It has its faults, however. It can escape to lawns, and in hot, dry weather it may die out at the center. If it isn't watered in such weather, it may just die out, period. It is a plant that somehow invites neglect, seems not to mind for a time, and then perishes of thirst. But ajuga also will die from crown rot or root rot in overly moist soil: it's one of those damned-if-you-do-and-damned-if-you-don't plants.

Rumor has it that in addition to spreading by the runners that produce new rosettes of leaves in a widening circle around the mother plants, it is reproduced by ants that gather its seeds, start to haul them back to their nests, and then drop some en route. It could be so; cyclamen seeds are sometimes dispersed by forgetful ants.

In recent years, admirers of ajuga have been blessed by the addition of several new cultivars. Here are some of the best: 'Alba', with creamy flowers, has green leaves that turn purple in winter. 'Bronze Beauty', named for its lustrous bronze-purple foliage, has especially soft blue flowers. 'Gray Lady', with gray leaves and blue flowers, looks restful and dignified. 'Silver Beauty', which seems to be identical to 'Silver Carpet', is a very slow spreader with leaves of light gunmetal gray. 'Jungle Beauty', which may be a hybrid between *A. reptans* and *A. genevensis*, has blue-violet flowers, an upright habit, and thick and fleshy leaves. Allen Bush describes this cultivar as having flowers that look like "small birds flapping their wings." It is not much of a spreader. *A. genevensis* 'Pink Beauty' bears spikes of pink blooms abundantly in spring, then intermittently throughout the summer, but it is a temperamental performer that I have lost in a fairly mild winter. 'Catlin's Giant', the largest of the ajugas, has spikes of deep blue flowers that rise twelve inches above its shiny purple-bronze leaves.

Most plants have their stories behind them, but these are frequently lost. The plants make their way into the world, from one nursery to another, one garden to another, but in time the tale of how they originated or how they got their names is lost. By sheer accident, I found out who the Catlin of 'Catlin's Giant' was, and telephoned this well-known plantsman, Jack Catlin, in southern California at his home in La Cañada. He told this tale. Sometime in the middle 1970s, alarmed by the spread of a dwarf bamboo, he sprayed it with a devil's brew of two herbicides—2-4 D and amino triazole. A sudden breeze wafted the spray into a nearby patch of *Ajuga reptans*. Most of the ajuga perished in a few days. One plant remained, not only surviving but also growing lustily, with vigor never seen before. Its leaves grew thick and fleshy, and it lifted itself to a height previously unknown in ajugas. Apparently, the herbicides had conducted an unintended experiment in genetic engineering, producing a somatic variation that proved stable. Western Hills Nursery in California propagated it and sold it. Now it grows in gardens all over the United States and even in England.

Alchemilla

Alchemilla, or ladies mantle, is an heirloom plant, if any is. It has been grown in European gardens since the Middle Ages, possibly longer, although it was grown for its supposed uses as a medicinal

In late spring, the dramatic spikes of ajuga 'Catlin's Giant' (possibly a mutation brought into being by some chemical warfare in Jack Catlin's garden in California) command attention for their bold form and saturated color in a mixed pathway planting in the Beasley-Sampson garden in Oregon.

Ladies mantle and eryngiums flank a path leading to a sunny garden scene in Penelope Hobhouse's garden at Tintinhull House in Somerset.

herb, not for its delicate and singular beauty. In *The Herball* (1633), John Gerard wrote:

> Ladies mantle hath many round leaves, with five or six corners finely indented about the edges, which before they be opened are plaited and folded together [. . .]: among which rise up tender stalks set with the like leaves but much lesser: on the tops whereof grow small mossie floures clustering together, of a yellowish greene colour. The seed is small and yellow, inclosed in greene husks. The root is thicke, and full of threddy strings.

To this plant, which he also called Lyons foot, he attributed several "vertues," including these: "it stoppeth bleeding, and also the over-much flowing of the natural sicknesse: it keeps downe maidens paps or dugs, and when they be too great or flaggy it maketh them lesser or harder."

I think ladies mantle is no longer put to these uses. It is grown instead for its distinctive grace and elegance. There are several species that have considerable value in a garden, all of which prefer partial shade, dislike heat and humidity, and do not do well in the South. The most common is *Alchemilla mollis*, which makes an attractive low mound of downy, accordian-pleated, soft green leaves that capture individual drops of morning dew quite beautifully. It bears clouds of tiny, yellowish green flowers, just as Gerard described them, in early summer. *A. alpina*, mountain ladies' mantle, a more diminutive species, has silver-edged leaves that are silky on the back and catch the light very appealingly. Both of these species should be sheared back sharply as they finish blooming, to bring freshness to their leaves and to reduce self-seeding. *A. ellenbeckii* is a real charmer. A weaver that hugs the ground and requires full shade, it bears tiny pleated leaves on garnet stems and yellow-green flowers. I got a plant from Heronswood Nursery in Kingston, Washington, and fell in love with it as soon as I unpacked the box early one May. I gave it its own pot on our deck for the summer, to assure it a good start. Unfortunately, I also put it in full sun, not realizing its need for shade. It grew beautifully for two months, spreading over the rim of the pot in all directions. I checked every day to see how it was doing—and to admire, more each time, its tiny leaves and its garnet stems. Then, almost overnight, it croaked, turning to unrecognizable rot. I mean to try again. The standard rule here is not to give up on a plant until you have killed it three times.

Dainty, nearly prostrate *Alchemilla ellenbeckii* covers the ground around a dwarf species of maple at Dan Hinkley's Heronswood Nursery in Kingston, Washington.

Asarum

It took some time before I could lay claim to growing *Asarum europaeum*, or European wild ginger, as a groundcover. For some years, just one clump of this lovely, low plant with dark, semi-ever-green, very shiny kidney-shaped leaves grew in a somewhat shady spot near our deck, where we could keep an eye on it. It is handsome most of the year, but is especially lovely in late winter, when the snowdrops that have sown themselves in its midst raise their pearl white flowers above their gray-green leaves. The purplish brown juglike flowers of the wild ginger must be sought for since they are borne below and are completely concealed by the foliage. I wanted more, much more of it, a whole carpet in fact, but it spreads slowly, if at all. It is also fairly expensive, and nurseries tend to ration it out

European wild ginger (*Asarum europaeum*) carpets the ground at Wing Haven, the garden and private bird sanctuary developed beginning in the 1930s by Eddie and Elizabeth Clarkson in Charlotte, North Carolina, now maintained by the city for the enjoyment of the public.

The fresh and glossy new foliage of *Asarum shuttleworthii*, a native American wild ginger, is as intricately patterned as a rattlesnake's skin.

—"only three plants per customer." But gradually, three plants at a time from these ungenerous nurseries—with their ridiculous idea that those of us who hanker for 300 European wild gingers should defer to ninety-nine other people who would be content with their share of three—I built up a little patch, two by three feet, in front of ferns and hostas in a shady bed that stays reasonably moist.

In time, this species of wild ginger (whose roots have a gingery smell, although the plant is unrelated to the true gingers that are the source of the delicious spice used in cooking) got some company, and quite a cosmopolitan lot. From the woodlands of eastern North America, it was joined by *Asarum canadense*, a deciduous species with a more spreading habit, which I planted at some distance from its European cousin. From the southeastern United States came *A. shuttleworthii* 'Callaway', a selected form that tends to be evergreen and bears wonderfully patterned leaves marked with gray. I was reasonably happy with this little group of wild gingers, until word reached me that eastern Asia was home to a number of spectacular species that are almost impossible to obtain in America.

Obtaining what is impossible to obtain is one of the most powerful desires in a gardener's psyche. Finally, one of these Asian asarums reached me through circuitous channels. It is *A. splendens*, yet another of the many fine Asian plants that Barry Yinger has introduced to America. It is the most gorgeous foliage plant I know. (Specimens have been stolen from the Arnold Arboretum so often now that I hear the plant is kept in a secret location, so as not to tempt the avid but unscrupulous gardener.) The leaves, almost the size of a hand but shaped like angel wings, have great substance, and they are mottled with pewter and gray and several shades of green, something like an especially fine form of *Cyclamen hederifolium*.

Convallaria and Galium

If one sign of a groundcover's success is its ability to thrive with only minimal assistance from human beings, then an even greater sign of its success must be its ability to go on from year to year with no assistance whatsoever. My candidate for champion in this regard is the lily-of-the-valley (*Convallaria majalis*). It is one of those plants that have naturalized in wooded areas of southern New Jersey, on land once farmed. Little is left of the deserted farmhouses, but signs of their former habitation are evident hundreds of feet from where they once stood, where lily-of-the-valley, a native European plant, spreads out in dense, low-growing colonies that no weed has mastered. These are graceful plants, with their wide blades of leaves and their nodding and sweetly fragrant bells of purest white in early spring, which are sometimes followed in the fall by large round fruits the color of tangerines. They will grow in the sun, but their leaves burn at the tips, and they are happiest in shade. Lily-of-the-valley brings a bit of theology with it. In traditional Christian iconography, it was a symbol of both the Immaculate Conception of Mary and of Christ's Incarnation. It also symbolized the theological virtue of humility; Botticelli's painting "Judith Returning with the Head of Holofernes" in the Uffizi shows lilies-of-the-valley growing at Judith's feet, to show that she was humble in her grisly victory.

Unsuspected theological meanings also accompany another shade-loving groundcover: sweet woodruff, bedstraw, or lady's bedstraw (*Galium odoratum*). Medieval plant lore held that when Job lay down on his bed of dung after his affliction with boils, the dung was mixed with bedstraw. This plant was also believed to be the straw in the stable where Christ was born. Its scratchy texture when dried made it, furthermore, a traditional symbol of tribulation. It is nonetheless a pleasant plant, a low spreading herb about eight inches tall that enjoys moist soil. The white flowers in spring, used in Germany to flavor May wine, have a pleasant vanilla scent, and the tiered pale green foliage in whorls of six to eight leaves is attractive. The dried leaves were once used to freshen linens with a fragrance of new-mown hay.

Ferns

Ferns occupy their own special niche in the world of garden groundcovers. Their evolutionary history is much older than that of other garden plants. They reproduce themselves by spores rather than seeds, and they have no need of insect or other pollinators. The precise botanical language used to describe them differs from that used with other plants; the most obvious difference is in their foliage, which consists technically of fronds, not leaves. Ferns vary in size, color, form, preferred habitat, and their ability to tolerate extreme heat or extreme cold. Many revel in shade, but a few are genuine sun worshipers. Most ferns require moist soil and appreciate a bit of lime in the soil. Of a great many species that might be suitable for garden use, I restrict myself to those that are most likely to be available at a well-stocked, general-purpose nursery. I am leaving out of consideration cinnamon fern (*Osmunda cinnamonea*) and ostrich fern (*Matteuccia struthiopteris*), because their great height and spread disqualify them as groundcovers. And I am blackballing the sensitive fern (*Onoclea sensibilis*) and the hay-scented fern (*Dennstaedtia punctilobula*) for their poor citizenship in gardens. The former is sensitive only in the sense that the first frost of autumn gets it, not that it is delicate or dainty; it is an extremely aggressive spreader. The latter, which will grow in dry, sunny locations, has even more muscle, producing chemicals that are toxic to many other plants.

I also exclude any native North American fern that is rare and that may have been collected in the wild. This despicable practice, prevalent during the British fern mania of the nineteenth century, resulted in the extinction of some species in their native habitats.

I have reservations about recommending the lady fern (*Athyrium filix-femina*) as well, for it is not at all ladylike, but more hoydenish, in its aggression. At two feet high and three feet across, an established plant holds its territory in a commanding way. Specialty nurseries offer many cultivars, including dwarfs and forms with crinkled and crested—and otherwise oddball—fronds. But I have no reservations whatsoever about another member of the genus, *A. nipponicum* 'Pictum', the Japanese painted fern, a deciduous, densely spreading colonizer. This relatively new plant proves that "fern" is not necessarily synonymous with "green," for its fronds mingle subtle hues of raspberry, rose, pewter, gray, and olive to beautiful effect. It prefers moist shade, but will withstand some sun and drought. (The description may sound a bit like *Ajuga* 'Burgundy Glow', but the effect is very different—and very lovely.) There are a number of variant forms, and this fern breeds freely with its cousin, the lady fern, producing sometimes odd and puzzling progeny.

Another Asian fern with relatives in the West is *Dryopteris erythrospora*, which the British call the Japanese shield fern, although in America its common name is autumn fern. The name derives from the autumnal tints—copper with a somewhat pinkish cast—of its new fronds in the spring. The colors persist for several weeks before this fern of middle stature, which gets about twenty inches high and spreads as wide, assumes a more subdued green color. It stays green all winter, and it's the only evergreen fern I know whose fronds don't sink to half-mast or even lower when cold weather settles in for good. The related North American and European species *D. filix-mas*, the male fern, plays no springtime pranks of color, but like the lady

fern, it has many cultivars with crested and otherwise bizarre foliage forms.

The autumn fern is not the only one that's evergreen. Far more commonly grown is the Christmas fern (*Polystichum acrostichoides*), native to our eastern woodlands. It has beautiful long fronds, much like those of the Boston fern, which has been a favorite house plant since Victorian times. It prefers moist shade, although it can take some sun and is drought tolerant once established. Although its foliage stays green all year round, the old fronds are so lax in winter that they fairly hug the ground. To tell the truth, I mention the Christmas fern here only because I feel affection toward it. I would be foolish to plant it with the idea that it would do much in suppressing weeds.

The maidenhair fern (*Adiantum pedatum*) is as delicate and dainty as its name implies. Its semicircular whorls of shiny, fresh green fronds (distinctly pinkish when they first appear in spring) on eigh-

A carpet of sweet woodruff makes a beautiful foil in late spring for the enormous new fronds of a group of ostrich ferns in the Beasley-Sampson garden in Oregon. The delicate foliage of the sweet woodruff and its clouds of tiny flowers bespeak grace, and the ferns suggest force and power.

This combination of Japanese painted ferns, variegated giant solomon's seal, and hostas in a shady corner of the Conservatory Garden in Central Park shows a brilliant sense of design. The contrasting textures and forms of these plants will remain handsome all during the growing season.

Mixed ferns and yellow trilliums at Mt. Cuba, near Wilmington, Delaware—a garden that celebrates the beauty of the native woodland plants of the eastern United States.

Southern maidenhair ferns line the pleasant entrance to Patti McGee's garden on Church Street in Charleston, South Carolina, next to the Dock Street Theater.

In my garden and Hella's in southern New Jersey, life bursts forth in early May in a little bog garden tucked into a curve in a lilac hedge. Ferns, *Tradescantia subaspera*, heuchera 'Palace Purple', *Artemisia versicolor*, and *Primula japonica* make a fine ensemble. The ivy in the foreground is 'Gold Heart'.

teen-inch-wiry black stems are the embodiment of grace. The reference books say that it requires moist shade, but Edith Eddleman reports that it does quite nicely in her garden in dry shade on clay soil. I have found it difficult to please, however, and have replaced it on several occasions when it failed to appear in the spring. Equally lovely is *A. capillus-veneris*, the southern maidenhair fern, which is often grown as a houseplant for its pleasing filmy fronds to eighteen inches. It is, however, not winter-hardy above Zone 9. Another splendid fern for southern gardens, but well into the warmer reaches of Zone 7, is *Thelyphus kunthii*, the Florida shield fern. It grows two to three feet tall, with an equal spread, and it has a fine habit of constantly putting up fresh new fronds during the growing season.

Hellebores

Hellebores are not groundcovers for the impatient, for they are slow to spread. But once they get going and have established themselves, they seed themselves around prolifically. This habit is utterly delightful, for I have long been of the opinion that no one can possibly have too many hellebores in the garden. The easiest species in this genus to please is the Lenten rose (*Helleborus orientalis*). It is marvelous all year long for its dark, almost black evergreen foliage about fifteen inches tall. The large leaves are generally divided into five segments, two of which divide further into two halves. The leaves much resemble an outstretched hand, with fingers spread far apart. The true flowers of this hellebore are insignificant and bloom briefly in late winter, before the seed capsules that will ripen in early June begin to swell. But the "petals" of Lenten roses (actually floral bracts) last for many, many weeks. The effect is of single roses, wonderfully colored in a palette of mostly pastel shades of mauve, cream, straw, and flesh, with occasionally something that can fairly be called purple. The bracts are usually flecked, dappled, or stippled with other colors.

It seems to take several years before Lenten roses settle in, whereupon seedlings will germinate around the parent plants in mid-February. These can be left in place for a denser stand, or they may be transplanted to new locations. (Their best site is beneath deep-rooted deciduous trees that will give them summer shade and winter sun.) I have found it best to dig up such seedlings in April, when they have developed past the seed-leaf stage to produce true leaves. It is advisable to transplant them into six-inch pots filled with a soil-

less potting mix affording both humus and good drainage, and to keep them in a partially shaded cold frame until setting them in their permanent locations in early autumn. Particularly choice individual specimens can be increased by division while in bloom.

Lenten roses may have a delicate and soft-spoken kind of beauty, but they are far from frail in constitution. They take drought in their stride. They don't seem to have any insect enemies, probably because every part of the plant contains helleborin, a lethal poison that enjoyed some vogue in early Renaissance Florence. I have seen *Helleborus orientalis* sprout in tiny cracks between pavements and walls, then flourish and bloom as if growing in rich, deep alluvial soil.

There are other species. *Helleborus niger*, the Christmas rose (which seldom blooms at Christmas, and isn't a rose, of course) is on the tricky side. Like *H. orientalis*, it produces its flowers sparsely (only one to three to a stem), but other species are more generous. *Helleborus foetidus*—stinking hellebore is the literal translation of its specific name, although it's also called the bearsfoot hellebore—produces great clusters of little apple-green flowers in late winter

In a quiet nook of the Withers garden, pelargoniums fill a handsome urn underplanted with lamiums and hellebores. The garden was designed by Mrs. Withers' close friend, the pre-eminent garden writer Elizabeth Lawrence.

and early spring. There's also *Helleborus lividus*, again with green flowers. This species is somewhat tender and may be lost in a harsh winter with little protective snow cover.

There are several hybrid strains of Christmas and Lenten roses. They may be raised from seed, although the wait from seed to flower can be a long one. The seeds take their own time—often a year or more—to germinate, and the seedlings are slow to establish. But once a colony of hellebores is happy, it is virtually permanent. As Elizabeth Lawrence wrote in *A Southern Garden* (1942), "An established plant becomes an heirloom, for in all likelihood it will outlive the gardener who plants it."

Miss Lawrence might have added that over the years, a mixed planting of hellebores will hybridize among themselves, producing many beautiful surprises in their progeny. And the excess plants will go on from garden to garden. We gardeners are a friendly and a sharing lot. Many of my own hellebores have their special history. Elizabeth Lawrence gave them long ago to her friend Hannah Withers in Charlotte, North Carolina. From Mrs. Withers, who is also my friend, they came to my own garden in New Jersey.

As for hostas, we Americans are far ahead of our British cousins in breeding and selecting new cultivars. Not so with hellebores. Working with *Helleborus orientalis* and a few other species, British breeders like Elizabeth Strangman and Eric Smith have in recent years brought forth such luscious hybrids as 'Queen of the Night' (a

Lenten roses may have subtle and delicately-patterned flowers, but they are long lasting and the plants are tough. In the Withers garden volunteer seedlings thrive in the cracks between a flagstone walk and a brick wall. ALLEN LACY

dark reddish purple with overtones of black), 'Pluto' (even darker), and 'Cosmos' (creamy pink flowers intensely freckled with raspberry). I have heard of double hellebores and fragrant ones, and of some advancement toward shades of yellow. A slender few, including 'Wesker Flisk', a form of *H. foetidus* that has red-purple stems and comes reasonably true from seed, have been imported to America by private gardeners, but none has yet become commercially available. I know at least two people who are hybridizing hellebores, in an attempt to close the great transatlantic hellebore gap. I have seen some promising developments—darker, stronger colors, for one thing. And work is being done to overcome one of the few defects in this genus, although it's a defect from a gardener's point of view, not a hellebore's. Hellebores hold their blossoms downward, so that to see into the beautiful heart of one, it's necessary either to pick it or to crawl under the plant and look up, an uncomfortable posture when the ground is still cold and damp. I have seen some recent seedlings, however, that face outward. It's a huge improvement.

Heucheras

It has taken *Heuchera* 'Palace Purple', whose exact species has been such a matter of debate that I dare offer no opinion, an amazingly short time to emerge into great popularity. Allen Bush brought seeds from England in the early 1980s and introduced it in the 1986 catalog of Holbrook Farm and Nursery. In 1991 it was named plant of the year by the Perennial Plant Association, and it would be much easier to list the nurseries that do not sell it than those that do. It produces dainty sprays of creamy flowers in midsummer above clumps of leaves about fourteen inches high, but its foliage is its great attraction. Since it is a seed-grown strain, colors can veer toward green, but in the best plants the crinkled, corduroyed leaves are a rich bronze-purple. In my garden, this heuchera can take full sun; in the South, light shade protects its leaves from sun-scorch. It holds its own as a specimen plant near the front of a border, but it also looks fine in a small colony of a dozen or so plants set about a foot apart.

'Palace Purple' also has started a little family. The tale is told in the 1991 spring catalog of Montrose Nursery, which I chronicle here. Dale Hendricks found, in the mountains of North Carolina, a form of *Heuchera americana* with somewhat dark silvery leaves. He gave

it to Allen Bush, who christened it 'Dale's Strain'. 'Palace Purple' and 'Dale's Strain' both made their way to Montrose, producing a hybrid form, *Heuchera* X 'Montrose Ruby', which is described by Nancy Goodwin as having "dark purple leaves, mottled with silver."

I grow all three plants next to one another, partly for reasons of sentimentality about close ties between members of a family, and partly because they just look good together. Another selection of *Heuchera americana*, 'Garnet', which is bound to be widely grown in the future, has splendid dark green leaves overlaid with the red tones of the gemstone that gives it its name. This selection comes from Mt. Cuba in Delaware.

Heuchera X *brizoides*, or coral bells, is a group of cultivars derived from complicated crosses involving at least three species in this North American genus. All are useful and lovely for their mounds of persistent, often dappled foliage and for their spikes of colorful blooms over several weeks in late spring and early summer. Cultivars include 'Chatterbox' (pink flowers), 'June Bride' (white flowers), and 'Queen of Hearts' (salmon flowers). 'Snowstorm' is especially fine for its leaves tinged with white and its abundant spikes of red flowers from early to mid summer.

Hostas

Among the most indispensable groundcovers for gardens, especially shady ones, are the diverse species in the genus *Hosta* and the numerous cultivars developed from them, either by deliberate hybridization or by selection of the mutations, which are especially common in these plants of east Asian origin.

I have never encountered a hosta that could be confused with anything else, but within the genus there is a truly enormous variety of characteristics. The size of individual mature plants varies from huge ('Sum and Substance' eventually gets larger than a couple of washtubs) to tiny (*H. venusta* is only three inches tall and four inches across, with flower scapes under ten inches high), with every size in between these extremes. Leaves vary in color from deep green, to green with a distinctly bluish overtone early in the growing season, to chartreuse and gold. Variegation is quite common, taking the form of margins of white or cream or gold, or irregular splashes of one or more colors across the middle portion of the leaves. The leaves can be large and bold—big enough to serve as a plate for food at a luau

In the Beasley-Sampson garden in Oregon, white groundcover comfrey (*Symphytum grandiflorum*) sits peacefully amidst a superbly choreographed planting of an unusual form of *Helleborus foetidus* that is striking for its black-toned foliage and its pale green open spikes of flowers and bracts.

Heuchera 'Palace Purple', a seed-grown strain from England introduced in the early 1980s by Allen Bush of Holbrook Farm and Nursery in North Carolina, has quickly attained wide popularity. In the Beasley-Sampson garden it is combined with *Miscanthus sinensis* var. *purpurescens*, ligularia 'Desdemona', and *Ilex crenata* 'Green Island'.

—or they can be delicate and dainty. Some leaves are salver-shaped, others long and attenuated. They may bend down gracefully, or they may stand erect, as in the cultivars 'Spritzer' and (sorry, but this is its name) 'Eager Bridegroom'. In texture, they may be smooth or heavily ribbed or deeply puckered, like seersucker. The seersuckered leaves of *Hosta tokudama* and its cultivars are so deeply cupped that they can hold water for a day after a good rain. In one of the best shady gardens I have seen in the United States—that of John Elsley in Greenwood, South Carolina, which demonstrates sheer imaginative genius in its use of many different hostas—the owner's cat makes free use of these leaves as a drinking bowl.

Almost all hostas are clump-forming, but there are a few that show tendencies to spread by underground stems. These include *H. clausa* var. *clausa* (so named because its flowers, like those of bottle gentians, do not open), *H. clausa* var. *stolonifera* (which does not bloom at all), 'Abiqua Ground Cover', and 'Vera Verde'.

The foliage of hostas is their main attraction, not their flowers, as I pointed out earlier. But there is considerable variation in flowering habit. Bloom may occur early, in mid-season, or late. The scapes may barely rise above the mounds of foliage, or they may tower to almost dizzying height; 'Tall Boy' produces flower stalks that sometimes stand six feet high. Flower color also varies, but within the narrow range between white and shades of blue-violet or blue-purple. I can think of only two hostas worth growing entirely for their flowers. One is the old-fashioned plantain lily or August lily, *H. plantaginea*. The first hosta to reach Europe, late in the eighteenth century, it was grown at Malmaison by the Empress Josephine and soon found great public favor under the invalid genus name *Funkia*.

Hosta fluctuans 'Variegata', although still rare and uncommonly grown, obviously has a great future before it. A plant of enormous dignity, it would make a superb accent in a mixed shady border.

It is notable for its very large waxen-white bell-shaped flowers flaring from long tubes in late summer and for its strong, sweet perfume. Its beauty is undeniable, but outstripped by its double-flowered cultivar, 'Aphrodite', whose blossoms look like small gardenias.

Like daylilies, irises, orchids, and roses, hostas are addictive plants. A reasonable appreciation of them and their uses in the garden can become a ruling passion, a deep obsession, a mania. The first symptoms of pathological hostaphilia generally occur when someone has collected around twenty different hostas, knows the name of each by sight, thinks that another twenty would still be too few, doesn't think spending $125 on just one rare new cultivar is excessive, and considers joining the American Hosta Society in order to attend conventions, find additional hostas to covet, and enjoy the company of similarly afflicted people. The malady reaches its height when the hostaphile divides the plant kingdom into two categories: hostas and "companion plants."

My own collection of hostas now numbers slightly under fifty cultivars, which pretty well represent all the pleasing variations the genus offers. I have deliberately tried to avoid true hostamania by simply trying not to know them all by name. When I plant a new one, I write its name in indelible ink on a plastic label, which I then bury just in front of the plant. In this way, if I really need to know what something is, I can dig around, find the label, and make the identification. Nevertheless, certain hostas are so distinctive that their names cannot be forgotten.

Here are a few of my own favorites. 'Sum and Substance', bred, like a great many other fine new hostas, by the American hybridizer Paul Aden, is at the top of the list. It has, quite simply, an enormous

At Sheila Macqueen's Westwick Cottage, Leverstock Green, Hertfordshire, the golden foliage of *Ribes sanguineum* comports itself splendidly with hostas *H. sieboldiana* 'Elegans', 'Frances Williams', and other bold cultivars with variegated or blue-gray leaves.

presence in the garden. A mature plant stands well over four feet tall and stretches three feet in diameter if grown well. The leaves are fourteen inches wide and twenty inches long. They are pale lime to chartreuse as they expand, then turn somewhat golden yellow, provided they receive some direct sun during the day. The pale lilac-blue flowers in August are highly attractive. My plant is in a spot below a paulownia tree and a dogwood, where it gets morning sun. In the afternoon, as the spot becomes densely shaded, 'Sum and Substance' pumps light and rich color into an area that otherwise would be without interest and even dreary. Flanking it are two other behemoths. 'Big Mama' is roughly the same size as 'Sum and Substance', but has slightly smaller blue-green leaves. 'Aurora Borealis', which much resembles the widely grown, very popular cultivar 'Frances Williams', is slightly shorter and more compact than the two other members of this dramatic, back-of-the-border trio, but it shows up well thanks to the margins and splashings of yellow against the basic blue-green of its forceful leaves. I generally tuck a few red caladiums around the skirts of 'Sum and Substance' for a little splash of salsa.

The hosta that everyone knows, even if not by name—the small, fairly spreading one with green-and-white variegated foliage—is described in several reference books as the species *H. undulata*, with several variant forms. But in his exhaustive monograph, *The Genus Hosta* (1991), George Schmid calls it *H.* 'Undulata', denying it the italics that would indicate that it was a genuine species. It is, instead, a plant originating in cultivation that is generally sterile and unstable, meaning that it often produces plain green leaves in summer and that plants will eventually revert through a series of intermediate

In the Greenwood, South Carolina garden of John and Billie Elsley, hostas 'Sum and Substance' on right and 'Sun Power' on left flank the entrance to a path of pine straw, with 'Hilda Nisbett' and other groundcover azaleas in the background. JOHN ELSLEY

changes to entirely green and unvariegated leaves. It hardly matters whether it is *Hosta undulata* or *H.* 'Undulata' that many gardeners start out with, often as an over-the-fence gift from a neighbor, since it is not the one that gardeners end with, once they have discovered the multitudinous delights of the genus. They will want the golds, of all sizes, such as 'Golden Scepter', 'Golden Tiara', 'Zounds', and many others. They will covet the blues—'Blue Angel', 'Blue Umbrellas', 'Hadspen Heron', for starters. They will go for the elegantly variegated ones, such as 'Sugar and Cream', 'Tambourine', and 'Wide Brim'. They will learn to appreciate the enormous diversity of form of hostas that are content to be just plain green—'Birchwood Elegance', 'Green Piecrust', 'Leather Sheen'. They will have lust in their hearts for 'Big John', 'Dick Ward', 'Don Stevens', 'Mildred Seaver', 'Polly Bishop', and maybe even 'Emily Dickinson'.

There are good nurseries, in well-heeled suburban areas where an interest in gardening is keen, that carry twenty or more cultivars, already grown in containers to fairly reasonable size. But local nurseries that sell a wide range of plants, including a few hostas, are not the best sources. The way to acquire hostas is to seek out more specialized nurseries, such as the Klehm Nursery in Illinois, Andre Viette Farm and Nursery in Virginia, or Hatfield Gardens in Ohio. Plants can be selected in person, or they can be bought by mail order. Some nurseries ship them, either dormant or in active growth, in containers. Others will ship bareroot plants. With hostas, bareroot shipment is no problem. During my most recent attack of hostaphilia, caused by the realization that my garden was in serious need of a lot more golden foliage, I ordered fifteen plants from Hatfield Gardens. They arrived in mid-May, bareroot and in full leaf. I set

Although it is very common, and not a plant that will quicken the pulse of the collector, hosta 'Undulata' still has solid merit. At the Bishop's Close in Portland, Oregon, it makes a pleasant spring picture with lily-of-the-valley, ferns, and *Anemone nemerosa*.

In the Frederick garden in Delaware, the low mounds of hosta 'Kabitan' face down a clump of spent tulips. This hosta, which grows under a foot high, bearing arched, lance-shaped yellow leaves with thin margins of dark green, is effective either as an edging or planted in a mass.

them out immediately and watered them in well. They looked like they had been growing there for a year or more.

But a caveat is in order concerning mail-order nurseries and hostas. These plants are, to an increasing extent, being micropropagated in tissue-culture labs. The benefits of this technology to gardeners are obvious. The older method of propagating hostas, by dividing clumps, increased them perhaps tenfold per year. Tissue-culture increases plants by many thousands at a time, thus lowering prices and decreasing the waiting time to acquire whatever delicious new hosta the eye lusts after. Good mail-order nurseries buy tiny plants from these laboratories (if they don't maintain their own labs) and grow them to a respectable size before selling them retail. I have been burnt a couple of times paying hefty prices for hostas and then receiving tiny plantlets barely out of the test tube. When dealing for the first time with an unfamiliar nursery, it is wise to place only a small order. Then, if the plants are puny, you can chalk it up to experience and scratch the nursery off the list of ones that are fair, honest, and determined to give good value for money received.

One of the very best traits of hostas, especially for gardeners severely pressed for time in spring or for those who elevate procrastination to a fine art, is their utter indifference to transplanting. A clump can be lifted and dug and then replanted all during the growing season, without wilting or even sulking. This amiable temperament makes it possible to lift several clumps at a time and to play with siting them where they work best together. (They can also be dug and moved during winter dormancy when the ground is not frozen, but it may be difficult to tell exactly where the plants are.) Early spring or mid-fall is probably the optimum time to divide clumps of hostas, but I have divided them in midsummer without visible damage to their well-being.

For gardeners who have reached that stage of hostaphilia when it seems only reasonable to shell out $100 for some new cultivar that simply cannot wait until the supply increases and the price drops, I pass an excellent suggestion from George Schmid's book: *Buy two*. One of them can be put in a place of special honor in the garden, then left alone to see how it performs in the two or three years it will take it to reach maturity. The other can be divided relentlessly, by cutting away each little plantlet as it appears and setting it in a nursery row in some out-of-the-way spot in the garden. These can be traded with other hosta fanciers for divisions from their own special new acquisitions.

Liriope and Ophiopogon

I like *Liriope muscari* (syn. *L. platyphylla*) a whole lot, which is good, because I have plenty of it. The ordinary species entered our garden as a small clump donated many years ago by our neighbor Ed Plantan. It has been repeatedly divided, and now it stretches along both sidewalks at the edge of our property. If I kept dividing it until the end of my life, and then my sons did the same thing, and then passed the task on to our grandchildren, I suspect that before their hair turned gray this one original clump would have produced enough liriope to girdle the globe at the Equator.

If there's a perfect groundcover, this is it. Its graceful, strappy, dark green foliage looks fine throughout the year, until very late winter, when it gets a bit ragged and can be chopped back hard to let the fresh new growth take over in early spring. Liriope is the epitome of toughness. It grows well in fairly deep shade, and can also take a sunny location, although in the South it may burn there. I have never seen any damage on it from insects or slugs, nor have I observed signs of disease. The tuberous structures in its root system,

like those of *Asparagus sprengeri*, store moisture that enables it to laugh at drought. It is hardy from central Texas to coastal New England. Even if it didn't bloom, I would prize it for its tailored look, but the flowers in late summer are nothing to scoff at, and they are followed by dark jade berries that turn black-purple in the late fall and often remain through the winter. It stays in clumps and will seed itself about a bit, but the seedlings are distinctive and can be pulled up where they're not wanted. (A warning is in order about another species, *L. spicata*, which is winter-hardy to Zone 5. It looks much like nut grass, and it is a vicious spreading perennial weed that is almost impossible to eradicate.)

The flower spikes of ordinary *Liriope muscari* are a rather pallid lavender-purple, but 'Majestic' has very tall spikes of rich purple, and 'Monroe White' has blossoms like little pearls. There is one form with gold and green variegation, and 'Silvery Sunproof' sports green-and-silver-striped leaves. 'PeeDee Ingot', which was introduced a few years ago by Coastal Gardens in Myrtle Beach, South Carolina, is my favorite. Its bright chartreuse leaves seem to radiate light. It is absolutely sensational combined with the black mondo—or monkey—grass, *Ophiopogon planiscapus* 'Nigrescens' (sometimes sold under the commercial name 'Ebony Knight'). The contrast between the dour charcoal foliage of the mondo grass and the pale bright foliage of 'PeeDee Ingot' is elegant and jazzy. I like these two plants together so well that, in addition to using them as groundcovers, I have been them growing in a large clay dish on the deck, in a neat little planting with a creeping green-and-white dwarf euonymus and *Rubus nepalensis*, a charming low bramble.

Other species and cultivars of *Ophiopogon* are also highly garden-worthy. I have from J. C. Raulston a handsome variegated monkey grass, *O. jaburan*, collected in Korea in 1985. It is a maddeningly slow increaser, but the bold white-and-green variegated foliage is striking and worth the wait. It grows about a foot tall and has white summer flowers followed by gorgeous lapis-lazuli fruits in the fall. The fruits, unfortunately, are borne so far down in the leaves that they may escape notice. Two dwarf forms of *O. japonicus* also commend themselves; 'Gyoku' is deep green, 'Kyoto Dwarf' is black-purple, and both grow in tufted little fans. These grow to about four inches tall, spread slowly into mats, and can withstand some foot traffic.

Ophiopogon and *Liriope* are so similar in their foliage and their effect that they would seem to be in the same genus, but the differ-

In Frances Parker's lush garden in Beaufort, South Carolina, a tall form of *Ophiopogon japonicus* edges plantings of spring phloxes and irises. The variegated ivy on the tree to the rear of the garden is the aromatic *Hedera colchica* 'Dentata-variegata'.

ences are clear in their flowers. *Liriope*, incidentally, was named for a Greek forest nymph—and why not? *Ophiopogon* derives its name from two Greek words meaning "the beard of a serpent." I suspect that the botanist who dreamed this one up must have had recent contact with some other, highly hallucinogenic plant.

Spring Woodland Echoes

If the late spring and early summer roadsides of Texas provide keen inspiration (and many plants) for the sunny summer herbaceous border, it is equally true that our eastern woodlands have lessons— and plants—that can guide us in the making of spring gardens of surpassing loveliness. Such a woodland in late April and May is a model for a style of planting that is natural, harmonious, and in keeping with much of the larger American landscape. Before oaks, beeches, and other hardwoods have leafed out fully to form a dense canopy overhead, there is a brief time of dappled shade, when the play of light is constantly changing. The new growth overhead is fresh and vivid, the blue sky still shows through, and the forest floor is alive with wildflowers in bloom—claytonias, trilliums, hepaticas, native terrestrial orchids, aquilegias.

Not every wildflower that grows in the light, but quickly deepening shade of a spring woodland adapts itself easily to life in a garden. The showy pink lady's slipper and many other native orchids are best left alone, for they thrive only in complicated symbiosis with certain soil fungi. Most trilliums are difficult to transplant. From seed, they may take as long as ten years to flower. Any nursery that offers lady's slippers or trilliums should probably be regarded as guilty of collecting these plants (and others on its list) from the wild until proven innocent. And if the price of any wildflower sounds like a bargain or too good to be true, the plant probably has been collected. It costs just as much, and sometimes more, for a nursery to propagate perennial wildflowers as it does any other perennials. Low prices for plants are good tip-offs to unscrupulous ethics, even lawbreaking.

A number of native north American perennials qualify for the shady garden in spring. *Phlox* is a particularly rich genus. The word first calls to mind the buxom tall cultivars of *P. paniculata* of the mid- and late-summer sunny border, one of its mainstays with their thunderhead-shaped clusters of long-lasting flowers in a wide range of colors, but the more modest woodland phlox of spring have great charm. *P. divaricata*, the wild sweet william (but not a dianthus), occurs naturally in pale blue, icy white, or mauve. *P. stolonifera*, the creeping phlox, blooms in late spring, well after daffodils have finished. It can stand full sun, but appreciates at least partial shade. 'Blue Ridge', a pale blue cultivar, is excellent, as is 'Bruce's White'. Sydney Eddison has great affection for the cultivar 'Homefires'. "Not everyone will like it for its magenta-pink color," she says, "but it makes a knockout groundcover under maples, and even goes so far as to sweep up the boles of the trees with its leafy runners." Regarding the parentage of another spring-blooming phlox, 'Chattahoochee', there is a controversy of opinion. I will take my courageous stand with Allen Bush, who offers the hypothesis that it's a cross between *P. divaricata* and the milkman. It blooms later than *P. divaricata*, bearing blue flowers with red eyes. Nancy Goodwin is especially keen on *Phlox pilosa*. She writes in the 1992 Montrose catalog, "This native phlox is one of our favorites, blooming as it does in late spring with soft pink flowers. It is disease resistant and spreads by root stolons, making a good clump in a fairly short time. It is a superb weaver and can keep a border from looking too spotty." And I am equally keen on *P*. X 'Millstream Jupiter'. It is sometimes described as a hybrid between the very early, sun-loving, evergreen species *P. subulata* (thrift, or mountain pink) and *P. nivalis*, but the noted American rock garden expert H. Lincoln Foster said that the parentage was *P. subulata* X *P. bifida*. I take his word, for he hybridized it. It is stunning in William Frederick's garden in Delaware, planted below flowering quinces in several pastel shades. This soft blue phlox may rebloom in the fall, but its superb showing in late April is sufficient to earn its keep. It is happy in partial shade, but can also stand full sun.

Stylophorum diphyllum, the celandine poppy, is one of the greater glories of our eastern woodlands, particularly if it is grown with *Mertensia virginica*, or Virginia bluebells, in the moist, shady spots both plants prefer. The poppy cheers the heart in April with its radiant yellow flowers. As for Virginia bluebells, they are surely one of the loveliest and most garden-worthy of American wildflowers. The tubular blossoms, flared at their ends like a skirt, open soft pink, then change to blue. Everything about this plant bespeaks softness, including the pale green of its handsome leaves. White- and pink-flowered variants will often appear among those with blue flowers, since plants self-seed to form spreading colonies where conditions are to their liking. Virginia bluebells go dormant in early

Phlox divaricata 'Fuller's White' at the Bishop's Close, Portland, Oregon.

summer, but they can be interplanted with ferns, caladiums, hellebores, or shade-loving annuals like impatiens to fill in the spots they have vacated.

No shady garden should go without tiarellas, or foamflowers. This genus of little native North American spring wildflowers offers delightful ten-inch spikes of white to extremely pale pink blossoms in late spring and slightly hairy, sometimes spotted leaves that persist into winter. *Tiarella cordifolia* can be stoloniferous and a fair spreader, although the species varies greatly in this trait. One form, *T. cordifolia* var. *collina*, reliably stays in a clump, to the delight of gardeners who are unnerved by foamflowers that wander. (I don't care a bit if they do.) Another cultivar, *T. cordifolia* 'Montrose Selection', also a clump-former, blooms later than the rest. It has slightly pink flowers and dark-centered leaves. Tiarellas are superb plants for lining a path of soft pine straw.

Our native eastern columbine (*Aquilegia canadensis*) also deserves a place in every shady garden. Its gray-green foliage is delicate, and its pale yellow and red flowers nod on two-foot plants very agreeably. The selection 'Nana' is a miniature duplicate of the regular species, and 'Corbett' is entirely yellow. Not a believer in horticultural chauvinism, I see no reason not to plant species of columbine originating elsewhere than in North America. For over twenty years I have been enamored of the dwarf Japanese fan columbine (*A. plabellata* 'Nana'), a low, mounding plant with blue-green foliage and plump-looking teal or creamy white flowers that appear in early spring. All columbines are short-lived perennials, but they self-seed so freely that I've never gone without them in spring.

My candidate for the most satisfactory native American wildflower for year-round groundcover is *Iris cristata*. It has beautiful little blue (occasionally white) flowers on short stems in mid-spring. The low, dense mat of foliage blades is evergreen and spreads into ever-widening colonies without making a pest of itself.

Some friends may think me crazy, but I'm willing to allow a little buttercup, the lesser celandine (*Ranunculus ficaria*), room in the shady parts of my garden in spring. It looks like a native woodland wildflower, and in fact has naturalized itself in much of the United States. Some hold that it is an unmitigated weed; perhaps it is, for it self-seeds prodigiously, popping up everywhere it can get a toehold. But its bright yellow flowers, so shiny that they seem to have been given a coat of shellac, are abundant and radiate good cheer. Its glossy, deep green leaves are pretty, and the lesser celandine lapses peacefully into dormancy with the first warm weather, no matter how rambunctious it may have been during cool spring days. There are forms with pale, almost creamy white flowers. The double variety *R. ficaria* 'Flore Pleno' has perfect manners, staying where it has been planted. One cultivar, 'Brazen Hussy', has superb bronze foliage.

Another non-native spring-blooming genus that combines well with American woodland plants is *Epimedium*, or barrenwort. These semi-evergreen Old World plants benefit from a late-winter shearing so that the delicately beautiful little flowers can be seen. The genus is tolerant of even heavy shade and competition from tree roots. Most of the species and cultivars grow about ten inches tall and cover an area twelve inches wide. *E.* X 'Rubrum' has garnet-red flowers; *E. grandiflorum*, white flowers tinged with yellow and rose; and *E. perralderianum* 'Frohnleiten', showy yellow flowers above reddish new leaves. The slightly smaller hybrid *E.* X *youngianum* 'Niveum' bears white flowers, its sister cultivar, 'Roseum', pink ones. The best epimedium for use as a groundcover may be *E. pinnatum colchicum*, with bronze-edged, nearly evergreen foliage and fairly large, bright yellow spurred flowers in spring.

A closely related genus to the epimediums, the Pacific Northwest native *Vancouveria hexandra*, or American barrenwort, has a similar appearance and uses. It grows twelve inches high and as much across in its first season or so. Sydney Eddison praises this plant to the skies as one of very few perennials that will thrive in the dry

In Genie White's garden in Charlotte, North Carolina in mid-April, foam flower (*Tiarella cordifolia*) and celandine poppies (*Stylophorum diphyllum*), both native woodland plants of eastern North America, provide delicately contrasting forms and color. When spring marches to its conclusion and shade closes in, ferns and variegated liriope will keep this garden-vignette interesting.

shade of eleven mature maples in her Connecticut garden. It has pleasant, ferny foliage that persists well into winter. American barrenwort spreads at a steady pace by underground stems and makes a fine edging for hosta beds. Eddison says that the tiny white flowers in late spring or early summer "look as if they had opened in a wind tunnel."

Bold Strokes, Delicate Touches

It is one of my most settled hunches that much that passes for deliberate design in the making of gardens originates in accident. For example, this color lands next to that, possibly in that feverish rush to get everything in the ground right away on an early spring day when orders arrive simultaneously from three different mail-order nurseries. Often the result is dreadful and must be corrected as soon as possible. But sometimes there's a surprisingly pleasant accident, a combination of colors that begs to be repeated, but the next time with forethought. (By way of digression as regards color, I pass on here the best advice about color combinations I have ever heard. It comes from Douglas Ruhren, who has developed a shortcut in the process of trial and error. Instead of planting X, Y, and Z together and then waiting another growing season to see how they actually work, he just gathers a few flowers and scraps of colored foliage, takes them into the shade—sun won't do, he says—and studies them. Then he knows whether a particular daylily with apricot flowers will or will not look fine with purple perilla planted around it. Doug's brilliantly worked-out color schemes are based on solid empirical ground—and on the testimony of his own eyes.)

As with color, so with texture. Accidental combinations beg to be repeated. Among the most powerful of these are the juxtaposition of the bold and the delicate. Such a juxtaposition may occur at every level in a garden. It is very common in the South for a southern magnolia (*Magnolia grandiflora*) to grow near a mimosa tree (*Albizia julibrissin*). The two trees contrast in many ways. Magnolia's growth is columnar, and until the tree has reached great age its lower branches sweep the ground, giving it powerful mass and volume. Mimosa grows upward and then outward, in a spreading canopy that provides cooling shade that is open enough to allow many plants to grow under it. Magnolia's leaves are large and so shiny that they seem varnished. They are stiff, and it takes an equally stiff wind to move them. Mimosa's leaves are finely cut, feathery, and ferny. The slightest breeze makes them dance, and at dusk they fold up, becoming even more insubstantial. The magnolia's flowers are immense cups or chalices, snow white fading to old gold. The flowers of mimosa are little rosy pink powder puffs. Both trees are fragrant in flower, but the scent of magnolia is sharp and heavy with lemon, and that of mimosa is a faint but memorable sweet spice. "Bold" sums up one, "delicate" (or "tender," which is what *mimosa* means) the other.

I have no southern magnolia, nor mimosa either. Both trees will grow in southern New Jersey, but the magnolia is faint-hearted this far north, and mimosa is plagued by blight throughout most of its range. But in the highest tier of my garden—by accident, not forethought—there is a similar combination of boldness and delicacy, where two very fast-growing trees sit adjacent to each other. One is an empress tree (*Paulownia tomentosa*), now fifty feet high. Its broad leaves are not evergreen, but they are large and bold. The other, even taller at seventy-five feet, is a dawn redwood (*Metasequoia glyptostroboides*), a living fossil thought to be extinct until it was discovered in a remote province of China right after World War II, then propagated from seeds and distributed by the Arnold Arboretum. This deciduous conifer, with leaves that turn a beautiful rosy shade of apricot in autumn, is very graceful, delicate, and ferny in its foliage, which contrasts beautifully with the more stolid leaves of the paulownia. This contrast has to do not only with the size of the

At Hidcote Manor, a slightly curving path of worn stone passes by a massed planting of epimediums punctuated by ferns on the left, and tall ferns behind an imposing clump of a euphorbia on the right.

Brunnera macrophylla at Hidcote combines bold foliage with delicate sprays of forget-me-not-flowers in high spring, just as celandine poppies are putting in their last golden words of the season.

leaves, but also (and more importantly) with what they do in light—or what light does with them. Large leaves mostly reflect light. Tiny, intricately constructed foliage allows the light to play on it and through it. It shimmers and it dances in sunlight as well as in the least breeze.

Once this combination is understood, it can be repeated at every tier in a garden space, as in the juxtaposition of cannas and purple fennel, which are shoulder- or head-high at Montrose. And it can be carried on down into the lowest tier of the garden, into its tapestry of groundcovers.

Plants with bold and striking foliage are notable for the drama they bring to mixed plantings. Most gardens are too small to accommodate plants like gunneras, whose leaves are large enough that I have seen them used in Costa Rica as makeshift umbrellas. But effective use can be made of castor beans, cannas, Scotch thistles, acanthus, and other plants that aren't the least bit shy about proclaiming their presence. Some groundcovers fit in this category, especially the largest hostas and *Petasites japonicus* (which, for excellent reasons, I will hold off discussing until much later).

The really big hostas have pre-eminence, but other bold plants are worth considering—always with the idea of seeking out more delicate companions to set them off.

One is *Symplocarpus foetidus*, but there's a warning in its common names, skunk cabbage and polecat weed. It is one of the first plants to bloom in the moist woodlands and along the margins of streams in the eastern United States. Its large flowers are strange rather than beautiful, and one of the peculiarities about this plant is that it generates its own heat—enough to melt snow so that it can get on with the business of blooming without waiting for a thaw. (According to some sources, with the ground frozen all around the plant, the temperature of the emerging flower is slightly over 60 degrees F.) The leaf rosettes that develop later are gigantic, giving it something of the look of a bright green hosta on steroids. It is, by any reckoning, a beautiful foliage plant—to look at. Its not inconsiderable defect is that its foliage has an extremely unpleasant odor when bruised. I am content simply to admire this plant out in the countryside, not invite it into the garden, but I have friends with greater olfactory daring who grow it.

The hybrid forms of the *Bergenia* that was such a favorite of Gertrude Jekyll's for the moist border have advanced considerably since her time. Many new cultivars have been bred in both Great

Britain and Germany, and their origins betrayed by names like 'Bressingham Bountiful', 'Bressingham White', and 'Margery Fish', or like 'Abendglut', 'Morgenrote', and 'Silberlicht'. Some of these imports are increasingly available from American nurseries, with more surely to come. They are valuable for their little towers (if, however, leaning towers) of pastel flowers in early spring, and for their persistent fleshy foliage, which in winter often veers from green to shades of red or purple. Bergenias are not at all fond of torrid summer weather, and they appreciate a little lime in the soil. Their common name, pigsqueak—well, no one has ever satisfactorily explained it to me.

Brunnera macrophylla does double duty in the moist and shady spots where it is happy. In the spring and early summer, it bears abundant sprays of tiny, rich blue, forget-me-not flowers. After it blooms, the leaves increase in size, making it effective in keeping down weeds. It is not at all happy in my light soil—it prefers clay— so I don't grow it any longer. I could keep the ordinary species growing for two years at most. A cream-and-white variegated form died at my hands in about a month. If I ever tried this species again, I'd go for a cultivar called 'Langtrees', which has wonderful spatterings and splashings of silver around the edges of its dark green, somewhat heart-shaped leaves.

I'm not sure that *Pulmonaria saccharata*, or lungwort, really qualifies as bold, but it certainly is one of the most striking plants in the garden almost year round, as its foliage departs in very late autumn and reappears in latest winter or earliest spring. Its blue, pink, or pink-changing-to-blue flowers in spring, which closely resemble those of Virginia bluebells, are welcome, but the foliage is really what counts; it endures, though bloom is brief. It is wonderfully spotted, marbled, mottled, and otherwise marked with cream, gray, or silver. American plantsmen like Henry Ross of Ohio have been busy with the genus, coming up with fine new cultivars like 'British Sterling', which has much more silvery white in it than green. But so far, the greatest number of interesting cultivars have originated in Great Britain—'Janet Fisk', 'Margery Fish', 'Mrs. Moon', 'Sissinghurst White', and others. All make beautiful mounds of foliage that, because of their silvery markings, do not fade into dimness in shade. They all are built to the same model, with minor variations in length, width, or shape of the leaves, and in their degree of variegation. The nursery which thus far has imported more of these cultivars is Klehm Nursery of Illinois, which made its name in peonies, iris, hemerocallis, and hostas (roughly in that order, over its long history) and which of late has introduced to America many fine plants of European origin, in several genera. But delightful confusion is in store for gardeners who plant as many of the new pulmonarias as they can lay their hands on. These cultivars are vegetatively propagated—'Janet Fisk', divided or increased by tissue-culture, will provide endless replicas of herself. But like columbines, tricyrtis, hellebores, and some other plants with slack sexual mores, pulmonarias reproduce by seeds as if they had no respect for their separate identities. Plant 'Mrs. Moon', 'Margery Fish', 'British Sterling', and other new pulmonarias in your garden now, and there's no telling what may crop up later in another corner. The sexual lives of plants—and their outcome—are much more thrilling than . . . (readers are invited to finish this sentence any way they like).

A final word on pulmonarias is in order. Almost all are clump formers, but a new one, 'Kingswood', from Ohio, spreads by underground stems. I hear that it is beautiful, but what excites me is its genetic capability of mothering (or fathering) new forms of pulmonaria that will roam and wander in shady spots, with fine results.

The quintessential plants of delicate tracery to combine with bolder things are, of course, the ferns, but "ferniness," a characteristic of foliage that is finely dissected to a greater or a lesser degree, can come from flowering plants as well.

Two of the best of these, both North American natives and both members of the fumitory family, are *Corydalis* and *Dicentra eximia*. They are also the same size—about twelve by twelve inches—and their blossoms show the family resemblance. *Corydalis lutea* has attractive light green foliage and bears a steady crop of little tubular golden yellow flowers steadily from late spring to fall. Another species, *C. cheilanthefolia*, blooms yellow in May and June. It remains attractive after blooming has ceased, with foliage that could easily be mistaken for the fronds of a small fern, as the foliage of *C. lutea* could not. There is a bronze form that keeps its foliage color into midsummer, when it reverts to green. *Dicentra eximia*, the fringed bleeding heart, has nicely cut blue-green foliage and abundant flowers in spring that are miniature versions of the lockets of the more spectacular Asian bleeding heart (widely regarded as a very old-fashioned plant, although it didn't reach gardens in America and Europe until the first half of the nineteenth century). The fringed bleeding heart shuts up its florist shop in late spring, but some hybrid cultivars, possibly involving *D. formosa*, stay the course almost to

Beneath the clouds of pale straw-yellow flowers on the leafless branches of *Corylopsis parviflora* in early spring at the Bishop's Close in Oregon, a carpet of *Pulmonaria angustifolia* paints the earth in deepest azure.

fall, even if sporadically. 'Luxuriant' bears cherry-pink flowers, 'Zestful' is a paler pink, and 'Snowdrift' presents no puzzle as to its color. *D. formosa*, one of the putative parents of these hybrids, also grows about twelve by twelve inches, with a slight tendency to creep, and its pale pink flowers appear over a long season. Its cultivar 'Sweetheart' is white.

Goat's beard (*Aruncus dioicus*) is a Japanese plant of almost shrublike proportions. Where it's happy, it looks in midsummer like an enormous, well-fed astilbe, four feet high and as wide. Its creamy panicles are very attractive. Its groundcover equivalent is dwarf goat's beard, the Korean species *A. aethusifolius*, which bears ferny foliage and creamy white flower plumes in late spring. It loves moist shade, is temperamental in hot and humid summers, and is reportedly difficult to establish in the Pacific Northwest. I know for sure that it has repeatedly sulked, then died, in our garden in southern New Jersey. I know this plant mainly from tempting photographs in nursery catalogs, and from moribund scraps of vegetation under my hopeful care. New England, maybe?

Saxifraga stolonifera, whose common names include mother of thousands, strawberry begonia, and strawberry geranium (although it's neither a begonia nor a geranium), is one of those surprising houseplants that prove remarkably winter-hardy outdoors, right through Zone 6. It spreads, like most strawberries, by runners that grow new little plants on their tips. The fleshy, hairy, rounded leaves with scalloped edges stay close to the earth, gradually making a dense cover. They have grand elegance for the prominent silver veins that fan out from the leaf petiole, in a pattern reminiscent of a river delta. This saxifrage blooms gracefully in late spring and early summer, producing twelve-inch spikes of tiny white flowers.

In encouraging the idea of combining these plants of delicate leaf with bolder ones, I hope I have not discouraged the idea of planting several of them together. They can echo each other's forms, and there is sufficient contrast of texture in having, let's say, a couple of hostas nearby—maybe one that is bold, but not overpowering, like a form of *Hosta tokudama*.

The clusters of deep blue flowers of agapanthus are beautifully set off by the swirling foliage and yellow button flowers of gray santolina. Pelargoniums and pale yellow achilleas complete this satisfying scene in the garden that Chris Rosmini designed for Ruth Borun in Brentwood, California.

4 Woody Plants as Groundcovers

The great peril in making a new garden lies in unfortunate or unwise choices of its woody plants. The corollary is that in inheriting a garden already made by someone else, the greatest problems will likely concern the woody plants established there. The only difference is that in the first case, you regret your own choices; in the second, you can blame another party.

Obviously, the biggest headaches as a garden matures will be its large trees. They may have seemed paltry at first, but trees grow up. A red maple looks harmless as a sapling, but in time becomes an enormous tree with voracious surface roots that spread everywhere, greedy for moisture and nourishment. A four-foot-tall blue Colorado spruce, so perky and perfectly conical, just like the perfect little

Christmas tree, looks cute next to a front sidewalk. But in twenty years it will be a very large tree, entirely out of scale for the garden of only moderate size. Nobody seems to realize until too late that a blue Atlas cedar planted next to a house is genetically programmed to grow fifty feet high and thirty feet wide in no time flat—and not to stop there, either. Copper beeches may grow fairly slowly, but they do grow, and with time, one is sufficient to hog almost all the space in a front yard of modest size. Weeping willows are seductively beautiful, but they grow rapidly, a school of woes swimming in their wake—brittle branches that snap in wind or ice storms, and thirsty roots that clog septic tanks and sewer lines.

When it comes to large woody plants, the best advice I know—based, alas, on my own long litany of mistakes—is to *think small about big trees.* Don't plant a red maple; plant a Japanese maple instead. You will thank yourself in years to come. Don't plant a spruce or a fir, unless it is a genetic dwarf. Go easy on oaks. Plant sourwoods, hybrid witch hazels, bayberries, and vitex instead, if you live where vitex is winter-hardy. I planted two ordinary mock oranges in the wrong spot, early in the making of my garden. They were too close to the house. I had to remove them only six years later, in three days of sweating and cursing, with pick, mattock, spade, and saw. I got the smaller one out finally, but the larger was more determined to hold on. I wrapped a chain around it, fastened the chain to the rear bumper of my car, and drove forward slowly and carefully. In a sudden lurch, the mock orange tottered and then broke loose. The bumper lay on the ground, still attached to the chain—but not to the car.

I don't regret planting every woody plant that got enormous. The dawn redwood at one corner of my back garden stands over sixty feet tall now, and it pleases me whenever I look at it. A ginkgo is on the muscle in just seven years, but I have no regrets. The shape of a ginkgo leaf is one of the most elegant forms in nature, and the radiant gold foliage in autumn is a final blessing at the end of the liturgy of the growing season.

There is another benefit to thinking small about woody plants. Big plants take up lots of room, excluding other plants you might like to have. Conversely, small plants take up less room, so there's more space for other plants. The obvious conclusion is that in a garden of modest size like mine, choosing smaller plants means that I can grow more plants than would otherwise be possible. The result is that I can have a garden of great diversity.

രാമ

Trouble at the Foundations—An American Misfortune

In my neighborhood, in one of several adjacent towns between Great Egg Bay and the Mullica River, residential development has been slow and steady since the early nineteenth century. The pleasant result is that Federal-style houses mingle with Victorian carpenter-gothic ones, bungalows from the 1920s, ranch houses from the 1950s, and the pseudo-Palladian dwellings that are the current local fad. New houses still go up on the remaining vacant lots, providing a chance to observe the early evolution of the landscaping that homeowners either do themselves or hire others to do. It is generally a series of early mistakes that either will have to be corrected somewhere down the line, at considerable expense in labor and money, or must simply be lived with, not very happily.

Here's the common pattern. The first order of business, either on the part of the developer who built the house or its maiden owners, is to put in a lawn, by seeding or by sodding. Some minimal, token gestures at "landscaping" may be carried out, with a few small conifers or broad-leafed evergreen shrubs randomly planted near the house. But the house still looks naked and bare. Its foundations show, and Americans hold an almost religious belief that foundation plantings—a mixed grouping of woody plants close to the house—are part of the moral order of the cosmos.

The assertion about a connection between foundation plantings and morality is neither fancy nor hyperbole. It is explicitly set forth in theories about domestic landscape architecture that have long since escaped into the public mind from their original source, as did Frank J. Scott's theories about suburban lawns.

A leading proponent of foundation plantings was Frank A. Waugh, a professor of landscape architecture at the University of Massachusetts in Amherst, who fully supported Scott's doctrine about lawns and the lack of enclosure. Writing in 1927, in a preface to Leonard H. Johnson's *Foundation Planting*, he concurred with Scott. "In the Old Country the primary planting which gives a home its individuality is a hedge all along the street front," he wrote. "The American house is characteristically different in that it is open to the street." But he went further. In what he called "the ideal American home," the "plantings, instead of forming a hedge on the street line, are pushed back against the foundations of the house. They are foundation plantings." Such plantings, Waugh argued, were "fundamental to the whole of American domestic architecture." They "both protect and express the family life." They turned mere houses into real homes. They had a moral and a civic value. "Promoting this campaign of planting," he preached, was "patriotic duty."

Waugh's ideas triumphed, as did Scott's. Let us consider further the common pattern when people first occupy a new house.

On the first sunny and halfway warm Saturday in spring, the typical new homeowners make a beeline for a local garden center, where for weeks trucks from the major wholesale nurseries specializing in woody plants have been disgorging their cargoes of shrubs and trees.

They are about to dress up the foundations of their house. Pushing a large hand truck, they go up and down the aisles of nursery stock making their selections. They pick up a white fir (*Abies concolor*) that stands about four feet tall. They like its blue-gray needles and its pleasing conical shape. They go for a deodar cedar (*Cedrus deodara*), a pyramidal plant some five feet tall, with blue-green needles, a soft texture, and graceful, slightly weeping branches. They select a couple of fat little mugo pines. They load onto their truck one or two plants of *Rhododendron catawbiense*—healthy-looking plants already three feet tall and wide, and loaded with flower buds. They throw in some yews, both columnar and spreading forms, as well as some large barberries and a dirt-cheap forsythia just coming into flower. There has to be holly, of course, so 'Blue Prince' and 'Blue Princess' go on the second hand truck now needed to haul their selections up to the cash register and out to the car.

Once home, in a bed that was previously prepared around the house foundations, they unload their shrubbery and begin to arrange it, standing back with a critical eye, and then moving the rhododendron where the deodar cedar has been, and vice versa. They want a pleasing combination: plants with vertical habits contrasting nicely with ones that are more spreading and horizontal. Everything is set in place where it is to grow, but there are still gaps. The plants have a stingy look somehow, so it's back to the garden center for another rhododendron, a Japanese black pine, a bridal wreath spiraea, and three mophead hydrangeas. By Sunday evening, everything has been planted, watered, and mulched. Everything looks just wonderful, as if it had been growing there forever.

It will continue to look wonderful—for three years, five at the most. It is in the nature of almost all of these plants to grow large, or

to grow very large indeed. Deodar cedar matures at a final height of anywhere between forty-five and seventy feet, white fir, between thirty and fifty-five. There are rhododendrons that stay demure all their lives, but *Rhododendron catawbiense* is not among them. It is a hog for territory. The selection of plants described here will fight with one another. They will block windows and head for the eaves. They will quickly be out of scale with themselves and with the house behind them that they are swallowing up. Pruning may keep them in check, but not very successfully, and it will distort the beauty of the natural forms that they would have if planted in a more appropriate location.

What has gone wrong here? One answer is haste. It is virtually impossible to plant so many woody plants in one place on a spring weekend and have a satisfactory result for long. Another answer is convenience. Many garden centers deal mostly in very common woody plants that can be easily and economically propagated by large wholesale nurseries, and a preponderance of these plants have gargantuan tendencies. Homeowner greed, sorry to say, probably played its part. That garden center may have had *Abies balsamea* 'Nana', the dwarf balsam fir, sitting in its container just down the aisle from the white fir. Both cost the same, but the dwarf fir was only ten inches high and the white fir was over four times as big. When moved by the principle "more bang for the buck," we often get into trouble.

In Geof Beasley and Jim Sampson's Oregon garden, a low, spreading planting of *Oxalis oregana* is pierced by the bold leaf-blades and nodding white flowers of lily-of-the-valley. Added luster comes from *Dicentra eximia* in the background, offering ferny bluish-green leaves and locket flowers of soft rose.

This well-known garden of Mrs. Emily Whaley, enclosed in the style characteristic of Charleston's Historic District, is one of very few there that is regularly open to the public. Visitors may leave donations to one of the owner's favorite charities, such as a fund to restore the steeple of St. Philip's Episcopal Church that was damaged by Hurricane Hugo. Seen here is a corner of the garden with dwarf boxwood and *Saxifraga stolonifera.*

Furthermore, the conventional wisdom about much in life can often stand some scrutiny. The conventional wisdom in America during much of the twentieth century has been that a house must have foundation plantings. I'm not at all convinced. Unlike Frank Waugh, I see no moral or patriotic imperative here. Cramming as many woody things as possible right next to the house may bring on problems with excessive moisture and rot. There are alternatives. One very pleasant one is to leave a broad path next to the house, putting groups of woody plants beyond the path. They will eventually lend privacy, yet allow sunlight to stream through first-floor windows in the winter, and breezes to flow in them in the summer. Another alternative is generous decking next to the house, perhaps on two or even three sides. A deck conceals a foundation as well as any plant can, and it won't grow up to the eaves or ever need to be pruned. It can be home to many plants in containers, and it provides a very civilized transitional space between house and garden. But even if there's no deck, another question pops up: What's wrong with the entire facade of a building, bottom to top, being open to view instead of partially concealed by a mass of vegetation? Quite a few houses in France, Spain, Italy, and a few cities in the United States such as Charleston, South Carolina, sit right on the sidewalk, their only horticultural adornment a flower box or two. They look just fine, sans shrubbery. No one rushes by, eyes averted, to avoid the dwelling's indecent exposure in its lower part.

Knowledge and a willingness to go to some trouble to learn the ways of woody plants are important tools in making a garden that will bring satisfaction over many years. Anyone who regularly visits the many public arboreta that America is blessed with will benefit from the experience in his or her own garden. Once someone sees a magnificent *Cedrus deodora* growing to a great height out in the open at the Arnold Arboretum, the sight of a small specimen on sale at a garden center will not be much of a temptation. A visit to the National Arboretum in Washington, home to the Gotelli collection of dwarf conifers, probably will convince the homeowner with a small garden that these are the ones to seek out. Mail-order nurseries—the really good ones—have highly educational catalogs. They also sell many rare and unusual plants that are difficult to obtain elsewhere.

I have on my desk at the moment two such catalogs. One is from Heronswood Nursery, in Kingston, Washington. The other is from Roslyn Nursery in Dix Hills, New York.

The Heronswood catalog is loaded, among other things, with unfamiliar genera of woody plants that sound terrific even in the understated prose of a catalog devoid of hyperbole or hard sell. (I will eventually get around to how I discovered some species of *Rubus* for groundcover, thanks to this nursery.) It also offers rare and exotic species of genera I do know, in their more common forms. There are eight barberries I've never heard of, ditto eight different boxwoods, five callicarpas or beauty berries, thirteen hypericums, and so on. Fine small nurseries like this one offer a treasure trove of plants few local nurseries can match, because they can't afford to; the average local customer wants plants that are familiar, not something that is strange or bizarre.

The Roslyn catalog is equally fine, especially for its dwarf conifers, dwarf forms of broad-leafed evergreens that usually are much larger, and woody groundcovers.

Before detailing some of the temptations in this catalog, I must digress. When looking for plants of manageable ultimate size for small gardens, it helps to know a little Latin. Some of the species names, or epithets, are *adpressus* (lying flat), *compactus* (compact— or thick), *parvulus* (quite small), *parvus* (small), *pygmaeus* (small for its genus), *pumilus* (dwarf), *repens* (creeping), and *reptans* (creeping). Cultivar names also can be useful tips on size. *Ilex opaca*, or American holly, is a sizable tree, but the cultivar 'Maryland Dwarf' isn't (it tops off at three feet or under).

Skating on Thin Ice, Helped by a Nursery Catalog

When writing about gardening, I have a terrible handicap. I don't feel comfortable writing about something that I have not grown long enough to know, or that I have no trustworthy testimony about from other gardeners. When it comes to the topic of woody groundcover plants, I have another handicap, dictated by the modest dimensions of the home ground where Hella and I have been gardening for many years. There seem to be no limits to the number of herbaceous perennials or bulbs that we can grow, and we can experiment with new annuals each year. There is always room for another container on the deck or in one of the side yards, where we can grow plants with special needs or plants that would be dangerous to set loose in the garden.

Woody plants are another matter. We have stretched to the limit our ability to accommodate any more large trees or big shrubs. There wasn't even much room left for small woody plants not too long ago, and now there is none. I placed a hefty order for quite a few, from Roslyn and some other nurseries. They are growing and doing well. But all I can do for now, hewing to actual experience, is to talk about why I planted them and about my hopes. What follows is a small part of some large nursery orders, with comments. I skate on thin ice, because it will be a few years before there is the thicker ice of experience to skate on.

Arctostaphylos uvi-ursi 'Massachusetts' and 'Vancouver Jade'. These are selected forms of the native bearberry, or kinnikinick. They form creeping mats of very glossy, dark green leaves.

Azalea 'Joseph Hill'. Using seed of a low-growing *Rhododendron* species from Japan, Polly Hill has, for over two decades, bred virtually a new race of very late-blooming semi-evergreen hybrid azaleas eminently suitable for groundcover use. Collectively known as the North Tisbury azaleas, these include such cultivars as 'Hill's Single Red', 'Marilee', and 'Michael Hill'. 'Joseph Hill' is one of the best known. It has intense red flowers, reaches between six and fourteen inches in height, and may eventually spread to four feet.

Chamaecyparis obtusa 'Little Marky'. This conifer is supposed to make a chartreuse pyramid that soars to thirty inches tall in about fifteen years. Doesn't sound like it will ever make much of a nuisance of itself.

Forsythia viridissima 'Bronxensis'. Forsythias are sprawling, unkempt large shrubs, bright in their brief bloom in early spring, but offering little to the garden the rest of the year. This one, which is supposed to stay at two feet or under, may turn out fine. I suspect, however, that it will be a sparse bloomer.

Leiophyllum buxifolium var. *prostratum*. Box sand myrtle, native to sandy habitats from New Jersey to Florida, is a sun-loving, low creeping evergreen whose foliage assumes bronzed tints in winter. It blooms freely in May, with copious clusters of small, pinkish white flowers.

Microbiota decussata. I have heard a lot of praise for this Siberian evergreen, unusual among conifers in that shade is its preference, although it can take sun, too. Its maximum height is said to be two feet or less, with a possible spread of five feet or more. Its bright green foliage is plumy or feathery.

Salix yezoalpina. I do have an early report on this deciduous shrub, a prostrate willow with silvery down on its pale green leaves, and erect snowy white catkins that stand upright above the low branches in mid-spring. Barry Yinger had praised it to the skies, and I was eager to see it. It seemed to be everything that he had promised. But when I planted it, it died right away. I think it does not like full sun and sandy soil. Willows tend to be creatures of huge thirst. I will try again, in a moister and more protected spot.

Sarcocca hookeriana var. *humilis.* Sweet box, native to cold provinces of China, is an evergreen that grows to about two feet tall and suckers to form colonies as much across. The tiny evergreen leaves are glossy and attractive. Clusters of tiny white flowers borne in the leaf axils are inconspicuous, but sweetly fragrant and, on female plants, are followed by purple berries.

Skimmia japonica 'Rubella'. This fairly low-growing evergreen shrub, a male cultivar, shows clusters of deep red buds in late fall, accompanied by red-tinged foliage. The white flowers in the spring are quite fragrant.

Vaccinium crassifolium 'Well's Delight'. This creeping blueberry has pink bell-like flowers in spring, followed by edible dark purple-black flowers.

I'm off the thin ice. Now I can go on to things I can speak of with more confidence (with a little help from my friends).

Junipers Afoot

In an earlier chapter, I let it slip out that the widely used, multitudinous cultivars of our native *Juniperus horizontalis*, a low, spreading evergreen conifer that is one real toughie among woody groundcovers, was not quite as dear to my heart as some other plants (as dear as, say, some species of *Rubus* and a little spreading rose called 'Snow Carpet'). It is often better to turn to someone else to make the best possible case for a plant that one is not enthusiastic about. My Virgil through the world of low, carpeting junipers is Kim Tripp, Curator of Conifers of the Arboretum at the North Carolina State University in Raleigh, which has probably the world's largest collection of these plants, started some years ago by a graduate student, Larry Hatch. Carpet junipers are, after all, extremely popular in this country, and they deserve their day in court.

Kim was a little surprised when I confessed that my enthusiasm for these conifers had always been at a low ebb, with no likelihood that it would ever reach high tide. We batted the matter about a bit. She asked me if I was perhaps thinking of these junipers as "mono-clonal plantings"—as plantings of just one clone or cultivar. Did I have in mind "mono-clonal plantings that simply fill space that is not physically appropriate for a lawn?"

In Ann Armstrong's garden in Charlotte, azaleas and Japanese maples provide a woody backdrop for hostas and *Aquilegia canadensis*.

That was exactly what I had in mind, and that was exactly how carpet junipers were usually used. A sea of them between a bank and a parking lot. A whole gaggle of them, all one kind, underneath the lighted sign in front of a Holiday Inn.

That was not what Kim Tripp had in mind. *That* was a failure of imagination. Didn't I realize that *"Juniperus horizontalis* cultivars may be successfully combined in a mosaic of textures, forms, and colors to create a living carpet of pattern in the landscape?" she asked. Her enthusiasm was infectious. "The soft gold of 'Mother Lode' curling through the silvery foliage of 'Jade River', or the play of textures when 'Watnong' and 'Heidi' intertwine, cannot be duplicated by any other kind of planting."

I got the picture. And Kim went on to suggest that I might get a bit beyond carpet juniper cultivars like 'Blue Rug' and 'Bar Harbor' —the staples of every garden center in the land each spring—to explore some of those on display at the Arboretum. She suggested several, chosen for their disease resistance, winter hardiness, and ability to withstand torrid, muggy southern summers, as well as for good color year round and availability from nurseries. (Some of the best, however, she said might take a little searching to locate.)

Here are some of her recommendations and what she liked about each:

'Argenteus'. "It's a rich blue-green form, with contrasting gray new growth in spring, and it gets eleven inches high, spreading to five feet."

'Blue Horizon'. "It's an exceptionally flat form, with intense blue foliage that turns an attractive bronze-green in winter. It stays about seven inches tall and spreads to five feet."

'Heidi'. "This one spreads very slowly to only three feet, gets fifteen inches tall, and has handsome gray-green foliage. Put it where you can enjoy it up close for its unusually striking fernlike foliage."

'Jade River'. "This cultivar has beautiful blue-green foliage with a slight silvery cast on long, spreading leaders over a low, tight mat. It grows between eight and ten inches high, and spreads six feet, with a softly undulating appearance."

'Mother Lode'. "This patented cultivar from Iseli Nurseries in Oregon is relatively slow growing and

low, with twelve inches probably the maximum
height. The plumy-textured foliage is unbelievably
bright gold."

'Watnong'. "This one is very low and tight, has
clear green beadlike foliage, and gets only six
inches high. Very dense growth."

Kim also had high praise for 'Blue Forest', 'Douglasii' (a.k.a.
'Waukegan'), 'Lime Glow', 'Prince of Wales', 'Turquoise Spreader',
and 'Yukon Belle'.

I then brought up *Juniperus conferta*, the shore juniper from Japan
that I have grown and admired in my garden for years. Wanting to
make amends for being so backward about *J. horizontalis*, I said I
liked this one. She asked if I had seen its cultivar 'Silver Mist'. I
hadn't. She said I had to try it as soon as possible: it's well-
mannered; it makes a lovely silvery gray mound in the garden; it
would do well in the sandy soil of my coastal garden; it's the best.

I'll take her advice. When it comes to low junipers and many other
woody plants, I trust Kim Tripp a lot.

Little Crape Myrtles

I garden near the northernmost range of winter hardiness for one
of the most glorious of all the woody plants that blossom in the
summer, crape myrtle, or *Lagerstroemia indica*. It grows here, but
only to about ten feet tall, not the twenty feet that is more typical in
Norfolk, Virginia, or the thirty-five feet I have seen on outstanding
specimens in Beaufort, South Carolina. It blooms here, and anyone
would think it surpassingly lovely through all of July and August,
unless he or she had seen it growing in the South. Crape myrtle is
the most magnificent plant of summer. It thrives on heat and sun.
Its dark and glossy little leaves are handsome enough that they would
probably be sufficient reason to grow it. They also turn orange-red,
yellow, maroon, or purple in the fall, depending on the cultivar. The
exfoliating bark, which peels off in long strips to reveal interesting
patches of gray and russet below, is beautiful. My friend Hannah
Withers, in Charlotte, North Carolina, has showed me a little trick
she plays with the trunks of the several big crape myrtles in her
beautiful enclosed back garden. She polishes the trunks with flannel
rags until they turn a pale grayish tan, with a waxy sheen. The colors
of crape myrtles are pure magic—big billowing clouds of watermelon

red, deep pink, pale and delicate pink, lavender, lilac, magenta, and winy purple. The rounded seed-pods, which are beaked where they have opened to release the seeds, remain through the winter, giving these small trees seasonal interest even then.

Northerners, even those who live much farther north than I, don't have to live without crape myrtles. In colder regions, the plants die back to the ground in the winter, but they sprout new stems late the following spring. Since they bloom on new wood, they become, in effect, herbaceous perennials. But it's a far different matter to wander beneath the rows of crape myrtles lining the street of a city like Norfolk, and to look up through those clouds of color to the blue sky above.

When I lived in the South, I never knew there was any such thing as a crape myrtle groundcover. But there is. I grew a dozen plants in mixed colors from seed in 1977, and they have been with me ever since, in a little massed planting adjacent to the step that leads from our side garden to the deck. The seed came from Park's in South Carolina, under a name that embarrasses me—"crapemyrtlettes." Diminutives are fine in Spanish or Italian, but they sound cutesy and contrived in English. So let's have none of this "-ettes" stuff, and call them what they are: little lagerstroemias.

I don't think I've ever planted a package of seeds that brought such pleasure for so many years as did that package of little lagerstroemias. They germinated well, and they bloomed their first summer, on plants that reached about a foot tall. In their second year, they reached their mature size, anywhere from fifteen to twenty-four inches high. Their habit varies; some are upright, some more low and slouching. The colors are good—lavenders, several shades of pink, and a watermelon red. They show the usual range of leaf color in the autumn. They have never died back to the roots in the winter, and I think that with a little protection they would be wood-hardy to Zone 6, root-hardy to Zone 5. Once established, they are very effective as weed-suppressing groundcovers.

A Rose that Creeps

Perhaps the most surprising groundcover I grow is a rose—surprising because finding a rose that's a groundcover sounds as peculiar as a heavy snowfall in June. Appropriately, the name of the rose is 'Snow Carpet', bred in England by the prominent rosarian Sam McGredy. It stays low, to about ten inches tall, and it spreads far and wide by trailing prostrate canes that root every so often to form

Mixed dwarf conifers, other small evergreens, and dianthus form a pleasing combination on this slope at the University of British Columbia Botanical Garden.

new plants. It may be hard to find, but it's worth the search, for it's a dandy plant in every way, except for its prickles (which are vicious, but in no way approach those of *Rosa rugosa* in their ability to stab the unwary).

'Snow Carpet' produces just one main flush of bloom, for about two weeks in June, with occasional sporadic flowers appearing during the rest of the summer. The flowers are flat, not buxomly rounded, and they are about the size of a quarter. They are white with creamy centers, slightly fragrant, and so abundant during the peak of bloom that they almost conceal the leaves. The foliage is a glossy dark green, and in five years I have never found a trace of black spot, mildew, or any of the other loathsome diseases and afflictions that prey on other roses. The leaves persist into very late autumn, and in the winter the stems remain green, offering with their prickles an interesting texture.

This small-flowered, low-growing rose has a lot of muscle. In five years it spread six feet in every direction, smothering every plant in its path, including weeds. It grows on its own roots, not on a grafted rootstock. Propagation is dirt-simple. Put a brick down on a runner, and in a couple of months a new plant will have rooted and be ready to separate from its mother and conquer a new site.

The Cheering Hypericums

The genus *Hypericum* is well inhabited, with many species distributed over a vast range extending from Japan to Eurasia, and a number of North American natives as well. The range of winter hardiness is extremely wide: the Asian species *H. perforatum* is hardy to Zone 3, but *H. revolutum*, whose native habitat extends from Saudi Arabia to South Africa, will survive only in frost-free regions. All are instantly recognizable for their golden yellow flowers with prominent whiskery stamens that make them seem as though they'd be usable, in a pinch, as powder puffs. The blossoms vary in size from truly tiny (those of *H. densiflorum* check in at half an inch across) to quite large (those of *H. calycinum* can exceed three inches). Some well-known cultivars, such as 'Hidcote', are large shrubs, to four feet or more, and so do not qualify as groundcovers in the strict sense. Others, however, are more diminutive.

Hypericums are largely summer bloomers over a long season, although the first to flower in my garden, *H. olympicum*, blooms for only two weeks, if that, starting in late May. It is nonetheless a little

Dwarf sweet box (*Sarcococca hookeriana* var. *humilis*), a low woody evergreen from Hupeh, China, seen here in the Platt garden in Portland in mid-winter, spreads by suckering, but not uncontrollably.

charmer, with lemon-yellow flowers about an inch in diameter. It does not exceed eight inches in height, and its spread—to about a foot—is modest. Its tiny, gray-green leaves grow on stems that curve in a tight arc, as if the plant were hugging itself.

A more serious contender as a groundcover is *Hypericum calycinum*, or Aaron's beard, a Eurasian species that grows between twelve and eighteen inches tall. It covers a large area quickly, for its stems root as they run. Its slightly blue-green foliage is attractive most of the growing season, and it flowers prolifically from late June up to the end of August. It may not flower well in the Deep South, and it can be plagued by rust diseases. The somewhat shorter native North American species, *Hypericum bucklei*, is more reliable. Its season of bloom in early summer lasts only a month or so, but there's a bonus late in the year, when its gray-green foliage turns toward crimson.

Santolinas

There are almost twenty species in the genus *Santolina*, most of them native to Spain or Italy. There are some cultivars circulating among British gardeners, but for the moment, Americans need bother their heads about only two of these low, woody subshrubs, which look great almost all year long and have a pleasantly pungent scent. One is *Santolina chamaecyparissus*, or lavender cotton, a silvery gray plant that stays under twenty inches. It has been grown in America since early colonial times; John Josselyn noted in *New England's Rarities Discovered*, the book he published in 1674 detailing his voyages from England to New England in 1638 and 1663, that lavender cotton "groweth pretty well . . . But Lavender is not for the Climate." (Despite their Mediterranean origin, santolinas are winter-hardy to Zone 5.) The other species is listed in virtually every catalog for the time being as *S. virens*, but taxonomical sticklers will insist that it's really a form of *S. rosmarinifolia*. It is a brilliant green, and it is this one that provided the genus its name, which comes from the Latin words for "holy flax." I have never been able to decipher the reasons that green santolina should be holy flax, or gray santolina, lavender cotton, but we are sometimes left with names after whoever dreamed them up has departed this earth, leaving no explanation. I do know that in the herbal traditions of ancient Rome, santolina mulled in wine was regarded as an excellent antidote for viper bites.

Rose 'Snow Carpet' makes
an attractive, trouble-free, low
and spreading groundcover,
with a heavy flush of flowers in
June, sporadic blooms the rest
of the summer.

Some hypericums, like this
unidentified hybrid, display
attractive fruits and flowers at
the same time.

Hypericum 'Hidcote'
displays the large, showy flower
of one of the most popular and
spectacular cultivars in this
genus.

These two santolinas combine beautifully together. The gray one has coarser, needlelike foliage, and its texture is reminiscent of a coral reef. Green santolina has much finer, smaller, more densely packed leaves. Both bloom in midsummer with a huge crop of little pompom flowers—deep gold on the gray species, pale lemon on the other. They associate beautifully with lavender, lamb's ears, and ornamental blue fescue grass, and this particular grouping of plants becomes even more sensational when tall golden anthemis is placed in the background with the immensely shrubby *Lavatera* 'Barnsley'. The small golden daisies of the anthemis echo the gold of gray santolina's little buttony flowers, and the pink mallowlike flowers of the lavatera are set off well by the vivid green and the soft gray of the santolinas in the front of this planting.

Mosaics of Woody Groundcovers

I will borrow here Kim Tripp's point about carpet junipers—that they can be used "mono-clonally" (meaning that a single kind is planted en masse to fill a space), or they can be combined in different forms to make a pleasing tapestry or mosaic. This same principle applies equally to other small woody plants, including santolinas, hypericums, rose 'Snow Carpet', and dwarf crape myrtles. These plants are lovely and useful individually. Several plants of the same kind can be planted together to fill a space. But they can also be combined with one another in various ways, since they share the same need for full sun without copious watering.

For sunny places that are not overly blessed with moisture, many other low woody plants can serve as tesserae in a mosaic, or as threads in a tapestry. The list is not infinite, but it is so extensive that I can only scratch the surface here with a few examples.

Nandina domestica, as ordinarily encountered, is by no means a groundcover, as it grows upward of six feet. It is, however, entirely admirable. Its somewhat ferny leaves have a graceful, airy texture. Its long-lasting panicles of white flowers in midsummer give it distinction, and are followed by deep red or occasionally yellow fruits that may not fall off until early spring. (Birds seem to disdain them.) Its leaves persist well into winter, tending in the South to be evergreen. In colder areas where it is winter-hardy, at least as far north as New York City, they turn a bronzed shade of henna with purple overtones. There is only one species in the genus, but several much smaller cultivars have come along of late. The smallest is 'San Gabriel', which in my garden stays under ten inches. Its deeply dissected leaves give it a wispy look. 'Atropurpurea Nana' makes a little mound about a foot high. It neither flowers nor fruits, but in full sun in winter its foliage blazes a brilliant red or smolders in shades of red and wine. Neither of these cultivars is prone to wander, but 'Harbor Dwarf' spreads by underground stems. It is a two-foot version of the common species, a dead look-alike in foliage, flowers, and fruit. Other cultivars are available on the West Coast, but these are the ones most commonly sold in the East.

Some small spring-flowering shrubs are, like the dwarf nandinas, scaled-down versions of larger plants. Three of them are andromedas, or *Pieris japonica*. The smallest, 'Pygmaea', tops off at around ten inches. 'Bisbee Dwarf' exceeds it in height by a few inches. The largest of this trio, 'Little Heath Green', eventually makes it to three feet, but it is still diminutive compared to larger cultivars that range from six to ten feet. These three shrubs all have the characteristic flowering habit of andromedas, producing, in late winter or early spring, cascades of numerous white or pink-tinged cream bell-like flowers reminiscent of the florets of lily-of-the-valley.

Later in the spring comes another dwarf version of a much rangier shrub, *Deutzia gracilis* 'Nikko', a recent import from a Japanese nursery. 'Nikko', which can be kept to a height of about two feet with modest pruning right after it blooms, absolutely covers itself with a foam of small flowers of the purest white imaginable. A second season of spectacle occurs in fall, when the foliage turns a stunning red-purple.

Then there are the little brooms of spring. *Genista pilosa* 'Vancouver Gold' is a six-inch tall ground-hugger that spreads to about thirty inches. *G. tinctoria* 'Flore Pleno', slightly taller, rises to ten inches but spreads less widely. *G. lydia*, the largest of these little yellow-flowered shrubby legumes, grows to about two feet. Its arching green branches stay virtually leafless, resulting in a bizarre but fascinating effect. These brooms have in common a very nonplussing trait: they may die in winter, for no discernible reason. The best attitude toward them is to enjoy them while they live, rejoice if they make it back in spring, and remain stoic in the face of their demise.

Daphnes are also spring shrubs with morbid tendencies. They can be murdered (dry soil will do it), but they can also just commit hara-kiri, even when kept moist. They are wonderful nonetheless. *Daphne cneorum* 'Eximia', which stays under ten inches, delights the eye and nose alike when its clusters of crimson buds open into deep pink flowers with exquisite perfume. *D. retusa*, larger at twenty-four inches in height, bears clusters of sweetly fragrant white flowers. 'Carol Mackie' offers variegated green-and-white foliage and very sweet-smelling pink flowers. I take the view that a dead daphne should be replaced immediately, because it would be painful to be without one.

I hate to continue what sounds like a forecast of floral obituaries, but heaths and heathers aren't exactly Methuselahs, either. These small evergreen shrubs are short-lived. The best way to cope with the brevity of their sojourns among the living is to plant a couple of new ones every year. They don't die en masse, like lemmings rushing over a cliff into the sea. It's simply that the occasional heath or heather will look sickly, die back at the tips, then die back by the branch, until finally what's left is a dead plant. Just pull it up, and be glad that there's a little one coming along to take its place.

Specialized nurseries offer heathers (cultivars of *Calluna vulgaris*) in great numbers. It isn't unusual to find over 100 different kinds of these summer-blooming low shrubs in a catalog. The colors of their flowers cover a wide gamut in the white-to-purple range, including mauve, pink, lilac, lavender, purple, and crimson. Foliage color is extremely diverse, including gray, blue-gray, copper, and yellow, as well as many different hues of green. Of those I have grown, I especially like 'Robert Chapman', for its chartreuse foliage that changes to orange in cold weather, and 'Sir John Charringon', for its orange-tipped, primrose-yellow branches that turn deep red in the fall. These changes of leaf color lend additional interest just as the Darleyensis winter heaths, hybrids of *Erica carnea* and *E. erigena*, begin to chime in. There aren't as many hybrid winter heath cultivars as there are of heathers, but there are still plenty. The two most common are 'Mediterranean White' and 'Mediterranean Pink', both of which may even turn up in garden centers, but it is well worth the effort to seek out other cultivars such as 'Ada S. Collins', 'Arthur Johnson', and 'Jack Brummage' from mail-order sources, including Heaths and Heathers in Elma, Washington. All of these hybrid winter heaths stay in constant bloom from November through March.

Heathers and heaths combine beautifully with other small shrubs that share their preferences for full sun and lean, slightly acidic, well-drained soil. But heathers and heaths can also be combined splendidly to make an entirely bi-generic garden. Inspiring examples of such plantings can be found at Kew and at the botanical gardens in Edinburgh and Zurich. A warning is in order, however. A few

heathers and heaths can lead to delightful obsession; some gardeners go on from *Calluna vulgaris* (Scotch heather) to related genera and species such as *Erica vagans* (Cornish heath), *Daboecia cantabrica* (Irish heath), *Bruckenthalia spiculifolia* (Balkan heath), and more. The obsession becomes hopeless once *Erica cinerea* (bell or twisted heath) is discovered, for its several cultivars have unusually intense floral color, often combined with striking foliage. Unusually fine are 'Golden Drop' (mauve flowers, copper foliage), 'Pink Ice' (deep pink flowers, silvery leaves), and 'Velvet Night' (flowers the color of beets, dark green foliage).

Except for *Nandina* 'Harbor Dwarf', all the woody plants for a low mosaic or tapestry garden of groundcovers are stay-at-homes. They may enlarge and spread outward, but they do not roam or suffer from wanderlust. I see no reason, however, to exclude as threads in a tapestry a few plants that weave.

Some of the best of these are found among the small cotoneasters —*Cotoneaster adpressus* 'Little Gem', *C. apiculatus*, *C. dammeri* 'Coral Beauty', *C. horizontalis*, *C. salicifolius*, and other kinds in this genus, which also includes some very large shrubs. The ankle-to knee-level kinds are notably drought resistant, and some are ever-green. They make an almost impenetrable groundcover, yet they will share space with other woody plants. I have *C. apiculatus* growing

Heaths, heathers, and low conifers complement one another most handsomely in the Edinburgh Botanical Garden.

with *Juniperus conferta* in the same bed, and they seem amiably wed. Cotoneasters bloom pleasantly, if not spectacularly, in late spring, and they have colorful fruits in late summer and fall. These merits, combined with the plants' diversity in height and growth habit, suggest that it is unnecessary to search for more woody groundcovers. But the susceptibility of cotoneasters to fire blight makes it advisable not to go overboard on them. The diverse garden stands the best chance of surviving the assault of diseases and harmful insects.

Euonymus fortunei is a low evergreen shrub that creeps, weaves, and sometimes climbs. There are many cultivars, but I'll just go for the best. 'Harlequin' has beautiful small green-and-white leaves that look fresh all year, and the new growth in spring is tinged with pink. It's one more of the many East Asian plants we can thank Barry Yinger for.

The Little Bramble Cousins

In 1990, on a visit to Dan Hinkley's exciting Heronswood Nursery in Kingston, Washington, I loaded the car up with many rare and unusual treasures. One was a little groundcover in the genus *Rubus*, whose many species include some spectacularly prickly plants like raspberries and blackberries. But this plant was only lightly armed, and it looked nothing like a blackberry bush. Its rich green leaves, shaped something like the club suit in a deck of cards, were crisp green, slightly deckle-edged, and pebbly in texture. It was *Rubus calycinoides*, which is fairly common in the Pacific Northwest, but not often seen on the East Coast. I liked it, and I liked what it started to do in my garden, spreading out in all directions by runners that rooted as they went, staying quite close to the ground. That fall I noticed that the leaves, which persist all winter, assumed tones of cordovan red with hints of copper—very pretty. The plant greened up beautifully in the spring and continued to spread. But its spread was well-mannered. This new groundcover in my garden wasn't going to make a pest of itself, or shove anything else aside.

In 1992, when the Heronswood catalog arrived in February, fatter and more tempting than ever, I noted that there was an even larger number of species of *Rubus* than before. Their listings and descriptions were prefaced by Dan Hinkley's remark that he was in the middle of a craze for the genus. *Rubus nepalensis*, another groundcover species, sounded especially fine, and so I ordered one.

This border of heaths and heathers at Wakehurst Place possesses subtle beauty throughout the year.

Low heaths and heathers fill the lower tier of this part of Dr. Jack Elliott's garden in Kent, with purple barberry occupying the middle tier, beneath an *Acer griseum*.

Aurelian hybrid lilies in mixed colors rising out of low spreading cotoneasters, with yellow broom above the lilies, makes an unforgettably winning garden picture at Tintinhull. The rhythm of this combination makes it worth imitating.

I liked it just as well as *R. calycinoides*, but it had different characteristics. Its trifoliate leaves, like those of strawberry, were glossy. And the plant spread outward in a widening clump, instead of sending out runners. I thought it had great promise.

By then, Dan and I were friends, and both of us were members of a National Campaign Steering Committee to raise funds for the Arboretum at North Carolina State University. After the committee's spring meeting, I asked him to give me his assessment of these and other species in the genus that might make good groundcovers. He wrote:

Collectively, the *Rubi* I grow in my garden, which number forty-five species to date, are all movers and shakers. Yet it is the groundcovering species which are the most civilized, as they inform you as to their directions and intentions, rather than startling you with a stem arising 6 feet away from the mother plant.

Rubus parvus grows in my rock garden, and I admire this plant that gets no more than four inches tall for the bramble it pretends not to be. With jagged-toothed edges of finger shape and length, it forms an impenetrable groundcover, yet remains politely non-invasive. The dark green leaves take on a bronzed russet in the winter months. Though it is a New Zealand native, it has experienced an extended punishment of 5 degrees F. and survived, yet would probably be damaged without protection below zero. This species and *R. calycinoides* and *R. nepalensis* are the exceptions rather than the rule in their tendency to produce solid carpets of groundcovering leaves and stems. By far the majority of low-growing species of *Rubus* glide along at ground level, forming pieces of the puzzle that collectively is called the forest floor. While it is the utility of the former species that I admire, it is the knitters and gliders that both challenge and delight me in my garden. They teach me the concept of contrived naturalness—and demand the discipline to say enough is enough as you subdue the rampage. *Rubus tricolor* is a dazzling species, yet I have seen it used by too many designers who expected it to perform as a carpet maker rather than simply a marvelous triad of colors in the multicolored tapestry. The specific epithet is derived from the translucent red bristly hairs on the young stems in combination with glossy green leaves undercoated with a glaucous bloom.

At Heronswood Nursery in Kingston, Washington, *Rubus nepalensis* shows off as a new groundcover of high merit and promise alike. The crinkled trifoliate leaves and the creeping growth habit are the main attractions, the small white flowers a bonus.

Rubus chamaemorus, dubbed the cloudberry, has formed a reasonably sized colony in a dry section of a mixed border where many other groundcovers are found. The leaves are delicately strawberry-like, and copious flowers of very soft pink are produced at ground level. It, too, knits through its neighboring groundcovers, in this case, several species of *Gaultheria*, but by underground stolons rather than above-ground stems. In demeanor, it resembles our most beautiful native species, *Rubus pedatus*, known commonly as the mountain raspberry. Delicate leaves and flowers of white are found lacing through and above mosses and ferns in coniferous forests at moderate elevations in the Northwest. It has established itself well in my woodland garden, and I have found it to be a good groundcover for many of the diminutive woodland plants in my collection. Tiny plants of *Soldanella alpina*, *Homogyne alpina*, and several species of hardy cyclamen are easily swamped by a vigorous groundcover. *Rubus pedatus* excuses itself as it steps aside and passes by.

Fresh new growth from a recently clipped mass planting of *Erica carnea* 'Springwood White' at the Platt garden gleams a rich green, on plants that billow like ocean waves far offshore.

I know that I have quoted from Dan Hinkley at length, but I have my reasons. My love affair with the groundcovers in the genus *Rubus* has just started; his is far advanced. Little crushes on this plant or that one must stand aside when grand passion speaks.

Louise Beebe Wilder once wrote of autumn's colchicums that "they come blowing out of the earth with all the verve and enthusiasm that we associate with spring's manifestations."

5 Groundcovers with Bulbs

An area occupied by groundcovers need not be static and unchanging throughout the seasons of the year. Indeed, the thoughtful gardener will contrive it so that even the year-round evergreen groundcovers like *Vinca minor* or the various cultivars of *Lamium maculatum* will provide a backdrop for other flowering plants. Bulbs are especially well suited for this use.

First come the bulbs that break dormancy in early spring, bloom at its height, and then return to dormancy in summer. Many of the spring bulbs that are unfairly tagged as "minor" (meaning only that they are smaller than tall tulips like the Darwin hybrids and large daffodils with boastful names like 'Unsurpassable') become the jewels of the garden in high spring when they rise above a carpet of appropriate groundcovers. Glory of the snow (*Chionodoxa luciliae*), with its open and upward-facing sky-blue blossoms with silvery highlights, is heartstoppingly beautiful in such a setting, especially when combined with cobalt blue *Scilla sibirica*, milky white, silvery blue striated *Puschkinia libanotica*, and the starry, daisylike *Anemone blanda* in white or pink or blue. As for grape hyacinths, I suspect that they are the first plants many gardeners learn to love in earliest childhood, and the affection does not die after many a spring has passed. Those with pearly white flowers deserve a place in any garden, but the commoner sort, with grapelike clusters of blue-violet florets, each a little bell that is almost closed at its end, are an unfailing joy. They earn their common name not only by looking like a bunch of grapes, but also by bearing the sweet piercing fragrance of a vineyard ripening in September.

Judging from my own neighborhood and other places where I have lived, few gardens go without grape hyacinths, but I believe most of us are far too neglectful of *Ipheion uniflorum*. It is winter-hardy at least to Zone 6, although where winters are prolonged, it benefits from mulch and a location where it is sheltered from frosty winds. This South American bulb bears wide, rather grassy foliage in abundance, topped in early to mid spring with a host of pale blue starry flowers that make a great show when planted in a mass. Its strange lack of popularity may be due to its lack of a common name in

Sheer flamboyant genius is the only way to describe Mary Keen's pyrotechnic juxtaposition of Rembrandt tulips and a golden variegated mint at St. Mary's Farm, Beenham, Berkshire. The spectacle may be brief, but it lingers in the mind.

general use in America. (But in Charlotte, North Carolina, where it is widely planted to beautiful effect when it blooms in mid-March, some of my gardening friends call it the "Charlotte onion," for two reasons: first, it escapes to lawns, where it forms clumps somewhat reminiscent of wild onions, but far lovelier; and second, the foliage, if crushed, has an odor midway between onions and garlic.)

"Charlotte onion," however, is not exactly the kind of common name that will urge more of us to plant *Ipheion*. Perhaps it would receive more attention if our bulb catalogs adopted the name sometimes used for it in Great Britain—spring starflower. The cultivar 'Wisley Blue' is superior to the species.

One of the best spring bulbs to combine with groundcovers also has problematic nomenclature. The problems arise, however, not with its common name, since either wood hyacinths or Spanish bluebells will do, but with its scientific name. I grew up believing that it was *Scilla campanulata*, but then heard that it had been yanked from the scillas and put in another genus and species altogether, *Endymion hispanica*—or, quite possibly *E. non-scriptus*. Depending on the mail-order bulb catalog consulted, it may still be found under any of these names. But taxonomists, as mentioned before, do change names on gardeners, and they are restless and name-scrupulous souls. High authority now has passed on the news that all of these names are on the scrap heap. Wood hyacinths are now regarded as cultivars of either *Hyacinthoides hispanica* or *H. non-*

In Portland, Cynthia Woodyard interplants *Anemone blanda* with *Ipheion uniflorum* to superb effect. In a cool spring the combination remains lovely for two weeks or more.

In the garden of Marguerite Norrbo in Portland, masses of blue scillas lead the eye forward toward bright azaleas and somber purple barberries.

scripta—or else hybrids between these species. I will just stick with wood hyacinths, but they are marvelous under any name. Among the very latest spring bulbs, they bloom just as daffodils begin to go by and as lilacs begin to fill the garden with their ineffable perfume. They form graceful clumps of arching, dark green foliage, topped in mid-May with equally graceful spikes of nodding pink, blue, or white bells. They are happy in shade, and they are one of very few bulbs that can hold their own year after year in a dense planting of English ivy, cheerfully oblivious to its smothering inclinations. Even in a sea of ivy, they thrive perpetually, their clumps getting larger and more floriferous with each new spring.

All of these bulbs self-seed abundantly where they are happy. I still recall two Aprils I spent many years ago in Clinton, New York, where the woods below Hamilton College on College Hill were a solid sea of self-sown glory-of-the-snow covering an acre or more, so blue that it looked as if heaven had fallen to the earth—just like wild bluebonnets in Texas. In my own garden in southern New Jersey, grape hyacinths, glory-of-the-snow, Siberian squills, spring star-flowers, puschkinias, and wood hyacinths thrive in places where they were never planted, as highly welcome volunteers. The most generous self-seeder, however, is a blue *Anemone blanda*. It has cropped up everywhere, and it is lovely indeed for its richly colored flowers, each on a stem only a couple of inches tall and each surrounded by a little collar of foliage that seems to deck it out in Elizabethan costume. It is too dainty to survive a battle with English ivy, but it has a great affinity for spreading sheets of low and prostrate evergreen *Sedum acre*. In a particularly cool spring, as in 1992 in the Northeast, it can stay in bloom for almost two months—the longest season of any bulb.

The bulbs of spring combine extraordinarily well with hostas and with ferns, in spots in the garden where deciduous trees allow sunshine throughout the winter well into spring, but then leaf out into cool shade during the summer. Since hostas go dormant in the fall and do not put up new foliage until mid-spring, and since many choice ferns are also deciduous, the bulbs can enjoy the spotlight during their brief but cheering season. Hosta leaves and fern fronds then help conceal the yellowing bulb foliage in very early summer.

I know of no better bulbs for combining with summer groundcovers than the little daffodils, which, experience has taught me, are much better garden plants than their taller and more assertive brothers. Tall daffodils with huge trumpet or flatcup flowers look wonderful in vases inside a house, and grassy meadows where they have been naturalized in huge drifts lift the spirits from afar. But in a garden, tall daffodils are easy prey to wind and rain that can leave them prostrate and stained with mud. And after they bloom, the agony of their dying foliage is prolonged. The little daffodils—'Hawera', 'Lintie', 'Jack Snipe', 'Quince', and all the rest—are much better behaved. Because of their modest height of twelve inches or less, and because of their diminutive flower size, they do not go to earth in spring storms. They are, however, even more colorful than the larger daffodils, since many of them bear two or three flowers per stem, and since they can be planted very close together. In mid-April in my own back garden, there is a river of little daffodils about eighteen inches wide that curves in a grand sweep across an entire border of shade-tolerant perennials, including hostas and ferns. Most years, their peak of bloom comes in the final week of April, just as the new shoots of hostas are beginning to break ground and the crosiers of ferns are beginning to unfurl into fresh new fronds. By the middle of May, as the leaves of these daffodils of diminutive size but exuberant effect begin to ripen, their unsightliness is largely concealed by the more luxuriant foliage of the other plants.

Besides ferns and hostas, there are other perennials that are spring sleepyheads—quite late in breaking winter dormancy—and thus are ideal in combination with spring bulbs. Three that I like especially are blue leadwort (*Ceratostigma plumbaginoides*), hardy ageratum (an ageratum imposter, as it's really *Eupatorium coelestinum*), and dwarf astilbe (*Astilbe chinensis* 'Pumila'). All three will thrive in either full sun or partial shade.

Leadwort's foliage doesn't appear until the tulip leaves have already started to yellow, and it really gets going only when the soil loses all hint of coolness. The plant is stoloniferous, but only a mild spreader. If planted in quantity, with the young plants set about eight inches apart, it is an effective groundcover in its first couple of years, forming a mat of lustrous, deep green foliage that stays under seven inches high. The flowers are such a deep shade of cobalt that when they first appear in late summer, it seems as though you could fall into another world if you looked at them too long. The bloom continues well into autumn, becoming even more beautiful as the nights lengthen and cool and leadwort's stems turn to glowing red.

I know of no fault in this indispensable groundcover, but cannot say the same of *Eupatorium coelestinum*. It shows itself even later than *Ceratostigma*, but then it romps, spreading far and wide, weav-

Ceratostigma plumbaginoides or blue leadwort makes an ideal groundcover for spring bulbs. It emerges late, as they begin to go dormant. It flowers from late summer well into fall, when its stems turn a handsome shade of garnet.

It spreads slowly, but evenually just one plant of *Astilbe chinensis* 'Pumila' will form a colony that serves well as a groundcover for spring bulbs. It is not nearly as thirsty as other astilbes, and its spikes of flowers in midsummer cheer the heart.

ing itself among other plants. Lean, dry soil tames it somewhat, as does a fungal disease that often crops up in hot, humid weather, but enough of the plant pulls through for it still to be a presence in the garden. By early autumn, when it has reached about twenty inches tall, it beings producing masses of fluffy little soft blue flower clusters. They have such charm that I forgive this plant's trespassing ways.

As for *Astilbe chinensis* 'Pumila', I didn't plant it knowing that it would be a fine groundcover for combining with the bulbs of spring. Rather, it just revealed itself, in time, as a remarkable plant with spreading ways, quite capable of holding down the space it occupies. I planted it because it was an astilbe, but a distinctive one. It is low, forming a solid mat of somewhat ferny compound leaves that grow some eight inches tall. It blooms—with the much taller, spectacular deep pink *Astilbe tacquettii* 'Superba'—in late July and early August, long after the flower plumes of most other astilbes have faded. It is much more tolerant of drought than other cultivars, which are unforgiving in their thirst. Its own flower plumes are stubby, with a texture that is somewhere between pipe cleaners and woolly bear caterpillars, and their color is a vibrant electric pink with a faint suggestion of blue. I had this charming little plant for over three years before the obvious hit me: this thing loves to travel. It doesn't die out at its center, as some spreading plants, such as ajugas, can. It doesn't send out long restless stolons that creep underground for considerable distances, then leap up as an unpleasant surprise, far from its original location. It just makes an ever-widening stand of itself, adding a few more inches to the edge of its territory each year. It is happy in either sun or partial shade, and it produces more and more spikes of flowers each year, unlike other astilbes, which must be divided every three years to keep their blooms from deteriorating from overcrowding and competition for moisture and nutrients. I give it an A +, no question about it.

Very late spring—May into the first days of June—belongs to the genus *Allium*, which includes the wild onions that plague our lawns in cool weather and the chives that enliven our food throughout the growing season. Chives (*A. schoenoprasum*) does double duty, for in addition to its culinary uses, it is beautiful in early June for its handsome clusters of pale lilac-purple blossoms. Other alliums are strictly ornamental, contributing nothing to the kitchen but a great deal to the garden. The most familiar of these bulbs is *Allium giganteum*, which can reach sixty inches and is often shown in catalogs

with a child crouching below its enormous ball-shaped clusters of deep purple flowers.

But the alliums include many less dramatic and equally satisfying species to explore. In 1992, a temporary planting of twenty-six different species and cultivars, all growing with groundcovers, was on display at Brookside Gardens in Wheaton, Maryland, a public garden well known as a wonderful source of ideas for the home landscape. I made a lot of notes. Completely new to me was *A. aflatunense* 'Purple Sensation', similar in form to *A. giganteum*, but with smaller flower clusters on stems that reach only to thirty-six inches. The flowers are a glowing shade of violet-purple. *A. christophii*, planted at Brookside with lamb's ears, is an old friend. Rising only eighteen inches, its enormous globes of starry and slightly silvery pale amethyst flowers often rest in the middle of perennials of modest height. The most elegant combination of alliums with groundcovers that Brookside offered, however, was *A. karataviense* massed together with *Artemisia stelleriana* 'Silver Brocade'. Many alliums have the unfortunate habit of producing foliage that begins to ripen and brown off at the tips just as they come into bloom, but this particular one holds off a while. It produces only two very low and wide, arching, bluish green leaves, which show off the cluster of pale pink flowers—a globe five inches across on eight-inch stems—producing a very compact and tidy effect. *Artemisia* 'Silver Brocade', a low and silvery plant with a somewhat swirling habit of growth and with none of the invasive tendencies common in this genus, marries well with this allium. It grows to under ten inches tall as the summer progresses, but that's tall enough to conceal the foliage of the allium as it moves into dormancy.

Well before the daffodil foliage begins to ripen, some of the bulbs of summer begin to assert themselves. One of these, whose praise must be tempered with a warning, is the latest of the alliums, the late June–blooming *Allium scorodoprasum*. This plant, whose common names are sand leek and rocambole, produces large clusters of lilac-purple flowers on thirty-six-inch stems. The rounded flower heads seem to float through the garden like a multitude of tennis balls arrested in their flight. This allium looks best planted in a curving line threading like a river through small shrubs and perennials, against a background of taller, pale-colored things like variegated miscanthus grass or the golden-leafed form of the giant reed, *Arundo donax*. Like the wild onions that infest lawns in later winter and spring, however, this species produces a great many bulbils with its

At Brookside Gardens in Wheaton, Maryland, the pairs of broad gray leaves and the large old-rose spherical flowerheads of *Allium karavatiense* are well-married to the emerging spikes of the lambs ears that will fill the space once the alliums lapse into dormancy.

In Rosemary Verey's garden at Barnsley House in Gloucestershire, in the heart of the Cotswolds, the big purple globes of *Allium christophii* nestle against the thistle-like prickly flowers of eryngiums.

At Brookside Gardens, rosy-flowered little *Allium oreophilum* is paired with *Artemisia stelleriana* 'Silver Brocade'. Unlike many other artemisias this low cultivar is not bent on conquering the earth by rambunctious and questing stolons.

flowers, each one ready to root and start a plague of new plants. The subspecies *A. scorodoprasum rotundum* is worth seeking out, as its flowers are larger, deeper in color, and free of troublesome bulbils.

June also marks the advent of the lilies, whose stalks rise like pagodas above tides of *Vinca minor*, or periwinkle. Because periwinkle seems not to be an especially heavy feeder, it does not compete with lilies for nutrients (even though I always toss a little bulb fertilizer around the lilies when they first emerge). And there is no doubt that the vinca helps provide the lilies with the cool root zone they prefer for protection against summer heat. The lily season is a long one, and it is an orderly parade of hybrid types, each with its name. First come the Asiatic hybrids, ranging in height from two to three feet, seldom taller. Some are freckled, others have clear complexions. On some the flowers face downward, some outward, and still others upward. The color range is wide, including whites, lavenders, buffs, apricots, nasturtium oranges, and firecracker reds. Their season extends from late May through early July, with the main show in mid-June. July is the month for the tall Aurelian hybrids, with candelabra stems of trumpet-shaped flowers in pinks and buffs and greenish whites, a more muted palette than the Asiatics offer. The procession of lilies concludes in August and September with the Oriental hybrids, which bear huge, intensely fragrant, often exotically fringed and spotted flowers. These flowers are such show-offs that they hold their own with cattleya orchids—and certainly steal the thunder from vinca or any other groundcover that may be giving them their cool root run.

No less spectacular than lilies in a sunny spot rising out of a carpet of groundcovers is the *Crocosmia* X *crocosmiflora* cultivar 'Lucifer', one of the best plants to come to America from Britain since World War II. The first year I had it, it bloomed in late September, so I ticketed it as a fall bulb, but it soon settled in to reveal itself as a mid-July bloomer. Its foliage, swordlike leaves that fan out from the narrow base of the plant, is a rich green with a corduroy texture that makes it handsome even out of bloom. In bloom, the plant stands shoulder-high, with inflorescences bearing huge numbers of fair-sized tubular flowers with a slight flare to the lower petals. Each strong and wiry flower stem branches several times so that blossoms are borne near the middle of the plant as well as near the top of the leaves. The color of the flowers is difficult to describe. Call them, appropriately, the flames of hell, for they manage to seem scarlet, vermilion, and several other shades of red, and they also have a hint

In both form and color, no bulb of summer can match the drama of crocosmia 'Lucifer', seen here rising above mounds of lavender in the Platt garden.

of smoke to them. They increase in number and in splendor every year, for the corms multiply at a fair clip. I have read that the corms should be lifted and stored over the winter, but in the chillier parts of Zone 7, this does not seem to be necessary. 'Lucifer' is an apt name: this plant can take the hottest and driest July my garden will even know without flagging. It is a superb cut flower, but it was several years before I had it in sufficient quantity not to grudge its presence in a bouquet, instead of in the garden. Its height qualifies it for a place among dwarf hollies and other woody groundcovers, and it looks superb rising out of a solid sheet of *Liriope muscari*. Plant it emerging out of a huge clump of lavender, and the pagan gods will rejoice in this fallen angel.

Autumn, too, has its characteristic bulbs, two of which blow into the world so entirely naked of foliage that they are like the newborn Eves of the plant kingdom, although judiciously placed groundcovers serve well as their fig leaves. First comes *Lycoris*. I consider it one of my misfortunes as a southern boy gardening up north that I cannot have the spider lilies (*L. radiata*) that I remember from Texas and North Carolina. They explode into bloom sometime in August, usually after one of those cool, prolonged rains that promise the advent of autumn. Atop each leafless stem is a joyous carousel of soft red flowers, each with protruding stamens and pistils, which look more like cats' whiskers than like the legs of spiders that give this plant its common name. Spider lilies are not reliably winter-hardy in my part of Zone 7, so I make do with the equally naked "hardy amaryllis" (*Lycoris squamigera*), which does well in light shade and blooms in August with clusters of amaryllislike flowers that are a peculiar blue shade of pink. Next come the several species of *Colchicum* and their cultivars—huge bold chalices, in some forms double, of rich pink, lavender-violet, or sparkling white. They make their appearance as suddenly and as dramatically as any operatic diva. That these particular garden divas are also nudists is a fact concealed by the supporting cast of groundcovers thickly placed at the base of their blossoms. *Lycoris* and *Colchicum* do, of course have their own leaves, but these appear in the spring and then go dormant through the summer. Then—if it comes at all, for it is persnickety—comes *Sternbergia lutea*, spectacular for its huge golden cups, which are like enormous crocus flowers and so shiny that they seem to be varnished. This one does put up straplike leaves before it flowers, but a background of low groundcovers nevertheless enhances its performance in a garden. It is particularly lovely arising from a mat of leadwort (*Ceratostigma plumbaginoides*), with its cobalt blue flowers and its stems that turn cranberry red as the nights lengthen and turn cool.

Then there are the crocuses—those that bloom not in the spring, but in the fall. It is unfortunate that Americans have paid so little heed to these splendid bulbs, which pop up like an unexpected visit from an old friend. As a result of our inattention to them, bulb dealers offer only a handful of the many species and cultivars, if any at all. I have planted in my own garden as many kinds as I can find, and I always leap to order a new one when I find it in a catalog. The most common species and the earliest to bloom, sometimes in late August, is *C. speciosus*, which means "showy," not "specious" crocus. This one blooms profusely with soft blue-violet flowers. I like it growing out of a mat of golden creeping jenny; it creates a harmonious combination of colors just as creeping jenny begins to assume the reddish bronze tints it will carry through the winter. I am equally pleased by the rich lavender- and white-striped flowers of October-blooming *C. sativus*, although its sexual parts (the source of saffron) fall out of the blossoms in a way that is certain to displease prudes. I don't think I could easily do without *C. ochroleucus* and its ivory blossoms in November, but if I had to limit myself to just one autumn crocus, it would be *C. goulimyi*, for it bears, for several weeks in early fall, a profuse crop of little trim and rounded flowers whose color veers toward rose at times, toward blue at others, depending on the light. One of the pleasures of autumn crocuses is that they

seed themselves about, cropping up unexpectedly in new locations each year.

I can think of only one tuberous or bulbous plant that qualifies as a real groundcover in areas where winters are not a mere interlude. (Of course, a number of tender bulbs can be used as groundcovers in much milder climates, or by gardeners who are meteorologically challenged and are willing to lift them and store them as winter approaches.) *Arum italicum* 'Pictum' is a toughie—winter-hardy through Zone 6 and possibly into Zone 5. Its striking, arrow-shaped leaves marked with pewter and cream appear in the fall. The exact time their welcome new leaves unfurl can vary, depending on some particular combination of cool nights and prolonged gentle rains. This aroid is well suited to spots near deciduous trees, where it is shady in the summer and sunny from late fall through winter. It is very effective combined with hellebores during winter and early spring, and it is highly compatible with maidenhair and Japanese painted ferns, which flourish when it is dormant. The glory of this arum is its fresh foliage all during the winter, but it is also spectacular in late summer, when its jack-in-the-pulpit-like flowers leave behind stout spikes of bright orange-red fruits that shout out in shade.

In the Platt garden, a sea of white epimediums and a happy colony of pink trout lilies may not be a marriage arranged in heaven, but it was an inspired pairing by a superb plantswoman who knew what she was doing.

Crocus sativus, the saffron crocus, bursts like a September fanfare through a prostrate carpet of *Lysimachia nummularia* 'Aurea' just as it has begun its own autumnal change of color.

Among the tender bulbs usable as groundcovers, I am most partial to fancy-leafed caladiums, which won't get through winters except in Zone 10. These extremely colorful—even gaudy—foliage plants with elongated, heart-shaped leaves are hybrids of *Caladium bicolor* and other tropical species endemic from Panama southward to Brazil. The color range of their leaves extends from green to white to pink to red, with often intricate contrasting veining and splashings, and with many combinations and permutations of these hues. They exceed even hostas, their nearest competition, in pumping lively color into gloomy corners.

Not everyone likes caladiums. Some people shudder at the thought of growing them, taking their presence in a garden as prima facie testimony to the bad taste of its owner. I have one friend who insists they look just like the linoleum patterns so popular in the days when automobiles had tail fins and hairdos were beehives. Maybe. I still like them, and I still grow them—sometimes in masses of single colors or of mixed ones, sometimes in groups of three as accents. To work as a solid groundcover in cold regions, they must be started inside in pots, and if the temperature is much below 70 degrees they will rot. They like shade and average to moist soil, under which conditions they will grow about eighteen inches tall and spread ten inches wide. In very moist soil, they may reach thirty inches or higher.

The standard advice about caladiums is to lift them in the fall, dry off the tubers, and store them in a warm place over the winter. They are, however, so likely to rot in dormant storage (with a horrid stench when they do) that I treat them as annuals. Caladium World and other specialty growers in Florida offer them so inexpensively that I just buy new tubers each spring.

People with the good sense (or the bad taste: take your pick) to brighten up their summer gardens with the crazy-quilt colors of caladiums probably grow elephant ears—listed in the genus *Colocasia* in some sources, *Alocasia* in others—as well. Their common name involves no metaphorical daring, for elephant ears is just what they look like. They are bolder even than large hostas. Children love them, and so do grown-up children. Their huge leaves seem plain green from a distance, but on closer look they are often suffused with smoky tones and patterns of great subtlety.

And there is one "caladium" for those whose taste runs in other directions. It is actually a cultivar of the small elephant ear from Burma, *Colocasia affinis*, sold by a handful of small nurseries as the black caladium. It isn't black, but very dark green overlaid with blackish purple shades that are most prominent in full sun. It has nothing in it of linoleum patterns, and its most effective use is as an accent in a tapestry planting of mixed groundcovers.

As for another popular tender plant of summer, the tuberous begonia, I like it, but have seldom grown it, except in hanging baskets above our deck. Its flowers are flouncy, splashy, abundant, and huge, as begonia flowers go. The color range is wide—clean whites, glowing reds and scarlets, soft apricots, good crisp yellows, covering among them much of the spectrum except violet, purple, and blue. I have admired the tuberous begonia in such public gardens as Butchart Gardens in Victoria, British Columbia. It is obviously a great crowd-pleaser, which only a true garden snob would hold against it.

If I ever get around to growing these begonias except on our deck, I would probably not grow them en masse in the ground, but in large pots scattered through our back border. That's my preferred way of treating the one tender bulb that I will never have enough of— *Agapanthus africanus*, or blue lily-of-the-Nile. I call it love flower, not only because of my strong affection for it, but also because that's what the Greek roots of its scientific name mean. One strain of agapanthus, the Headbourne Hybrids, is reported to be winter-hardy in Zone 7, but my experience has been that it is not so in my part of this zone. My wife and I tried for years to grow this bulb as a houseplant, with no success. Finally, in a garden center in Delaware, we found a large clump of it in a clay planter of some considerable size, brought it home, gave it a place of honor in the sun next to a potted gardenia, and were rewarded in July with twenty-five stems, each bearing fifty or more flowers of the purest and deepest blue I know. In my mind's eye, I multiply that pot and its glorious flowers fiftyfold, marching in a sweeping curve along that border, from one end to the other.

One day we will do it. And it will be a pretty sight indeed.

Clematis montana var. *rubens* has smallish flowers, but they are borne in huge profusion on vines of vaulting ambition. At the Van Duzen Botanical Garden in Vancouver, British Columbia they spill from a tall conifer like a foaming cataract, filling the air with their delicious light scent of vanilla.

6 Vines for Utility and Delight

Although many groundcovers are defined by the uses to which gardeners put them, it is another story with vines, plants whose nature is to climb and clamber and lift themselves aloft. No one can make a hosta take to a trellis or a tree; it is earthbound. And no one can persuade a wisteria or a trumpet vine to remain in a tight vegetative lump. It is commanded in their genes: "Thou shalt climb."

The ways plants climb vary. Some, like grapes, put forth from their leaf axils soft tendrils that search the air until they find something solid, and quickly coil around it, hardening into woody tissue and losing their original pliability. The tender climbing gloriosa lily (*Gloriosa superba* 'Rothschildiana') has no separate tendrils, but the

Euonymus fortunei 'Silver Queen', like other cultivars of this species, is amiably tractable. Unsupported, it will scramble across the ground, as a shrub with prostrate tendencies, like a guest at an ancient Roman banquet. But it will clamber upwards to modest height when it finds a vertical surface to attach itself to.

tips of its leaves serve as such, coiling around anything that will support the vine in its upward progress before it begins to produce its large and spectacular fiery red and yellow blossoms, with their six petals swept back elegantly and dramatically. Some vines such as *Euonymus fortunei*, trumpet vine, and English ivy (in its juvenile or climbing stage) put forth, along their stems, rootlets that can cement themselves to perfectly vertical surfaces of stone or wood. Virginia creeper climbs by similar means. In *The Movement and Habits of Climbing Plants* (1888), Charles Darwin closely observed the mechanisms of support on this vine growing on his house in Kent:

> In the course of about two days after a tendril has arranged its branches so as to press on any surface, the curved tips swell, become bright red, and form on their undersides the well-known discs or cushions with which they adhere firmly. In one case the tips were slightly swollen in 38 hours after coming in contact with a brick, in another case they were considerably swollen in 48 hours and in an additional 24 hours were firmly attached to a smooth board.

The stems of some vines like wisteria twine themselves around their supports (and one of the curious facts about wisterias is that some species twine clockwise, others counterclockwise, by an odd genetic quirk). Clematis weaves itself through trellises or in the branches of small trees. Some climbing plants, such as roses, just hurl themselves upward as high as they can and then lean on any convenient support.

Occasionally, vines are considered useful for screening off from sight something that is ugly, offensive, or distracting, but somehow they are a trifle disreputable in themselves. This attitude was perfectly expressed by William Atherton DuPuy in *Our Plant Friends and Foes* (1930): "Almost any plant family is likely to find that it has a vine in it and may be excused if it feels a bit ashamed of this member. A vine, if the truth must be told, is a plant that has lost its backbone. At one time it may have been quite upstanding and self-reliant but it acquired the habit of leaning on a prop and so lost the power to support itself." In these words, there is a sneering tone: vines are shiftless moochers with none of the classic Emersonian virtues, such as self-reliance. I believe that there's an egregious anthropomorphic fallacy in attempting to draw moral lessons from

plants, but if one must be drawn from vines, I would part from Mr. DuPuy's company by pointing out that dependency and co-dependency are part of both the moral and the natural orders. Besides, I wonder if Mr. DuPuy ever looked a fine clematis in the face?

Covering something unsightly is, of course, one of the uses to which vines are put, but only one of many. Some vines are better suited to this purpose than others. Golden European hops (*Humulus lupulus* 'Aureus'), which is used in this way more often in England than in America, is superb for screening or for covering a nondescript garden shed. Grapes, crossvine, and Boston ivy also are good at this kind of coverup operation, as is Dutchman's pipe (*Aristolochia macrophylla*, syn. *A. durior*). So is trumpet vine, but it is dangerous, as it can rip shingles loose. Cynthia Woodyard tells the tale of a trumpet vine that wandered in through the window of her bedroom in her house in Oregon. She says it kind of waved to her as it came in, attached itself to a wall, and started blooming. Some months later, she discovered that it had done a lot of damage to the window frame.

Golden hops (*Humulus lupulus* 'Aureus'), here seen at Butterstream Farm, Jim Reynolds' garden in Ireland, softens the lines of rustic buildings. Other gardeners may use it to hide genuine architectural eyesores, if they have any that embarrass them.

Sue Ryley in Victoria, British Columbia has allowed golden hops and *Clematis texensis* 'Pagoda' to become a two-part invention. I think that Johann Sebastian Bach himself would approve the resulting counterpoint.

The same dense and heavy vines that cover things up or screen them off from view are also valuable on porches, pergolas, and arbors for the welcome, cooling shade they bring. In *An Island Garden* (1894), a marvelous book about her garden on Appledore Island in the Isles of Shoals off Kittery, Maine, the American poet Celia Thaxter spoke appreciatively of the hops, honeysuckles, wisterias, morning glories, and other vines growing in a thick drapery around the broad piazza of her house. "The vines make a grateful green shade," she wrote, "doubly delightful for that there are no trees on my island, and the shade is most welcome in the wide brilliancy of sea and sky."

But not every vine is a plant for pure utility. Some can be simply enjoyed for their delicacy and grace, and for the beauty of their foliage or flowers.

Clematis and Roses

Even the smallest garden is unthinkable without a clematis vine and perhaps a climbing rose.

In my part of the country, sweet autumn clematis grows wild. It is among those vines of the railroad tracks, although it also has naturalized itself here at the fringes of marshes and woodlands, and in vacant lots, where it rises triumphantly above another Asian plant, Japanese knot weed, and native blackberry, ragweed, and pokeweed. It is an entirely forgivable plant for its aggressive ways (which are easily kept in check, since it flowers on new wood, and thus may be cut back ruthlessly in early spring). Starting in mid-August, it covers itself in a froth of pure white loveliness, a mass of tiny, four-sepaled flowers. It will grow into and over shrubs, or it will spread across the ground, where there are no heights to conquer. It has a delicate scent hinting of vanilla, and when it blooms, it proclaims, "Look at me!" Who could not—and in admiration?

Other clematis don't come unbidden; they must be sought in catalogs and invited into the garden. Although a handful of them are shrubby herbaceous perennials (some slouchy and flopping), by far the majority of species and cultivars are vines. For example, *C. armandii*, a Chinese species with handsome evergreen foliage and pleasantly fragrant white flowers in spring, can quickly reach twenty feet. Introduced by E. H. Wilson in 1900 and much planted in the South, it is, alas, not reliably winter-hardy much north of Raleigh, North Carolina. There is an uncommon pink cultivar, 'Apple Blossom', but the white is more spectacular. It will cover fences and walls, and, if given a chance will even leap into trees, then hang down in gorgeous swags of large and glistening flowers set off by the long, leathery black-green leaves. Even in Zone 8, a really severe winter may damage it or kill its top growth, but it will eventually recover to become one of the glories of earliest spring.

No other genus of ornamental plants comes close to offering the number of garden-worthy vines *Clematis* does. The genus is also remarkably far-flung in its geographical range. A large majority of its species are native to the north temperate zone—North America, Europe, and Asia—but there are species from New Zealand and even South Africa. Clematis have been extensively hybridized, first in Japan, and later in Great Britain, France, and other Western countries from the early nineteenth century until the present. Their colors virtually cover the spectrum except (as far as I know) bright orange. Pure white, rich purples and crimsons, blues, and pale yellows are all found. Flower size varies from the tiny white blossoms of my railroad vine to opulent blossoms measuring at least six inches across. Flower forms also vary. Most clematis have four or more sepals spread out in a flat disk or plate form, but *C. tangutica* and *C. orientalis* bear downward-facing, somewhat globular soft yellow blooms that look like little parasols or parachutes. The blooming season for the various species and cultivars differs as well. *C. cirrhosa*, a tender species from the Mediterranean area, blooms in early winter where winters are mild and it is hardy. In June, when roses are at their peak, there is an explosion of bloom among many clematis, some of which continue to blossom sporadically during the rest of the summer. Some cultivars bloom in two flushes: one in early summer, the other in the fall. And, of course, there are species that bloom in the fall, notably the sweet autumn clematis and *C. tangutica*.

Typically, clematis are tidy and undemanding. Most woody vines, as I have already pointed out, take up almost no ground space, and their foliage is sparse near the base. They are almost never greedy or out to swamp whatever supports them. Since they appreciate cool shade at their feet, they are ideal for planting with companionable large shrubs or small trees. I have a large cotoneaster that supports 'Niobe,' a dark red cultivar that spreads itself across the top of the shrub. I generally forget that it's there until one day in June the flowers, like a robe of deep ruby red velvet, come into view. The quince tree just outside our kitchen window is host to 'Henryi', which

Dutchman's pipe (*Aristolochia macrophylla*, syn. *A. durior*) grows lustily and quickly. It is a classic porch vine—and vine to cover a privy, in olden times. Its strange flowers have always struck me as having evolved to be pollinated by pterodactyls. Scientific botany does not support this opinion.

is dazzling for its crop of large, pure white single blossoms in June. Our twisted hazel is planted with 'Ville de Lyon', bearing rounded crimson flowers in early fall, and the Chinese witch hazel outside our dining room window is bedecked with 'Lady Betty Balfour', which blooms in September, producing a multitude of purple flowers that age to blue.

Combining shrubs or small trees with clematis follows a good horticultural principle for gardens, especially small ones: *always contrive to make things do double or even triple duty*. There's nothing wrong with putting a clematis on a trellis, but a quince tree swagged with a white clematis has three periods of appeal. In late April or early May, there are the large single quince flowers of palest pink, which I find lovelier by far than apple blossoms, especially against the soft, fresh gray-green quince leaves when they first appear. In June, when *Clematis* 'Henryi' blooms, it almost seems as if the quince has decided to flower again, but has new thoughts about what kind of blossoms it should sport. Then, in late summer, come the green quinces, so heavy that they cause the branches to arch down under their burden, even before they ripen to a golden tan.

I am sometimes tempted to plant a clematis under all the shrubs and small trees in my garden, but I know that Hella would say, as another friend once did, "There's such as thing as too much excess, you know."

Clematis 'Bees Jubilee', here growing at Bagatelle in Paris, is notable for its trifoliate leaves, intensity of color, and slightly ruffled petals and sepals.

Blooming in late winter and early spring, *Clematis armandii* is among the very noblest of evergreen flowering vines. Gardeners who live where winters are mild enough for it to thrive can count themselves among the blessed of this earth. ALLEN LACY

Clematis 'Niobe' and rose 'Opaline' are amicably paired at Bagatelle in Paris.

An unknown rose spills in profusion from a porch railing in the Georgetown section of the District of Columbia in late May.

Many people dream—or say they dream—of rose-covered cottages. Climbing roses cannot exactly be classified as vines, for they are really rambling woody shrubs with especially stiff, tall canes that can grow as pillars, or with lax and pliable branches that can be trained over walls or through supporting trellises. But they belong with vines as plants that lend a vertical dimension to the garden. Like true vines, they help cure the perceptual disease of "eye-level gardening." I do not worship at the shrine of the genus *Rosa* in my garden, although I could not easily forego the several rugosas, for they are disease resistant, flower beautifully over a long season, and thrive on sand. One, 'Fru Dagmar Hastrop', may even have, in a good year, wonderful purple, orange, and yellow autumn foliage.

The roses I am most partial to are the ramblers and climbers that take to walls and to the rooftops of garden sheds—roses we look through to the sky or that rain down their petals on warm days in late June. I agree entirely with the sound preferences expressed by Sir George Sitwell in *On the Making of Gardens* (1909):

> So, if it is to be a rose-garden, do not choose those stunted, unnatural, earth-loving strains, which have nothing of vigour and wildness in them. . . . Let climbing roses drop in a veil from the terrace and smother with flower-spangled embroidery the garden walls, run riot over vaulted arcades, clamber up the lofty obelisks of leaf-tangled trellises, twine themselves round the pillars of a rose-roofed temple, where little avalanches of sweetness shall rustle down at a touch and the dusty gold of the sunshine shall mingle with the summer snow of the flying petals. Let them leap in a great bow or fall in a creamy cataract to a foaming pool of flowers.

Sir George is not specific about which roses are to drop in veils from terraces, run riot over arcades, and plunge in creamy cataracts. Besides, many a new climbing or rambling rose has come along since his day. I will therefore fill in a bit with some names. 'New Dawn', introduced in 1930, is still hard to beat. It starts off as one of those "unnatural, earth-loving strains" that Sitwell beats up on, but eventually develops moderate aerial ambitions and ascends. It smothers itself in blush-pink double flowers in June, then blooms sporadically until frost. It has excellent, dark lustrous green foliage that is remarkably resistant to disease. 'Climbing Peace', a sport of 'Peace' that was introduced right after World War II and is probably the most popular rose yet, also has good foliage as well as blowsy, over-stuffed flowers that are an odd mix of cream, pink, and pale orange. 'Dortmund' is a pleasant crimson single with a white center. Another good single, 'American Pillar', is dark pink with a contrasting white eye. It was introduced in 1902, so Sitwell may have known it. Its canes can reach twenty feet, making it a fine plant to cover a low garden shed. It is subject to mildew in hot summers, and thus, ironically, it is grown much more widely in England than in America. One of the oldest climbers, 'Gloire de Dijon', originating in France in the 1850s, remains one of the best, for its double fleshy pink blossoms, its recurrent bloom, and its intense fragrance.

Although some cultivars and species of clematis do not bloom until late summer or fall, June is generally the month they make congress together with roses, in a spectacle of bloom that is incredibly rich because clematis contributes the purple and blues that are missing in roses. Correction: that are missing thus far. I hear reports that the

'Félicité et Perpétue' was introduced in France in 1827 by the head gardener of the Duc d'Orléans, A. A. Jacques, who named it for two martyrs who were thrown to the lions in 203 A.D. in Carthage. It blooms with spectacular beauty in the garden of Mrs. Ralph Merton, Old Rectory, Burghfield, in Berkshire.

Mixed climbing roses adorn this stone balustrade in Courances.

Rose 'Climbing Lady Hillington' in the garden of the eminent British rosarian and horticultural authority Graham Stuart Thomas.

genetic engineers are at work trying to splice into roses a gene that will produce the blue pigment delphinidin. Rumor has it they aim to sell, at $165 a stem, blue roses for Japanese electronic magnates to send as tokens of esteem to special clients. I take my stand with Hannah Withers on this possibility: "You might get used to it, but you really wouldn't want it." (But a blue rose would open new horizons in country and western music: "Blue Roses for a Blue Lady" might be a dandy song.)

A garden that used to be a few blocks down my street made excellent and ingenious use of roses and clematis in combination. There was a huge bed running from the street to the very back of the property. It was heavily planted in old-fashioned roses like 'Souvenir de la Malmaison'. Amongst these shrub roses, steel concrete-reinforcing rods were plunged into the earth, supporting great numbers of another old-fashioned favorite, the rich purple *C.* X *jackmanii*. The gardener's owner died some time ago, and the new owners ripped out the roses and clematis, replacing them with turf. I see no reason why other rose gardens might not make use of these rods for clematis, but to support more than one kind—say, *C.* X *durandii* (deep indigo), 'Polish Spirit' (dark purple with red stripes running down the center of each sepal), and 'Wada's Primrose' (pale creamy yellow).

Native Vines, Some with Asian Kin

When I was in college in the 1950s, I took courses in geology and botany, both subjects with some puzzles that have now been solved in a major overhaul of the earth sciences. In the geology class, I asked the professor what he made of the fact that pieces of some continents bulged in where pieces of others bulged out, as if they had once fit together as one landmass. He told me that I was voicing a crackpot idea that only a few geological loonies had ever espoused. Continents didn't roam around like nomads, and instead of idly speculating that they did, I should concentrate on getting the differences between the Mesozoic and the Cretaceous periods straight. In botany, I wondered about the odd analogues between the flora of parts of Eastern Asia and that of parts of North America. America had its hollies, rhododendrons, lilies, and other genera, and so did the Orient. I didn't ask why this was so; I was an English major and didn't want to be accused again of harboring harebrained ideas in the halls of science.

I take considerable satisfaction now in the triumph of those "geological loonies." The words "continental drift" give me pleasant goose bumps, and they also explain why I can grow two species of beauty berry side by side—one Asian, the other North American—and never know for sure which is which.

Some of these analogous American and Asian genera are vines. Virginia creeper (*Parthenocissus quinquefolia*) can get out of hand, but when its leaves turn brilliant crimson in September, it is one of the glories of the American landscape. This vine's blue berries are appealing, both to the human eye and to birds, which excrete the seeds everywhere, explaining what otherwise would seem to be Virginia creeper's apparent ability to propagate itself by spontaneous generation, cropping up where it was never planted. A related species is *P. tricuspidata*, commonly called Boston ivy not because it is native to coastal Massachusetts (it hails from China and Japan), but because it is so frequently planted in Boston, where public buildings are covered with it. Its bright green leaves in summer and its crimson ones in autumn are a joy to behold in a stiff breeze, for the buildings' walls seem to undulate as the foliage trembles. The small-leafed form 'Lowii' is especially fine. I have no use for Boston ivy in my own garden; it has a somewhat institutional air about it, but it has done yeoman's service in covering up many an architectural sin.

Ampelopsis arborea, commonly called peppervine or porchvine, deserves more attention than it gets. This native of the southeastern

Parthenocissus tricuspidata forms a leafy bower for this small statue of the Annunciation in Bellagio.

Parthenocissus tricuspidata has smothered a great deal of Western architecture since it arrived from the Orient and took on the misleading name, Boston ivy. But it hasn't quite triumphed yet over the Garibaldi Fort in Milan.

United States has lovely pink berries that ripen to a glistening blue-black. The handsome, shiny green leaves turn a fetching shade of red in late summer. It is somewhat tender in the North, requiring a protected spot in winter, but this tenderness can be an advantage, since a peppervine that is free of all danger from cold weather can run rampant. Its Asian counterpart, *Ampelopsis pedunculata* 'Elegans', behaves itself beautifully. Bearing smallish, three-lobed dark green foliage splashed with white and sometimes pink, it puts up with poor soil and will grow well in moderate shade, where the variegated leaves add a welcome note of light color. A modest vine, it climbs by means of tendrils, and weaves among other plants in tapestry style rather than blocking them from view. It achieves its final glory in the late summer and fall, when the abundant little yellow fruits change to a striking metallic shade of deep turquoise. Unfortunately, some birds find these fruits ambrosial, and they can strip a vine in no time flat. At their first sign of ripening, the fruit-bearing stems can be cut and brought inside for autumn arrangements, to which they lend a handsome touch.

A fern that climbs seems almost as outlandish an idea as continents wandering from here to there. But as David Hume pointed out, everything, before experience, is difficult; after experience, it becomes easy. There are two species of climbing ferns, both in the genus *Lygodium*. *L. palmatum* is native to the eastern United States, from northern Florida into Massachusetts, and thus is winter-hardy out of doors. I do not know of a commercial source for this fern, and sound policies of conservation call for foregoing it. It was threatened with extinction early in this century, thanks to the florists who over-collected its graceful fronds. The state of New York lists it as an endangered species. Its Asian analogue, *L. japonicum*, can be planted with a clear conscience, although it is not hardy much north of Zone 8. In the Deep South, this deciduous plant is a vigorous grower, with delicate, even dainty fronds (the spore-bearing ones are frilly and ruffled). It has an affinity for chain-link fences, whose harsh, dog-kennel look it helps to hide. I grow it outside in a pot on our deck, on a little trellis. During the cold months of the year it comes inside, where it remains evergreen.

I will not discuss here one Asian species in the genus *Lonicera*, which also has many North American species. It is *L. japonica*, or Japanese honeysuckle, which, despite some winning and agreeable traits, is a beast of a woody weed. It will be found later on, in a chapter about a whole rogue's gallery of thugs. But there are some

Gelsemium semper-virens, the Carolina jessamine, brightens a corner of the garden of Ann Armstrong in Charlotte, where it combines well with a pale lavender form of *Verbena canadensis*.

One of our most beautiful native vines, the red honeysuckle *Lonicera sempervirens*, blooms for most of the growing season. It here welcomes the passing stranger on a simple fence in Charleston's Historic District.

well-behaved vining forms of honeysuckles. *L. perfoliata* has fragrant pink blooms in summer, followed by orange berries. *L. sempervirens*, or trumpet honeysuckle, occurs naturally all along the eastern seaboard and flowers prolifically from late spring to autumn. Its blossoms are usually scarlet, but there are yellow forms as well. This honeysuckle lacks fragrance, but hummingbirds constantly flit among its tubular blossoms. A hybrid form, *L.* X *heckrottii* 'Goldflame', thought to be a cross between *L. sempervirens* and another native species, *L. americana*, blooms exuberantly from late spring to midsummer and then sporadically into autumn. In his *Manual of Woody Ornamental Plants*, Michael Dirr praises it for its carmine buds opening to yellow throats on flowers fading to pink on the outside. He calls the flowers "strikingly handsome," and judges this vine to be "the most handsome of the climbing honeysuckles."

There is at least one Southeast Asian vining species of *Gelsemium*, but either it is of no horticultural significance or Barry Yinger has not yet gotten around to ferreting it out and bringing it to us. But we are left with some fine native North American species. About *G. sempervirens*, Carolina jessamine or jasmine (which is not a true jasmine), there are just two pieces of bad news. It is poisonous in every part, and even honey made from its nectar may be toxic. I would grow it anyway, for it is one of the most beautiful of all American native plants, blooming profusely in spring and then sporadically well into autumn, with bright yellow, flaring tubular flowers that have an agreeable scent. One form has much paler, almost creamy petals, and the cultivar 'Pride of Augusta' shows off handsome double flowers. The rest of the bad news is that it is not reliably winter-hardy very far north; New York City is about the northern limit of its range (even there, it must be in a protected location), and it flowers most abundantly south of Maryland. Less common, but receiving increasing attention, is *G. rankanii*. It lacks fragrance but bursts into bloom in both fall and spring.

Ground nut vine (*Apios americana*) has its Asian cousin-species, too, but I know nothing at all about them. It's only by chance that I even know of the existence of this native vine. A friend dumped one in its pot on our doorstep one day while I was gone, unlabeled. It looked so alarmingly like a wisteria that I was about to compost it when its donor telephoned to tell me what it was. He said it was a shade-loving hardy vine that died back to the roots every year and never ran wild. A legume, it blooms with clusters of fragrant coral and white pealike flowers in mid-August. In the fall, it produces a

Crossvine (*Bignonia capreolata*) is handsome year round for its lustrous evergreen foliage, which veers toward purple in freezing weather, but it also blooms gorgeously in May, as here in William Frederick's garden in Delaware, above an enormous clump of *Hosta sieboldiana* 'Elegans'.

crop of edible nutty tubers, which native American tribes on the East Coast used to harvest for food. (It may be the mysterious "Indian potato" that Sir Walter Raleigh took back to England from Virginia.) My friend allowed as how the tubers weren't bad roasted or boiled and served forth with butter and salt, but that he wasn't at all tempted to forsake real potatoes and eat ground nuts instead.

The genus *Bignonia*, once rich in species native to North America, Asia, and other continents, is now a shadow of its former self. It looked fat and healthy in *Hortus III*, but now all but one species has been sent packing into other genera, such as *Campsis*, *Distictis*, and *Pandorea*. Just one species is left, *Bignonia capreolata*, our native crossvine—"cross," because the woody stems, when cut, reveal cross-shaped pulpy tissue at their centers. (As a boy, I sometimes cut off pieces of mature stem, set them afire at one end, and smoked them. I suspect that this childhood tradition has died out.) But the word takes on another meaning, since someone who tries to find a plant may get cross in the effort. More commonly grown in England than in America and not nearly as appreciated here as it deserves, it can be hard to locate. The search is worth it, for it's a noble plant and the only evergreen flowering vine that's winter-hardy in the North. Crossvine will grow in moderate shade, but bloom very sparsely; it requires full sun to bring on a heavy crop of its tubular, brown and buff-yellow flowers in mid-May. Its leaves are attractive year round. Pointed, oval, and somewhat leathery, they resemble those of the much more tender vine, *Clematis armandii*. In cold weather, the foliage takes on a purple cast.

The genus *Aster* includes some species from other parts of the world, but by and large, asters are North American herbaceous perennials. One, the quite remarkable Carolina climbing aster (*Aster carolinianus*), is woody, not herbaceous, and for best bloom it should not be cut to the ground in the fall or early spring. It is a vast, rangy plant that hurls itself up and then leans on the support of a lath house or other building in full sun. It bears hundreds of small, bluish pink flowers in November. It offers another surprise besides climbing: On warm and sunny afternoons, its intensely fragrant flowers fill the air with a strong scent of marzipan.

Annual Vines

Up to this point, all the vines and climbers I have touched on have been woody plants and perennials that come back every year, where

they happen to be winter-hardy. Annual vines, however, have their own place in the garden. Morning glories, moonflowers, scarlet runner beans, lablab beans, and others are all especially valuable to help dress and add bulk to a brand-new garden. A few packages of inexpensive seed are all that it takes in the spring to assure that fences and trellises will be covered at summer's end with luxuriant foliage and cheerful bright bloom.

As time passes and as gardeners presumably acquire more sophisticated tastes, they often grow forgetful of annuals. This forgetfulness is as sad as forgetting old friends who were simple and good and true. I am always unhappy when midsummer rolls around and I realize that once again I have forgotten to plant moonflowers and morning glories. In the North, both of these make lush growth and a huge crop of flowers from late summer well into autumn. (The season of bloom begins much earlier in the summer down South.) Between them, these two plants claim the evening and the forenoon. The moonflower's long, spiraling, greenish white buds, ballooning near their tips and then tapering to a fine point, open visibly near dusk, in under a minute, if the evening is warm. The large flat disks of the

Scarlet runner beans, quick-growing annual vines, have an old-fashioned quality that suits them perfectly to this old weathered barn in rural Vermont.

pure white flowers have a sweet fragrance that is irresistible to the night moths that seek their nectar well after dark. As for morning glories, there are rose ones and white ones and multicolored ones, but since childhood the cultivar 'Heavenly Blue' has owned my heart. Its name is not hyperbole but simple truth, for the multitudinous number of flowers borne by this plant, if grown in the lean soil it prefers, are as deep and pure a blue as the sky over Arizona in April. It epitomizes exuberant growth, for I have seen it climb a telephone pole and then, at the top, spread itself in both directions along the wire, as if to deny that it was earthbound by roots. Although it seems entirely blue from just a few feet away, its coloration is actually more complex. The creamy yellow throat at the center of the flower spreads itself out onto the base of the petals in a wash of white. The five veinlike depressed structures separating the petals are tinged with purple, and on the blue back of the flowers they are pearly white. These flowers are as pleasant to the hand as to the eye, as they have a soft and delicate silken texture.

The lablab bean, which is also commonly called hyacinth bean and bonavista vine, and which botanically is *Lablab purpureus* (syns. *Dipogon lablab, Dolichos lablab*), is hardly a novelty in American gardens. Thomas Jefferson grew it at Monticello, if it was the "purple bean" he referred to in his garden journals. But it has recently been rediscovered by gardeners in this country, in quite an infectious way; if you see it one year in someone else's garden, you will insist on having it the next year in your own. A lusty grower that quickly reaches ten feet or even higher where the soil is fairly rich and on the moist side, it should be started inside in peat pots in early April in the North. In the South, it may be sown directly in the ground once it has warmed. The three-lobed leaves have a smoky purple tint. The ten-inch clusters of white and lilac-purple pealike flowers look like those of wisteria, except that they stand erect instead of

Morning glories are lovely on fences, either solo or in combination with other vines, such as mandevilla 'Alice DuPont'.

drooping or hanging. The flowers are followed by seedpods much like those of lima beans, except that they have a varnished or waxy look and are a rich purple-red rather than green.

Lablab beans are not edible or even palatable, except to cattle, but scarlet runner beans are tasty, and when they are grown on a fence or trellis, the bright red blossoms are handsome. People who want a lot of green beans for the summer table had better plant bush beans instead, for scarlet runner beans are not highly prolific.

Cobaea scandens, or cup-and-saucer vine, is a tropical perennial grown as an annual in temperate regions. It was once widely planted in America, as it still is in northern Europe, but it has fallen out of fashion, perhaps because in areas where summer comes on late, it must be started inside in pots. It is, nonetheless, a delightful vine. The seeds I plant come from Central American seed farms, where the flowers are pollinated by bats—a fact that probably accounts for the huge size of the cup-shaped purple blossoms, sitting in their calyx saucers. There is a white form, but it is dingy. For quick cover of a fence, the side of a shed, or a trellis by a porch, this vine is ideal. As soon as the soil warms up, its growth is lickety-split. In the olden days, it was often used to grow on privies, and it is still used to screen an unwanted view.

Cypress vine (*Ipomoea quamoclit*) is in the same genus as morning glories, but it is as delicate as they are bold. The foliage is soft and ferny, and the flowers little bright red stars.

The strangest of all annual vines is one Hella and I stumbled on late one summer afternoon on the Olympic Peninsula, when we were suddenly socked in by fog, and had to stop in Sequim instead of driving on to Seattle. There was a little nursery next to the motel, and we picked up a hanging basket of *Rhodochiton atrosanguineum* to cart back on the plane to New Jersey the next night. It is a startling plant, to put it mildly. The heart-shaped leaves are edged in purple. Each flower emerges from a skirtlike red-violet calyx, which outlasts its flower for weeks. Before the long purple flower buds open, they are phalliform, to put it as delicately as possible, but when they flare open, they mirror the skirt shape of the calyces above them. Every year we try to remember to plant a few seeds in a big clay pot in a sunny spot on the deck, giving them a wicket or half-loop made of kiwi vine runners to cling to.

Cruel vine (*Araujia sericofera*), whose gentler common name is poor man's stephanotis, is a rampant Brazilian vine with clusters of fragrant white flowers. Its first common name comes from reports

Sweet peas grow beautifully near the edible kind in the kitchen garden of Barnsley House, Gloucestershire.

At Montrose in North Carolina on an October day lablab beans smolder with their purplish leaves and their pale purple and white flowers, above *Verbena bonariensis*, *Zinnia angustifolia*, and *Tradescantia pallida* 'Purple Heart'.
ALLEN LACY

Rhodochiton atrosanguineum, a vine native to Mexico, has a dark flower like a bell-clapper, hanging below a long-lasting fuchsia-colored set of bracts like a parachute. It has found a happy home in an orange tree above flamboyantly-colored pelargoniums.

that it traps moths inside its flowers at night, forcing them to pollinate it in their frantic efforts to escape, and then releasing them (looking, I presume, a little moth-eaten the next morning). I have grown this plant only once, and if it tortured any insects in its reproductive lust, I didn't see it. It makes large seedpods in the fall that look a bit like the fruits of cacao.

The squirting cucumber (*Ecballium elaterium*) is a joke plant, if there ever was one. I brought a few seeds of this annual back from England one year, and it reseeded for many years, until the spot where it grew got too shady. A cucumber relative, it is a vine that sprawls on the ground. At summer's end, it produces many hairy little fruits like footballs. The water pressure builds up inside the fruits as they ripen. Touched at just the right moment, the little fruits detach themselves and whoosh up in a great arc, as if jet-propelled, landing many feet away. There's nothing beautiful about squirting cucumbers, but in late August a few plants can keep a child's attention for a long, long time—ten minutes, at least.

Vines of Envy and Lust

Beginning gardeners have favorite plants, and if asked, they will tell you all about them. But as they continue to garden, they accumulate so many new favorites that the very word loses meaning. In time, they inevitably meet some earnest beginner (or worse, a chatterbox who has no interest in gardening but just wants to make idle conversation), who asks, "What is your favorite flower [daylily, rose, iris, etc.]?" Nancy Goodwin's honest and refreshing answer is "the one I happen to be looking at, at the time." I subscribe fully to both the essential truth and the courteous evasion of this answer. But I have a corollary answer, which comes from having lived first in the South and now in the North, and it is this: "My favorite flower, favorite rose, or whatever, is the one I can't grow where I live, but could grow where I used to live."

As useful as the distinctions between herbaceous and woody or other groups of plants may be, there's another distinction that's much nittier and a whole lot grittier. Wherever gardeners live, they see the world of plants as divided into two major classes: those they can grow because they live in the right place and climate, and those they can't grow because they live in the wrong place and climate.

I am now writing a catalog of regret, a catalog of the vines and other climbing plants I can't grow because I garden in New Jersey.

It's my personal view of things, and necessarily negative, but it has a positive side: people who live in some other places can grow plants I cannot. They may even despise some of them, but that's just an expression of common human depravity.

To go back to roses, I'd increase my annual charitable donations by $1,000 if I could grow the yellow climber 'Marechal Niel.' I can't. It hates winter cold that goes on for more than a few days at a time. I'd probably go up to $2,000 to grow the Lady Banks, or banksia, roses, which were brought from China to England in the early nineteenth century and then came to the warm regions of the United States shortly thereafter. The white form has a trace of fragrance that is lacking in the yellow form, but the yellows are magnificent—a cascade of bloom in the midst of spring or slightly later. It hardly matters that they bloom for only a few weeks and then become a mere leafy presence in the garden the rest of the year. During their brief reign, they flower more abundantly than any plant I know. I love them, but it's a star-crossed passion, unless I move back South. And I may. . . .

Then there are the jasmines. In a protected spot, next to the foundation on the south side of the house, I grow winter jasmine (*Jasminum nudiflorum*) passably well. It's a sprawling shrub, not a vine, and sniffing its blossoms is an olfactory dud, but it's bright and abundant in yellow flowers, tinged with scarlet on the backs of their petals, in January or February. I take what I can get, but I long for the fragrant white flowers of *Jasminum officinalis*, which grows well as far north as North Carolina. This vine will take to a trellis and then leap to the rooftop of a nearby house or a garage. I grow the more tender Arabian jasmine, *J. sambac*, inside in pots that come outside in summer, and I'm not about to say what crimes I might commit to have it outside all year and to delight in its intoxicating, but never cloying, sweetness. Confederate jasmine—not a true jasmine at all, but *Trachelospermum jasminoides*—we grow as a houseplant that summers outdoors, like Arabian jasmine. It's all we can do, but I'd love to have it curling around our doorway or taking to our lampposts, as it does in the South Carolina Low Country. This gorgeous creature bears propeller-shaped cream or white flowers of delicious scent and lustrous, dark evergreen leaves. It also makes a superb evergreen groundcover in warm regions.

Need I even mention *Bougainvillea?* The tender vining ornamental species of nightshade, or *Solanum?* Cat's claw vine? (But there's a cautionary tale about this vine, to be told in due course.)

Trachelospermum jasminoides, the sweetly fragrant Confederate jasmine that is a staple of southern gardens in the United States, puts on a fine show in Lucca, too, in the company of an opulent clematis.

The tip-off that this English-style house is not in England but in Los Angeles is the colorful bougainvillea, growing with parthenocissus, ivy, and the velvety flowers of tibouchina.

I lust for passion vines, too. Only two species, *Passiflora caerulea*, and *P. incarnata*, are marginally hardy where I live, although in the neighborhood there is one plant of the latter that not only flowers spectacularly but also produces large fruits in the fall, thanks to being planted on the south side of a house immediately above a heated basement. The fruits, however, never quite ripen enough to be edible. There is an Andean species, *P. mollissima*, which is winter-hardy to Zone 6 and bears delicious fruits with a bananalike taste, but I have never seen it offered in nursery catalogs.

The passifloras are mostly tropical or subtropical vines with large, exceedingly handsome flowers that are extremely complex in form and come in a spectacular array of colors, including brilliant scarlets, soft and glowing purples, and handsome bi-tones of white and violet or blue. They are called passion vines not because of any aphrodisiacal properties, but because Spanish missionary priests in the tropics of the New World saw them as emblematic of the Passion of Christ, finding in them symbolic representations of the crown of thorns, the hammer and nails employed in his Crucifixion, and assorted other theological imagery. The staunchly Anglican herbalist John Parkinson, who called passiflora "clematis," fulminated against such horticultural popery:

> Some superstituous Jesuite would fane make men beleeve, that in the flower of this plant are to be seene all the markes of our Saviours Passion. . . . and to that end have caused figures to be drawne, and printed, with all the parts proportioned out, as thornes, nailes, speare, whippe, pillar &c. in it . . . but these bee their advantagious lies (which with them are tolerable, or rather pious and meritorious) wherewith they use to instruct their people; but I dare say, God never willed his Priests to instruct his people with lyes, for they come from the Divell, the author of them . . . I must referre them to God, and hee knoweth the truth and will reforme or deforme them in his time.

Parkinson may have been unduly prejudiced against the Jesuit order, but I think he was on the right track in separating the plant kingdom from the realm of theology.

So far, the vines I lust for in vain I cannot grow because I don't live in Zone 9 or 10. But there's one—and it's a beauty that I can't grow because of summer heat and humidity. It grows very well indeed in parts of the Pacific Northwest and in Scotland, where it is called the Scotch flame flower. It is *Tropaeolum speciosum*, a herbaceous vining relative of nasturtiums. It dies back to the ground in the autumn, returning in the spring from rhizomes. Its foliage, like little five-leafed clover leaves, is exceedingly delicate and lovely, and its scarlet flowers marked with yellow are borne in profusion in late summer, followed by handsome little deep blue fruits. I have tried it a couple of times, in a pot in a shady spot on our deck, but as soon as the summer heat cranks up, the Scotch flame flower perishes almost overnight. (I must add that in the Pacific Northwest, where it is happy, it can also be a horrible pest, pulling down even substantial perennials under its weight.)

I have had no success whatsoever with *Hydrangea petiolaris*, (syn. *H. anomala* subsp. *petiolaris*), or climbing hydrangea. I can't blame the climate, for this exceedingly handsome plant thrives in both Litchfield, Connecticut, and Raleigh, North Carolina. It is hard to get established, and I do not really have a proper place for it, such as a brick or stucco wall, to which it may attach itself by the holdfasts

Solanum jasminoides 'Album', a member of the nightshade family and first cousin to the potato, is a lovely vine, but not winter-hardy in areas colder than Zone 9.

Lasting little over a day, *Passiflora caerulea* has perhaps the strangest, most intricately structured, and most beautiful of all flowers.

Passiflora coccinea, the red granadilla native to tropical South America, will produce delicious fruits, but only if hand-pollinated. It hardly matters, considering how sumptuous the flowers are for the eye to feast upon.

Still swelling toward ripeness, these passionvine fruits are as lovely as any jewel.

It is slow to get established, but *Hydrangea petiolaris*, the climbing hydrangea, is worth waiting for, as in this splendid specimen at the home of Mrs. Ralph Merton in Berkshire.

along its branches (which stick quickly with the strength of Crazy Glue). It is a gorgeous plant in every season, including winter, when its exfoliating cinnamon bark shows and the buds for next year's growth have already begun to swell. An easier substitute that I have admired in several gardens is *Schizophragma hydrangeoides*. It has handsome, rather downy leaves with notched edges, and many clusters of white or pale rose flower bracts in midsummer.

For Cool Shade and Good Fruit: Living with Hardy Kiwis

The vine I live with most intimately is the hardy kiwi (*Actinidia arguta*). There are four of them, in fact: three different female cultivars and one male, whose pollen is needed if there is to be fruit. (I did not know when I planted them that the cultivar 'Issai' is self-fruitful, which is good news for anyone with space enough for only one vine. 'Issai', a word which means one-year-old in Japanese, also bears fruit much sooner than other cultivars.) This species is not the kiwi vine that produces the brown fuzzy fruits with the juicy green flesh and the rings of black seeds at the center—the fruits we know from the grocery store. That one is *Actinidia chinensis*, a plant that is winter-hardy to Zone 6, but doesn't have time to ripen its fruits.

We planted our little seraglio of hardy kiwis in 1987—along one side of a trellis and on the posts of a fair-sized wooden pergola we added to our deck the year before—with visions of a heavy harvest of the smooth-skinned, grape-sized fruits our first fall. The plants were healthy and heavily rooted, growing in containers from Edible Landscaping, a nursery in Virginia that specializes in small fruits for home gardens. We had no fruit that year, but the vegetative growth was impressive. The vines grew twenty-seven feet in two months and branched out in many directions. There was a moderate amount of cool shade on the deck by August. But the vines are heavy, and we made the mistake of allowing some of them to ramble between the slats of the trellis, almost destroying it. I cut off the offending shoots that winter, and the following summer, the pergola was entirely covered, with long shoots waving in the breeze where the plants ran out of the pergola, as if they were looking for another world to conquer. No fruit, but the vines were still very handsome, for the contrast between their medium green large leaves and their garnet stems. The vines finally blossomed in May of 1990, with clusters of downward-facing, single pearly white blossoms that have a circle of black anthers at the base of their petals. The blossoms,

Tropaeolum speciosum, a perennial vine in the same genus as nasturtiums, combines handsome foliage like widespread fingers with the most intensely crimson flowers imaginable. Not everyone can grow it, but it thrives in Scotland and in the Pacific Northwest almost to the point of weediness.

Of similar uses to the climbing hydrangea, *Schizophragma hydrangeoides* grows far more easily and swiftly. It is seen here at the home of Princess Greta Sturdza near Dieppe.

which were pleasantly, if lightly lime-scented, looked like slightly smaller versions of the flowers on a nearby mock orange. We had fruit, but most of it dropped off in midsummer, and none of it ripened. We cut some of the fruits in half, and they were unmistakably kiwis, with that characteristic ring of black seeds. I decided to read up on kiwis. It turns out that they require heavy pruning in late winter to increase the fruiting spurs, and that in summer, those vagrant waving tips of the branches seeking new worlds to conquer need to be guillotined. I bought one of those extension-pole pruners with a rope and a pulley, started pruning, and ended up with a huge pile of both old and fresh new growth. Hella discovered that the prunings are pliable enough to make into informal wreaths, and the top of a picnic table under a nearby maple was soon covered with wreaths left to dry and harden.

Pruning kiwi vines is not a once-a-year job; it must be done every month during the summer to remove the long, loopy end growth.

Actinidia kolomikta, a species of hardy kiwi, seen here with hostas and ferns, bears leaves so splashed with hot pink and cream that from a distance they may be mistaken for flowers.

This practice increases the yield of fruit substantially. I have also found that the vines need to be thinned out several times during the summer. Left to themselves, they make a very dense canopy that produces heavy shade below them. Judicious editing of a branch here, a branch there, results in pleasantly dappled shade in which some of our flowering plants in hanging baskets will keep blooming.

Our kiwi vines contribute much to our lives in summer. They give us a pleasantly shady place to read, sit and talk with friends, or take meals, on a west-facing deck that would be too hot in the afternoons without the vines. We can sit in the shade, enjoying the abundant summer bloom of all the tender or tropical plants that come outside with us in late spring—the gardenias, hibiscus, plumbagos, mandevillas—and other colorful plants in pots, like geraniums, New Guinea impatiens, and heliotropes.

Actinidia arguta is not exactly new in America. At the turn of the century, it was widely planted as a landscaping vine on large private estates on Long Island and elsewhere. A male or a female plant was propagated by cuttings, in such a way that the sexes never got together to be fruitful and multiply sexually, in the best tradition of the Book of Genesis. No one then seemed to realize that it could bear delicious fruits, for it was not understood that it was dioecious, meaning that it takes two (or one and three, in our garden) to tango. Its new popularity comes from the interest in edible landscaping that writers like Rosaline Creasy and Lee Reich—and home gardeners getting bored with their lawns and their yews—have encouraged in recent years.

When I saw pictures in nursery catalogs of another hardy kiwi, *A. kolomikta*, I lusted for it, but knew I had no room for it left on the pergola. It looked luscious. Its variegated green, carmine, and white leaves looked in the pictures almost like flowers. So I gave a plant to Michael for his garden down the street from us. I haven't made up my mind yet whether I really like it. Some people hate it, others love it. Humans may be divided on this matter, but not their cats, to whom *A. kolomikta* is irresistible. They go crazy in the vine's presence—not a catnip kind of crazy that leaves them purring and rolling on their backs. They go berserk, racing around in a frenzy.

The Vine of Vines

Finally, there is the one true vine, the vine of vines, as it were—the grape, the common name for the several species in the genus

At John Greenlee's nursery in California, tassels of tall ornamental grass and clusters of ripe grapes paint a splendid autumn picture.

Vitis. The generic term "vine" is borrowed from a more specific use of the word to denote the wine grape or the vine grape, the Old World species *Vitis vinifera.* This plant, along with olives and wheat and barley, harkens back to the civilizations of Mesopotamia, Egypt, and classical Greece and Rome. It was sacred to Dionysus and other powerful gods of old who, I would hold, are still among us, but in hiding. Wine—with water, bread, olives, and cheese—is still part of the simple feast that sustains and celebrates our lives on this earth. The grape was domesticated in antiquity, and we continue to have our own roots in sweet-smelling vineyards in the season of harvest.

But North America also had its grapes, wild and undomesticated species—the fox grapes and the frost grapes, the riverbank grapes and the muscadines. These are all exuberant, bursting with life and full of the muscle that one of the great prophets of American agriculture and horticulture, Andrew Jackson Downing, celebrated in the middle of the nineteenth century in his *The Fruits and Fruit-Trees of America.* Here he wrote:

> The grape-vine is in all cases a trailing or climbing deciduous shrub, living to a great age, and, in its native forests, clambering over the tops of the tallest trees, in the deep rich alluvial soils. Several have been measured on the banks of the Ohio the stems of which were three feet in circumference, and the branches two hundred feet long, enwreathing and festooning the tops of huge poplars and sycamores.

Another American writer, Neltje Blanchan, wrote in 1900 in *Nature's Garden* of the joyful memories from her childhood of the native fox grape (*Vitus labrusca*):

> What fragrance is more delicious than that of the blossoming grape? To swing in a loop made by some strong old vine, when the air almost intoxicates one with its sweetness on a June evening, is many a country child's idea of perfect bliss. Not until about nine o'clock do the leaves "go to sleep" by becoming depressed in the center like saucers. This was the signal for bedtime that one child, at least, used to wait for.

Fox grapes not only take to the railroad tracks and the roadsides of the eastern United States, but also appear, unbidden, in gardens, planted by birds that feast on their fruits in wild places and then

Vitis coignetiae, an Asian species of grape, flames into color on a flint wall in England. There is no exaggeration whatsoever in its common name, crimson glory vine.

excrete their seeds wherever they fly. A summer seldom passes that I do not discover a fox grape that has grown immense in a single season, to be pulled out and coiled into wreaths.

I sometimes want to curse this plant when I see how much territory it has covered, but it has turned out to bring enormous blessings. The vineyards of Europe were almost wiped out in the nineteenth century by an epidemic of phylloxera, a disease caused by a tiny insect that attacked the root systems of the European wine grape. The days of wine, if not roses, were saved by North America's native fox, or labruscan, grape, whose roots were immune to phylloxera. European grape scions grafted on the roots of this American grape kept the vineyards of France, Spain, and Germany healthy and productive.

Wine grapes still have their ornamental uses, even in a small residential garden. They can cover a simple fence made of posts and wires in short order. If well chosen and well tended, they may yield clumps of delicious fragrant fruit for eating late in summer. The music and the dance of the wind rustling through their large, plentiful leaves is most agreeable. And there is even a Japanese species that brings a fine surprise as autumn arrives. *Vitis coignetiae* has splendid leaves all during the summer. Large and somewhat velvety to the touch, they glow pale green when they are backlit, and their stems are cranberry red. When the evenings begin to turn chilly and the nights frosty, this vine does not assume the yellow tones that are common to the rest of the genus, but turns bright crimson instead. Its common name is almost inevitable: the crimson glory vine.

On a January day at Montrose, in Hillsborough, North Carolina, an ancient grape vine embraces an even more ancient hackberry. This passionate relationship has lasted a century at least.
ALLEN LACY

William Frederick's strong hand with wisteria forces it to stay contained, looking something like a huge conifer on its restraining framework of steel girders.

7 Beautiful Thugs

In Eden, where all was perfect before the reckless conduct of our first parents, there can be no doubt that all plants behaved with fine restraint. Nothing grew out of bounds; no plant trespassed against another. But the tale in The Book of Genesis of this first of all gardens makes it plain that it was also the shortest-lived. After Eden, humans had to struggle with tares and weeds, fend off thistles and nettles, and fight with aggressive plants—some of them quite lovely. Every gardener knows that the worst weeds of all are those we plant deliberately, because we like them, and we do not understand how greedy and hard to control they may turn out to be.

Why do we plant things that turn out to be beautiful trouble?

There are two answers. One is that nursery catalogs often are written in a code that studiously avoids the word "invasive." Instead, a plant is a "strong grower," "lusty," and even "easy to grow." The other answer lies in the darker recesses of the human heart. Even if we are fully warned about the takeover tendencies of something like akebia, wisteria, or the showy evening primrose, the desire to grow them overtakes our good sense. Some of our worst weeds we are seduced to buy; others we choose out of free will, against good advice and our own better judgment. In one way or the other—or both—we invite these beautiful thugs into our gardens. I want to treat them in this chapter, partly as an antidote to the toxic snake oil of some catalogs, partly as a confession derived from my own experience and mistakes. To use a current term in academic jargon, this chapter's subtext is *Caveat emptor.*

Chief among these worst weeds of all are certain vines—a whole rogues' gallery of them.

Most people of my generation fed themselves on visual images not of tropical rainforests understood to be delicate ecosystems, but of *jungles*—steaming, unimaginably fertile places rank with vegetation, especially with vines and lianas plunging from the high canopy of trees to the forest floor beneath. Here, in loincloths and with machetes in hand, lived Bomba the Jungle Boy, Nyoka the Jungle Girl, and Tarzan—the half-wild, jungle-wise refugees from western white civilization who understood the ways of this tropical wilderness. Imbedded deeply in my own imagination are pictures from *National Geographic* of Buddhist temples in Burma and Thailand engulfed in luxuriant vines, and of abandoned Mayan cities in the Yucatan so swallowed up in these plants that almost nothing of their former human architecture could be seen in an aerial photograph. As a child, I understood very well that the devil's ivy that my mother grew as a trailing houseplant on a windowsill was, in its steaming native habitat near the equator, a truly demonic plant entirely worthy of its name.

The vocabulary attached to the subject of vines is neither tame nor pretty. I have already alluded to vines that *engulf* or *swallow up* buildings and entire cities. Vines *strangle*. They are *murderous, insidious,* and *sinister*. They *creep*, but then they *conquer*. By their very nature, vines are *dangerous*.

This vocabulary misses the mark. It attributes to the natural order a moral character and a system of intents and purposes it does not in fact possess. But as metaphor, it is understandable. Even in the earth's temperate regions, certain vines seem to be enemies not only of human beings but also of other plants they compete with and eventually destroy. It is an unfortunate but common experience that someone deliberately invites a vine into a habitat where it is not native, and then later discovers that this act was a horrible mistake, an ecological misfire, or even a disaster.

A prime case that will leap to the mind of any Southerner is kudzu (*Pueraria lobata*). I have to force myself to think of it as beautiful. I have seen the havoc it can wreak. When I lived in the South, I did hand-to-hand combat with it. But if I were seeing it for the first time —and seeing only one small plant, no more than fifteen feet high, working its way up a tree—I would covet it. Its leaves, an admirable shade of emerald and very dense, cast a cool shade on a boiling-hot day and flutter appealingly in a breeze.

But planting kudzu is one of those bright ideas that turns out, in hindsight, to have been really stupid. In *The World Was My Garden* (1938), a delightful memoir of his career as a plant collector for the U.S. Department of Agriculture, David Fairchild speaks of the use of kudzu in Japan as cattle fodder. His first attempts, in 1907, to establish it at his home in Washington, D.C., failed, but eventually he got viable seeds that germinated, bringing a quick and unpleasant surprise. "The seedlings all took root with a vengeance, grew over the bushes and climbed the pines, smothering them with masses of vegetation which bent them to the ground and became an awful, tangled nuisance," he wrote. In subsequent years, he spent over $200 trying to eradicate this vine from his property, without entire success. At the same time, the Soil Conservation Service was recommending kudzu "to control gullying and erosion throughout the South."

Despite his own experience, David Fairchild seems not to have foreseen the baleful consequences of the Soil Conservation Service's recommendation. Kudzu turned out to be the vine that ate the South. (Fairchild is sometimes blamed for importing this pest, but he is innocent. The culprit was Thomas Hogg, a United States consul to Japan who, before his death in 1892, introduced many Japanese plants, including kudzu, into American horticulture.) Today, this vine covers countless thousands of acres of fields and woodlands. It is a vegetative steamroller, capable of growing seventy feet in a single season. It gives no quarter to any other plant it encounters in its ruthless march forward. Where there is nothing to climb, it covers the ground with a deep cloak of green. When it finds something to

◀ A friendly green prince of an amphibian guards some steps in the Frederick garden against monsters and thugs.

◀ No Southerner will ever forgive the villains that brought us kudzu from Japan. Here it is gobbling up some roadside woodlands near Durham, North Carolina. ALLEN LACY

An unbridled menace in the eastern United States south of New York City, Japanese honeysuckle is relatively tamed in this village on Lago Iseo, where it has no room to wander sideways.

climb, it ascends immediately, throttling its unlucky host. Jack's beanstalk (like kudzu, a legume) is a piker by comparison. What appear to be pillars of shimmering green from afar turn out to be doomed trees, as enswathed in kudzu as a spider's prey in its silken trap. The pillars shimmer because the large leaves of kudzu catch the slightest breeze and seem to dance, as if in murderous glee. Mounds or hillocks of deep green in former fields now taken captive by this truly vicious weed conceal rusting junked cars or trucks. If kudzu finds an abandoned house, it will move right in, bursting through the windows and doors, pulling down dilapidated porches and roofs under its heavy weight and, within a few years, causing the entire building to collapse.

People who let kudzu get going in their gardens don't have another chore to do; they have a second career.

And the greatest pity in the tale of kudzu in the southern United States is that it proved to be virtually worthless in fighting soil erosion. It is a deciduous vine, with leaves so sensitive to frost that Southerners who wonder if last night brought the first frost of fall need only check the nearest patch of kudzu. (Contrary to popular opinion, this vine will grow north of the Mason-Dixon line, as it is fully winter-hardy to Zone 6. It is a menace in areas with milder winters because it does not die back to the roots, as it does where winters are more serious. Northerners, however, are wise to leave it alone and should resist the slightest temptation to use it as a fast-growing screen. There's always the possibility that the species might contain enough genetic variability to evolve toward more cold-resistant forms.)

No vine exceeds or even matches the power of kudzu, but it has some close rivals, most of which are also East Asian plants, that were deliberately imported to North America, or imported first to England and then crossed the Atlantic to the United States, where they found conditions rather too much to their liking. Historically, the first of these vines was Japanese honeysuckle (*Lonicera japonica*), which William Kerr selected at a nursery in Canton and sent back to Kew in England sometime after 1803. Other vines collected in East Asia and brought to England and then to America in the nineteenth century included chocolate vine (*Akebia quinata*), Oriental bittersweet (*Celastrus orbiculatus*), and wisteria (*W. floribunda* from Japan, *W. sinensis* from China). All of these plants, with the help of kudzu and *Rosa multiflora* (not, strictly speaking, a vine, but a mounded shrub that will climb into trees at the edges of woodlands), have changed the character of the native flora, in the South-eastern and Middle Atlantic states—and not to its improvement.

The case of Japanese honeysuckle is instructive, for it shows how little time it can take for an exotic plant to become a ubiquitous pest in much of the United States. Dr. Stephen A. Spongberg, the horticultural taxonomist of the Arnold Arboretum, details its comparatively short history in North America in *A Reunion of Trees* (1990). Even though honeysuckle reached England early in the nineteenth century, it came directly to the United States from Japan in 1862, in a collection of plants Dr. George Rogers Hall shipped from Yokohama to Francis Parkman, the eminent historian and a passionate horticulturist. It quickly became popular and was widely distributed in both the North and the South, where it escaped into the wild. Spongberg compares it aptly to the Norway rat that European explorers brought to North America.

If their considerable vices are overlooked, all of these plants obviously have their attractions; otherwise, no one would ever have gone to the trouble of collecting them and introducing them to Western gardens in the first place. Japanese honeysuckle is lovely for its oddly mixed cream and pure white flowers that appear in clusters during the summer, for its sweet perfume that carries far on the wind, and for the drop of delicious nectar deep within each blossom —nectar that most children know how to extract and sip. *Akebia quinata* and the related vine *A. trifoliata* bear modest but charming little blossoms in early spring, and the fresh new foliage is delicate, dainty, and quite elegant. The Asian wisterias are breathtaking in very late spring for their long, pendant clusters of pealike violet or white flowers, and *W. floribunda* has a heady perfume, like that of a ripening vineyard in August. (I can close my eyes and think back to my college days, during examination week in May at Duke University, when the night air was redolent of wisteria, honeysuckle, and magnolia, all with perfumes far more intense and sensual than they have in cooler climates.) The leaves of wisteria also turn a soft, glowing gold in autumn, and the thick, twisting, and gnarled trunk of this vine, as it grows to old age in well-matured gardens such as Dumbarton Oaks, bespeaks dignity and power. Oriental bittersweet, gathered in the fall, makes beautiful wreaths because of the candy-corn colors of its orange fruits and their paler yellow husks. As for the multiflora rose, it has no perfume worth mentioning, if any at all, but it grows quickly and produces a froth of tiny, single white flowers in early June. Only a couple of decades ago, it was being heavily

Wisteria, here seen at the Bishop's Close in Portland, is hauntingly beautiful and fragrant when it blooms in late spring, and it has a second season of loveliness when its foliage turns buttery yellow in autumn. It remains nonetheless a thug.

promoted as a living fence, a source of food for birds and other wildlife, and as a highway barrier so dense that it could prevent automobiles from crossing into oncoming lanes.

I have ransacked American gardening literature of the early twentieth century looking for negative remarks about any of these plants, but I haven't found any. Neltje Blanchan's *The American Flower Garden* (1927) antedates the craze for multiflora rose as a miracle plant, but it offers nothing but praise for wisteria, akebia, and bittersweet. (She does mention that honeysuckle, although "good for fences and walls," is "becoming a weed.") She proclaims kudzu as the "best very rapid growing foliage vine."

Nevertheless, the vices of all these plants outweigh their virtues. Japanese honeysuckle infests fields and woodlands southward from New Jersey like a plague of green. So does wisteria, a plant that people complain about at every stage of its existence. First it will not grow, or it grows slowly. Then it is stubborn, refusing to bloom for years. Then it blooms and seeds itself everywhere, as the vines gather strength and destructive power. (Wisteria will also pull down an abandoned house: A friend tells me of a house on Long Beach Island that virtually exploded from the wisteria that took over when people moved out and it moved in.) Bittersweet, once it fruits, sprouts everywhere. It is aggressive, and its twining, rapidly growing stems would make it necessary to invent the word "strangle," if we didn't already have it. Bittersweet eventually kills small trees by girdling them. Multiflora rose is fine food for birds, but they eat its hips, fly wherever they please, and excrete the seeds. Wherever it has become established, this shrubby weed has become a serious problem for farmers.

As mentioned already, the foliage of akebias looks dainty and delicate. The five leaflets of *Akebia quinata* and the three of *Akebia trifoliata* fan out at the end of their stems, with open space between each leaflet and the next. When akebia vines are young, they cast only mottled shade. Their first growth is so tentative that they seem shy and weak, perhaps destined for an early death. In fact, the first akebia I planted perished within a single season, just as it was about to twine its way into a lilac hedge. But the apparent delicacy of these Japanese vines is as dangerously deceptive as the Trojan horse. They have high territorial ambitions and murderous ways, with a knack for strangling. Nancy Goodwin has suggested that I skip akebias altogether, because of their boisterous ways and exceptional self-aggrandizement. They grow over, around, and in her pumphouse, coming in one window and then departing by another. She relates with some rue that she planted them, after being transfixed by the beauty of their flowers one late spring in Italy, where she saw them growing in splendid harmony with pink 'Mermaid' roses.

I have heard akebia called "gardener's revenge vines." There are tales down South of gardeners who, if they have a score to settle with someone, will present them with a plant of *Akebia quinata*, which is slightly the worse of the two species. They secretly dream that one day they may find their enemy's garden so swamped with akebia that he might have perished beneath it and that it might be years before his sorry remains are discovered.

It is worth noting that some of these East Asian plants have relatives that are far less invasive, in the same way that some generally nice families can have a nasty member or two. The greedy ways of Japanese honeysuckle, for example, should not cause gardeners to avoid other species in the genus that have merit. Not all, of course, are vines. Available from a few mail-order nurseries are at least eleven shrubby species, including *L. fragrantissima*, which is hardy to Zone 6, semi-evergreen, winter blooming, and, as its name suggests, sweet smelling. In the Northeast, it blooms in March, sometimes earlier. The cream-colored blossoms have a lemony scent, and the plants can be used in hedges. Among vining forms of honeysuckle, I have discussed earlier such desirable sorts as *L. perfoliata*, *L. sempervirens*, and *L.* X *heckrottii* 'Goldflame'.

American bittersweet (*Celastrus scandens*) seldom presents much of a problem, perhaps because, unlike its Asian counterpart, it bears male and female flowers on different plants and will not set seed unless plants of both sexes grow close to one another. As for *Wisteria frutescens* and *W. macrostachys*, these North American native species lack not only the spectacular beauty of their Far Eastern cousins, but also their vigor.

Among the exotic vines that have made themselves a bit too much at home on North American soil, *Wisteria floribunda* is arguably the most beautiful. But it has a very close rival in another vine that grows

Cat's claw vine, which is fortunately so tender that it grows only in places like Charleston and New Orleans, where winters are gentle, has gorgeous flowers but vicious manners.

Dwarf green-and-gold running bamboo is a temptation and a snare to the unwary. The wise gardener who grows it will contrive that it has no place to run to.

only where winters are mild—places where moderately harsh freezes are rare enough to stick in the memory for years. The plant is the cat's claw vine, or yellow bignonia, which is not actually a bignonia, although it is in the same family. It is *Macfadyena unguis-catis*, a native of the West Indies. In Charleston, South Carolina, it blooms in mid-April, and friends there report that it is only moderately troublesome, and even less so since Hurricane Hugo swept the city. It bears gorgeous golden chalices that invite the eye inward to its little folds and recesses. If I were a tiny elf, cat's claw vine might tempt me to take a nap inside its flowers.

But there is no such thing as advice about the ways of particular plants that is universally applicable. In New Orleans, cat's claw vine seems to be quite wicked, albeit beautiful. Charlotte Seidenberg has this to say about cat's claw vine in her fascinating book, *The New Orleans Garden* (1990):

> [An] evergreen vine which climbs to great heights with tropical rapidity, clinging with claw-like tendrils . . . It is my feeling that this plant's beautiful flowers do not come remotely close to redeeming it for its destructiveness. Its seeds are spread by the wind and sprout anywhere. Large tubers which extend deep

into the ground form on the roots and are difficult to dig out. The "claws" damage the surfaces on which they climb in addition to holding rain moisture, encouraging wood rot. The vine will smother other growth which tries to compete. I found one which had crept under my house and was growing up my livingroom fireplace chimney! Persistent pulling and the selective use of an herbicide will keep the beast somewhat under control until you get a new neighbor who sees it on his side of the fence and says: "What pretty flowers! I think I'll let it grow."

It is hard to believe, considering what Ms. Seidenberg says, but some nurseries actually sell this plant. A friend from New Orleans, Rebecca Freeman, has sent me this description of it from the catalog of Plumeria People:

An excellent choice for covering a fence, wall, or trellis. Due to the special "claws" (note how they will gently grab your finger), this vine needs no training and will cling to virtually any rough surface. Very easy to grow.

I'm inspired to try my hand at this sort of thing. Here goes:

This relative of sumac is a vigorous, easily grown vine or shrub native to North America. The British envy us because we can grow it and they cannot, although they have made the attempt. The handsome, deep green, trifoliate leaves are so glossy that they seem almost varnished. In a breeze, the whole plant shimmers, as if in pleasure and joy. This plant has no insect foes or other enemies to mar its beauty. It is highly drought resistant, requires no fertilizer, and will grow in full sun or partial shade. The brilliant foliage in autumn is followed by stunning gray-white fruits. Hardy from Zone 3 to Zone 10. Sturdy plants in one-gallon containers, $29.95 plus shipping.

What $29.95 plus shipping will get you is *Rhus radicans*—our gorgeous native poison ivy.

Comparatively few of our native vines are takeover artists. Poison ivy is a menace, of course. Trumpet vine (*Campsis radicans*) is extremely muscular, and it spreads by underground suckering as well as vaulting aerial maneuvers. Muscadines and other native grapes can cover a lot of territory in short order, and need to be watched and controlled. *Smilax rotundifolia* is tenacious and nasty, as its common names blaspheme vine, hellfetter, and tramp's trouble suggest. Virginia creeper (*Parthenocissus quinquefolia*), one of the loveliest of plants for its brilliant autumn foliage, looks fairly menacing where it drapes itself on buildings and takes to trees, hanging down from their crowns in graceful swags, but the best evidence suggests that it is fairly harmless. In a review of the scientific literature about Virginia creeper in *American Horticulturist* (September, 1986) Jeanne Goode concluded that it did not damage architecture and that it was a beneficial source of both shelter and food for songbirds and other wildlife.

If I had the power, I would cheerfully deport kudzu, Oriental bittersweet, multiflora rose, and probably akebia as well. But I make no final argument against either Japanese honeysuckle or wisteria, especially *Wisteria floribunda*. Despite its pushy ways, I still treasure honeysuckle for that piercingly sweet fragrance or that drop of nectar on a fresh cool morning in June. When planting any of these aggressive vines, the essential thing to keep in mind is that there is a hard bargain involved. Undeniable beauty must be paid for in substantial labor. I would not easily give up the form of our native trumpet vine with apricot blossoms I planted twenty years ago in my front garden, next to a tall and ancient Virginia juniper. The vine called no attention to itself for almost ten years, as its silvery-barked trunk blended in perfectly with the huge lower bole of the tree. Then one summer day I looked up, discovering a wonderful sight. The vine had reached the very crown of the tree, covering it with flowers attended by darting little specks against the sky—hummingbirds fighting for nectar. In the years that have intervened, the trumpet vine has suckered all around the juniper. It is hard work to remove the suckers, and contact with the foliage can cause dermatitis, but the work is worth it.

I have even acquired a second trumpet vine. So far, it is just a small rooted cutting in a pot on my deck, but it is a very special form of the Asian species, *Campsis grandiflora*. This species, collected in one of the warmer regions of China a century or more ago and one of the parents of the hybrid cultivar 'Mme Galen', is notably tender. But in 1985, Barry Yinger and Professor J. C. Raulston collected a much hardier form of the species in a region of Korea where winter is as severe as it is in the northeastern United States, and the plant has been passed on from one nurseryman to another. I got my first glimpse of it in July of 1991 at Holbrook Farm and Nursery near

Asheville, North Carolina. It was growing on a post by a fence next to the parking lot, and when I saw it, I almost drove through the fence. Its blossoms are huge, flaring trumpets. They are peachy pink, not orange, and they grow in dramatic inflorescences up to three feet long. The plant may turn out to be as horribly invasive as Japanese wisteria, but some forms of dangerous beauty are not to be resisted, and I hear reports that this species does not produce suckers.

It is probably politically unfashionable to confess any affection for circus lion tamers and tiger trainers, but as a child I loved their acts even better than the performances by clowns and trapeze artists. For me, the crack of the whip in the hands of a human being inside a cage with lions and tigers symbolized bravery in the face of danger. That said, I must go on to say that there are two horticultural lion tamers that I admire for their courage in taming or controlling akebia and wisteria, respectively.

One, Professor J. C. Raulston, has planted both *Akebia quinata* and *A. trifoliata*, as well as a hybrid between the two species, on an arbor above the walkway leading from the parking lot to the entrance to the North Carolina State University Arboretum in Raleigh. The plants have nowhere else to go, and thus are kept controlled. It is pleasant to walk under them in the spring and enjoy their chocolate-scented rose-purple flowers. Their dense shade in summer is pleasant and cooling. Akebias may not fruit in colder climates with shorter growing seasons, but here they bear handsome large purple or cream fruits that hang down and look a bit like mangoes. (I have another method of controlling this vine. My one akebia grows on the shady side of a wooden fence, under a large maple tree. The shade has kept it to only four feet, and it makes an appealing pattern on the fence, above a little bed of hostas and ferns. I know that if it ever grows just a couple of feet taller, reaches the top of the fence, and then spills over it into a neighboring yard, which is bright and sunny, it will be Katy-bar-the-door. But starving it of light has kept it looking shy and innocent.)

The other vine tamer, landscape architect William H. Frederick Jr., has invented the wisteria tree, but not in the usual sense of the words, referring to wisteria vines that have been pruned to develop a central trunk strong enough to support top growth, which is kept in check by frequent trimming. In his garden in Delaware, Frederick has two trees, made of Corten steel I-beams—the stuff of bridges and skyscrapers. These structures are actually garden sculptures that serve as support for *Wisteria floribunda* 'Macrobotrys', which is distinguished by exceptionally long racemes of fragrant violet-cobalt flowers. One specimen is twelve feet high and has a rounded crown, like a small shade tree. The other, thirty feet high, has the form of a tall conifer. In a triumph of human will over rambunctious plant nature, the wisterias are trained to the steel branches of the trees. They do what Bill Frederick wishes, for he had given them no alternative. It is a sight to gladden the heart of anyone who has ever done battle with wisteria, but lost.

The beautiful thugs among groundcovers cannot quite match the awesome power of their vining counterparts. Earthbound, they cannot crawl up, over, or into things. They are an infantry, not an air force. I suppose that any groundcover that spreads by underground stems or that roots as it goes has the potential for thuggery, as do weeds like crabgrass and chickweed. But there are a number of low and spreading plants that are such genuine thugs that they should be planted cautiously, if they are planted at all.

Some are grasses or grasslike plants. When the word "grass" is preceded by the adjective "spreading," little alarm bells go off in my head. I spent far too much time as a kid grubbing Bermuda grass out of flower beds to ignore these bells. In my New Jersey garden, I have nothing as horrid as Bermuda grass, but some things worry me. Blue lyme grass *(Elymus canadensis)* is notoriously invasive, but I have it in very dry shade under a royal privet. It has behaved itself beautifully for several years under these conditions. I think it's safe, and its cool gray-blue foliage is soothing. A little sedge, *Carex glauca*, has itchy feet, and I am keeping a wary eye on it.

But there are some other grassy plants that I would not dare set free. One is dwarf green-and-gold running bamboo, which grows to about eighteen inches tall. Its exact scientific name is a tangle of confusion. It used to be *Arundianaria viridistriata*, a name still used in most general nursery catalogs. Some nurseries specializing in bamboos, however, now list it as *Pleioblastus viridistriatus*, although *The New Royal Horticultural Society Dictionary of Gardening* claims that its valid name is *Pleioblastus auricoma*. I'll sit this one out until the taxonomists make up their minds, but no matter what it is called, it is one of the true beauties of this earth. Its variegation is so irregular that no two leaves are ever exactly alike. Their base color is pale gold verging on chartreuse, and the leaves are generally striped with dark green running parallel to the central vein. The stripes vary in

Equisetum hyemale and other species of horsetails have great elegance of form, but they need to be rigidly confined.

number and in width according to no discernible plan or pattern, and occasionally they are missing entirely. This bamboo changes hue with the light, and from a distance it seems to emanate a rich golden glow. It is gorgeous, but it is also dangerously invasive. The standard advice is to contain it, by such prophylactic means as surrounding it with metal shields running from just above the surface of the soil to a depth of two feet. This advice is hopelessly optimistic; dwarf green-and-gold bamboo is such a proficient escape artist that Houdini plant would be a fine common name for it. Having seen its ruthless spread in other gardens whose owners trusted in metal shields, I grow it on my deck, in a wooden half-barrel, where it cannot get loose and start to roam.

In a second barrel on the deck I have similarly confined gardener's garters (*Phalaris arundinacea picta*), a grass that grows about twenty inches high and is superbly striped white and green. It flags in late July, when the lower leaves crisp to parchment tones and the plant gets ungainly, but it comes back in a couple of weeks if sheared entirely to the ground and drenched with water. The cultivar 'Fleece's Form' has pink-tinted foliage in early spring and ivory rather than white stripes. Its great virtue is that it doesn't get ratty and require midsummer shearing. I am replacing my old gardener's garters with this obviously superior form.

On my deck, there are other prisoners. In several large terra cotta pots I have a collection of equisetums, which go under two common names: horsetail (for reasons I can't fathom) and scouring rush (because their high silica content made them suitable for cleaning pots, until steel wool came along). These extremely primitive plants from the age of the dinosaurs possess no leaves, and they reproduce from spores, not seeds. Their hollow green stems are wiry and flexible, but very tough. I grow three different kinds. *Equisetum hyemale* grows to two feet or slightly taller, and the form *E. hyemale* var. *robustum*, to four. Four feet, however, represents a distinct decline in the aerial ambitions of this genus; many of the long-extinct species of horsetail were towering treelike plants during their heyday in the Carboniferous era. (Their fossilized remains are an important source of coal.) My other horsetail, *E. scirpoides*, calls it quits at eight inches, forming a bristly, busy-looking mat of quill-like stems, which are not hollow in this species. I would hesitate to call any of the horsetails beautiful, but they are appealing. They have a sculptural quality, and they link my deck with life on earth long before the human race made its late appearance. They are also somewhat sinister. Livestock have been poisoned by eating hay contaminated with

Petasites japonicus in both its plain and variegated form, at the University of British Columbia Botanical Gardens, is in search of new worlds to conquer wherever it can.

their dried stems, and if they get loose in a garden, particularly in moist soil, they are the very dickens to get rid of. My sympathies go out to a gardener down the street who ordered three loads of topsoil for his perennial border, and then discovered that it was chockful of the rhizomatous roots of *Equisetum hyemale* and probably of its spores as well. Five years later, he still finds the stuff coming up while his back is turned.

Certain plants that are offered by nurseries as suitable groundcovers ought to come with warning labels, and I pride myself on having resisted three in particular.

One is crown vetch, *Coronilla varia* 'Penngift'. This plant has too strong an association with highway landscaping to be comfortably used in a home garden. It seems that the public authorities in one of the suburbs of Minneapolis feel the same way. There are rumors of an elderly woman there being cited for a misdemeanor when she ripped out her lawn and replaced it with crown vetch to reduce maintenance chores. It is unsurpassed for highway use, however, where it quickly covers steep, dry banks and smothers virtually any weed. Its abundant pink flowers are lovely to see on an interstate highway, even when one is speeding by at seventy-five miles per hour. But it often harbors rats and pine voles, says Barry Yinger, who despises it.

I have my own grave doubts about another plant that, by odd coincidence, was introduced into American horticulture from East Asia by none other than Barry Yinger. It is *Houttuynia cordata* 'Chameleon'. Barry gave this cultivar its name because of its different coloration in sun and shade. Its foliage is splashed with several shades of green, as well as cream and pink. It is happiest in moist to boggy soil, and it can take either full sun or shade. Highly invasive when it's happy with its home, it has somewhat better manners in dry soil. Some catalogs praise it for its orange-scented leaves. This claim is hogwash, although I once believed it. I crushed some leaves once and gave them a sniff; it was like being hit in the face. This plant is not only a thug but also afflicted with a repugnant odor.

The final member of the trio of things I have wisely not started in my garden is bishops weed, *Aegopodium podagraria* 'Variegatum', a vicious spreader from here to kingdom come. It might have some uses in difficult places in dry shade, and it is fairly pretty. Edith Eddleman reports that her grandmother has a planting of it that hasn't spread a millimeter in forty years, but this lady gardens on very heavy red clay, which seems to tame its territorial ambitions.

I do not want to give the impression that I am a gardener so knowing and wise that I have never let anything loose in my garden that I later regretted. Far from it. My garden is filled with thugs, great and small. I may keep that green-and-gold dwarf bamboo safely confined on the deck, but I planted a small piece of a larger species in one corner of the front garden in 1978, and since 1983, Hella and I have battled every spring with an asparagus knife to halt its advance. I rue the day I planted the ornamental grass *Miscanthus sinensis* 'Gracillimus', for it has seeded itself everywhere, including in the lawn, where it grows much more quickly than turf grass, to very odd effect. I happen to love *Gaura lindheimeri* for its tall graceful wands of tiny pink butterfly flowers from early July to frost, but Hella hates it, and I admit that it seeds itself around just a bit too exuberantly. We both agree that it was a black day when I bought

A rambling rose eats a garage and a
Bentley at Chris Rosmini's home in
southern California.

three hybrid tradescantias from White Flower Farm. On sandy soil, tradescantia is positively Dionysian in its reproductive energies, although it is not nearly so troublesome in clay. And we feel the same way about plume poppy, or *Macleaya cordata*. It is noble and imposing, and its silver-backed leaves are beautiful when they dance in the wind. But its underground roots seek new ground to conquer so rapidly that a new plant can suddenly appear fifteen feet away from the nearest one.

And some of my own thugs are groundcovers, or close to it. *Artemisia ludoviciana* 'Silver Queen' and 'Silver King', at thirty-three and twenty-eight inches respectively, are perhaps a trifle too tall to be groundcovers in the strictest sense, but in full sun they grow thickly enough to muscle aside anything else. There are some very well-behaved artemisias, but this species and its cultivars are as malicious in their spread as a small-town rumor. Their silvery foliage is very lovely, they are highly drought tolerant, and they are good in mixed bouquets. But I still didn't know what I was doing when I planted them.

I should have known what I was doing, however, when I planted *Oenothera speciosa*, the showy pink evening primrose. I saw it growing at the Andre Viette Farm and Nursery in Fisherville, Virginia, one summer. It was in full bloom—a spreading patch with hundreds of big pink flowers with lovely olive veins. I remembered it from my childhood in Texas, where it is abundant along highways and rural lanes. I begged Andre for a piece. "You don't want it," he said, "for it just takes over." I said I could control it. Pure hubris! It spreads everywhere, both by underground runners and by seeds. Roundup seems to check it, but then I turn my back and it's still in the garden, ready to gobble up more ground.

And now I'm smitten with something else: *Petasites japonicus*. This is an extremely bold plant that bears enormous, rounded, slightly heart-shaped, bluish green leaves that huddle together in thick colonies, looking somewhat like lotuses that have left the water to become terrestrial. It was much used in landscaping on large private estates earlier in this century, as was its only slightly less rambunctious kin, the winter heliotrope (*Petasites fragrans*). There is a new cultivar, *P. japonicus* 'Variegatus', that was collected in Japan and introduced by the University of British Columbia Botanical Garden. It has enjoyed increasing popularity among daring gardeners for its foliage, which is irregularly mottled, marbled, and stippled with creamy yellow markings. Gary Koller has written its

Is there a Grimm Brothers fairy tale about the unfortunate Prince who sat here one afternoon once upon a time to catch his breath, didn't notice *Campanula portenschlagiana* sprouting at his feet, and hasn't been seen since then? If not, there should be one.

praise in an article in *Arnoldia* about promising new and rare groundcovers. I have seen both the plain and the variegated forms growing side by side by a stream at Brookside Gardens in Wheaton, Maryland. I have also seen petasites at the Landscape Arboretum of the University of Minnesota. There it stretches back into the woodlands, almost to the horizon. It is, I think, a virtually unstoppable plant once it gets going.

I won't plant it. I think I won't plant it. I know I shouldn't plant it. I will be wise and reasonable, won't I?

I don't know.

The Prayer of General Confession in *The Book of Common Prayer* has my number. In the garden, as elsewhere, I have left undone those things that I ought to have done. I have also done those things that I ought not to have done.

Beautiful thugs give me a thrill.

Sources of Plants

A few lucky souls—people living in parts of the North Carolina Piedmont, eastern Long Island, California, and the thickly populated cities of the Pacific Northwest—can pretty much rely on local sources for their plants, including groundcovers and vines. These areas are horticulturally sophisticated enough that the demand is there to support fine nurseries to supply the plants. Most of us, however, have only run-of-the-mill to pretty decent garden centers to rely on. The chance of finding something rare and extraordinary in such a place is tiny. Among groundcovers, there is sure to be English ivy, vinca, pachysandra, and a few carpet junipers. *Rubus parvus* is just not going to turn up. Among vines, there may be some large-flowered hybrid clematis or red honeysuckles in containers. *Ampelopsis pedunculata* 'Elegans', crossvine, and ground-nut vine are not in the cards. Fortunately, however, the United States is increasingly blessed with splendid mail-order nurseries, most of them fairly small, with unillustrated catalogs that cost a dollar or two, where the rare and the unusual, as well as the old and familiar and dependable, can be found. In 1992, Dr. J. C. Raulston compiled a booklet called *North Carolina Grown*, which was published by the North Carolina State University Arboretum. It listed the plants in the catalogs of fifteen mail-order nurseries in the state—7,625 plants in all, from *Abeliophyllum distichum* to *Zizia trifoliata*. The overlap from nursery to nursery was small. Just eight of them offered one plant in common. Six of them converged on six plants. Some 6,481 plants were sold by only one nursery. North Carolina is a special case, for it is one of the true horticultural hot spots in America today, but even so, Raulston's statistics give some idea of the rich and diverse supply of uncommonly worthy plants to be had by gardeners willing to go to the trouble of sending for catalogs and following through with an order.

There follows an annotated list of some of the nurseries that I have dealt with satisfactorily over the years and that include in their offerings vines and plants suitable as groundcovers. No one should draw any conclusion from the absence of some nursery or other from the list. There are a few that aren't listed because I have had bad experiences with them and their plants. Some of these are notorious anyway, and they usually can be spotted for their hyperbolic ads in magazines—ads promising miraculous and sensational surprises for some plant that is really quite common and either unremarkable or else remarkably bad in behavior. But I have reason to believe that by far the majority of mail-order nurseries today are honorable and honest, and that they give good value for money received. Barbara Barton's *Gardening by Mail*, now in its third edition, is a good guide to America's great number of mail-order nurseries. I recommend it highly. My own list here reflects only my own experiences with several nurseries that have contributed to the garden Hella and I have been making for two decades.

B & D LILIES, 330 P Street, Port Townsend, Washington 98368 ($4.00). The color catalog is handsome and loaded with temptations. The selection of lilies is vast, and the bulbs are freshly dug and shipped with dispatch, to lessen the need for prolonged storage that can lead to shriveling and loss of vigor.

CALADIUM WORLD, P.O. Box 629, Sebring, Florida 33870 (free). This grower sells many different caladiums at rock-bottom prices, but their quality is high.

CANYON CREEK NURSERY, 3527 Dry Creek Road, Oroville, California 95965 ($2.00). This small, but highly choice nursery can always be counted on to offer perennials not easily found elsewhere, including some old-fashioned favorites that have virtually disappeared from commerce.

COASTAL GARDENS, 4611 Socastee Blvd., Myrtle Beach, South Carolina 29575 ($2.00). This nursery is the only source I know for "black" elephant ears and for the splendid chartreuse-leafed liriope cultivar 'PeeDee Ingot'.

DAFFODIL MART, Route 3, Box 794, Gloucester, Virginia 23062 ($1.00). For years, I have bought all my bulbs from this long-established firm in Tidewater Virginia. Its no-frills catalog is rich in small or miniature daffodils, in alliums, in fritillaries, and in many other genera of bulbs, and its prices are exceptionally reasonable for imported spring bulbs of top grade.

EDIBLE LANDSCAPING, P.O. Box 77, Afton, Virginia ($2.00). I acquired my several vines of hardy kiwi and different cultivars of *Actinidia arguta* here. The nursery also offers a wide variety of grapes for ornamental use as well as fruit.

FORESTFARM, 990 Tetherhod, Williams, Oregon 97544 ($2.00). The specialty here is rare woody plants, sold very inexpensively as rooted but established cuttings. Patient gardeners will be willing to grow them on to suitable size for use in the home landscape.

GLASSHOUSE WORKS, Church Street, P.O. Box 97, Stewart, Ohio 45779 ($2.00). Tropical plants are the main specialty here, but the thick, oversized, newsprint catalog bursts with rare hardy plants as well, including a heady assortment of low or dwarf conifers and dwarf nandinas and willows. Glasshouse, located in three carpenter-gothic houses and several greenhouses so crammed with plants that it's difficult to move down the aisles, is worth a special visit. Stewart is a tiny but beautiful town in the Hocking River Valley.

HATFIELD GARDENS, 22799 Ringgold Southern Road, Stoutsville, Ohio 43154 ($2.00). This splendid little home nursery, which has imaginative display gardens, sells daffodils, daylilies, and some other perennials, but its chief specialty is hostas—over 200 different species and cultivars in a recent catalog.

HEATHS AND HEATHERS, P.O. Box 850, Elma, Washington (SASE). This nursery specializes in species of *Erica* and *Calluna* and closely related genera. Hundreds of cultivars of these woody plants are offered. Display gardens show visitors how versatile heaths and heathers are in making, with little assistance from other plants, a landscape of great year-round beauty.

HERONSWOOD NURSERY, 7530 288th Street Northeast, Kingston, Washington 98346 ($2.00). Heronswood is a newcomer to the horticultural mail-order scene, but an exciting one for rare woody plants, vines, and herbaceous perennials. It emphasizes many plants of East Asian origin that simply aren't yet available anywhere else. Some things may be in short supply, so ordering as soon as Heronswood's catalog arrives is an excellent policy. The nursery's co-owners, Dan Hinkley and Robert Jones, offer the largest assortment in America and probably the whole world of species of *Rubus* suitable as woody groundcovers. The catalog lists an extraordinary number of vines, including species of *Clematis* that cannot at present be found anywhere else.

HOLBROOK FARM AND NURSERY, 115 Lance Road, P.O. Box 368, Fletcher, North Carolina 28732 (free). Allen Bush, Holbrook's founder and owner, is a person with great charm, good humor, and a passion for plants, and all of these qualities shine through the nursery's highly readable catalog.

KLEHM NURSERY, Route 5, Box 197, South Barrington, Illinois 60010 ($4.00). The Klehm family's nursery has long been known for its introductions of fine peonies, bearded iris, hemerocallis, and hostas, but in recent years it has branched out to include many superb perennials of European origin, such as several exciting new pulmonaria cultivars.

LAMB NURSERIES, East 101 Sharp Avenue, Spokane, Washington 99202 (free). Lamb sells some low woody plants suitable for groundcovers, as well as many herbaceous perennials. The selection of succulent plants, especially hens-and-chickens, is generous.

PARK SEED COMPANY, S. C. Highway 254N, Greenwood, South Carolina 29647 (free). Owned by the same family for generations, Park is an American horticultural tradition. A great many people depend on it for everything they grow from seed, from vegetables to annual vines.

PLANT DELIGHTS NURSERY, 9421 Sauls Road, Raleigh, North Carolina 26703 ($2.00). Hostas rule the roost here, but Tony Avent's small nursery also lists many other perennials and dwarf conifers in a choice selection.

ROSLYN NURSERY, 211 Burrs Lane, Dix Hills, New York 11746 ($3.00). The specialties here are rhododendrons, azaleas, andromedas, and mountain laurels, but other woody plants, many of them low or creeping, aren't neglected, nor are herbaceous perennial groundcovers.

SISKIYOU RARE PLANT NURSERY, 2825 Cummings Road, Medford, Oregon 97501 ($2.00). Siskiyou is excellent for alpines, both native and exotic, but it also offers a good selection of small woody plants and of native phlox.

ANDRE VIETTE FARM AND NURSERY, Route 1, Box 16, Fishersville, Virginia 22939 ($2.00). This family-run nursery is known for its wide selection of herbaceous perennials, especially daylilies and hostas. It sells from its shop on the premises, as well as by mail order. The display gardens, in a spectacular rolling setting in the Shenandoah Valley with a fine view of the Blue Ridge Mountains, are lovely and filled with ideas worth borrowing as regards plant combinations.

WAYSIDE GARDENS, Hodges, South Carolina 29695 (free). For generations, Wayside's catalog has been part of both the elementary and the higher education of many American gardeners. Its offerings cover a very wide range of plants, including many groundcovers and vines. Every year its catalogs can be counted on to offer new and often rare plants.

WE-DU NURSERY, Route 5, Box 724, Marion, North Carolina 28752 ($2.00). We-Du has a fine list of Asian plants, North American natives, and uncommon bulbs.

WOODLANDERS, 1128 Colleton Avenue, Aiken, South Carolina 29801 (business-size SASE). Woodlanders is a good place to look for plants native to the southeastern United States, especially vines. Gardeners in cold regions of the country are advised to order in the fall, as the nursery's spring shipping season does not extend beyond late March.

$\mathcal{A}ppendices$

INTRODUCTORY NOTE TO APPENDICES

In the following appendices, I offer information on the hardiness range, height, and spread of many of the groundcovers and vines discussed in the text. I have generally given the range of U.S.D.A. hardiness zones in which each plant may reasonably be expected to grow well. These zones are familiar to many gardeners, but they perhaps bear repeating here. The figures after each zone listed below represent the average annual minimum temperatures that define the zone.

Zone 1: Below $-50°$ F.
Zone 2: $-50°$ F. to $-40°$ F.
Zone 3: $-40°$ F. to $-30°$ F.
Zone 4: $-30°$ F. to $-20°$ F.
Zone 5: $-20°$ F. to $-10°$ F.
Zone 6: $-10°$ F. to $0°$ F.
Zone 7: $0°$ F. to $10°$ F.
Zone 8: $10°$ F. to $20°$ F.
Zone 9: $20°$ F. to $30°$ F.
Zone 10: $30°$ F. to $40°$ F.

It should be noted that these zones are derived from the map published by the U.S.D.A. in 1965. In 1990, the federal government issued a revised map, redefining each zone by dividing it in two, so that the former Zone 7 has now become Zones 7a ($0°$ F. to $5°$ F.) and 7b ($5°$ F. to $10°$ F.). This new system should prove to be a valuable improvement, but I have not followed it here for the simple reason that almost all published data on plant winter hardiness use the old system. It will take at least a generation of close observation of plants to bring this information up to date.

Not long ago, American gardening books and nursery catalogs gave plants only one zonal designation, indicating the average minimal annual temperature that they could be expected to survive. It is becoming more common now to offer a zonal range—for example, Zones 3–8, which suggests that a plant in this range might survive minimal annual average temperatures from $-40°$ to $20°$ F. I have followed this practice in the appendices. The reason for giving a higher zone designation as well as a lower one is that American gardeners are becoming increasingly aware that *summer hardiness is just as important as winter hardiness*. Plants are stressed by extreme and prolonged winter cold, but they may also be stressed by hot and humid summers that promote fungal diseases and by total annual heat accumulation. Prominent horticulturists in the southeastern United States, especially Professor J. C. Raulston of the North Carolina State University and Professors Allan M.

Armitage and Michael A. Dirr of the University of Georgia, have repeatedly and persuasively argued this point in recent years. The system is not entirely satisfactory, however. Giving a warmer zone as well as a colder one is a step in the right direction, but the zonal system, based as it is on average annual minimal temperatures, betrays a Northeastern bias. Furthermore, much of the evidence about plants' ability to thrive in prolonged hot and humid weather is anecdotal at best, pure guesswork at worst.

The philosopher Alfred North Whitehead warned of the perils of misplaced concreteness, which involves, among other things, the human tendency to take assertions for solid facts, and names for realities. The appendices that follow have a tidy look. For example, they seem to promise that *Alchemilla mollis* will do well in Zones 4 to 7, attaining a height of 12 inches and a spread of 18 inches, and that *Artemisia versicolor* will thrive in Zones 5 to 8, attaining a height of 10 inches and a spread of 12 inches. My garden in coastal southern New Jersey is in Zone 7, as is Hillsborough, North Carolina. This alchemilla, or ladies mantle, does well for me (rather too well in fact) but it is worse than iffy in Hillsborough, where the hot, humid summers make a large difference. As for this particular artemisia, which is one of my favorite plants, I may be somewhat generous in maintaining that it spreads to 12 inches. Friends in Oregon tell me that it can quickly spread to 36 inches across. And my friend Tony Avent in Raleigh, North Carolina, estimates its typical height at 6 inches, but agrees with me that it spreads very slowly. It may be hard for dogmatists and the literal-minded to accept, but the same plant can behave very differently in different places—and even in the same place in different years. Gardeners cannot live without making generalizations, but reality has a way of overturning them. Averages are only roughly descriptive of what has happened in the past; they have no true predictive reliability. I live in the upper reaches of Zone 7. Camellias, crape myrtles, and wax-leafed ligustrums are at their margins of winter hardiness here, but in the winter of 1985–86, they suffered no injury. In contrast, a balmy, lingering fall in Zone 8 to the south ended with a sudden plunge from 70° F. in mid-December to 10° or below. Growth there had not yet hardened off, and this precipitous drop in temperature was followed by a prolonged cold wave, with record low temperatures for the region. Camellias, crape myrtles, wax-leafed ligustrums, and other shrubs and trees such as boxwoods died back to the ground throughout the Southeast.

I offer zonal ranges, heights, and estimated spreads of plants only as very rough guides. They should not be taken as revealed truth, which is the territory of theology, not of horticulture. Nor should they limit gardeners who lust to grow some plant that "won't grow" in the zones where they live. I have long-standing affection for the Indian hawthorn *(Raphiolepis indica)* I grew up with in Texas. It is a fine evergreen shrub with many clusters of beautiful pink flowers in the spring, followed by handsome black fruits. The standard reference books all call it a Zone 8–9 plant. I bought one in North Carolina and brought it home, giving it a slightly protected, sunny location on the south side of the house. That was many years ago. My hawthorn has reached 3 feet, not the 5 feet it would where winters are warmer, on average.

But it has not only survived but also thrived, and if I had been intimidated by what the books said, I would miss the pleasure of those lovely pink flowers in early May.

An explanation is in order about the expected spread given for each plant. For plants that remain basically in clumps, the spread indicates the estimated planting distance needed between several individuals of the same plant for them to close ranks and serve as groundcover. For plants whose tendency is to spread far and wide, the number indicates an estimate of the proper distance between individual plants to achieve *quick* groundcover. The point cannot be reiterated too often: in a country as large as the United States and with such enormous variations in climate and soils, the same plant will often behave in different ways in different places.

For the information about size and hardiness of herbaceous plants, I am indebted to two excellent recent reference texts: Allan M. Armitage's *Herbaceous Perennial Plants*, and Ruth Rogers Clausen and Nicolas H. Ekstrom's *Perennials for American Gardens*. Where these sources disagree, I have split the difference or followed my hunches. For similar information about woody plants—both groundcovers and vines—I owe a considerable debt to J. C. Raulston's newsletters published by the North Carolina State University Arboretum, and to Michael A. Dirr's formidably authoritative *Manual of Woody Landscape Plants*, currently in its fourth edition.

APPENDIX A:
Selected Herbaceous Perennial Groundcovers

Adiantum capillis-veneris, Southern maidenhair fern, Z. 9, 12″–12″; *A. pedatum*, maidenhair fern, Z. 3–8, 12″–16″.

Aegopodium podagraria 'Variegatum', bishops weed, Z. 3–9, 6″ to the horizon; highly invasive in sun or shade.

Ajuga species and cultivars, bugle or bugleweed, Z. 5–8, vary widely in height, spread, and color of foliage and flowers.

Alchemilla, ladies mantle: *A. alpina*, mountain ladies mantle, Z. 3–7, 8″ x 12″; *A. ellenbeckii*, Z. 7–8 (with protected location in winter), 8″ x 12″; *A. mollis*, Z. 4–7, 12″ x 18″.

Arabis, rock cress: *A. blepharophylla* 'Spring Charm', Z. 3–7, 6″ x 12″; *A. caucasica*, Z. 4–7, 4″ x 12″; *A. fernandi-coburgii* 'Variegata', Z. 5–8, 1″ x 12″; *A. procurrens*, Z. 3–9, 2″ x 9″; *A. sturii*, Z. 4–8, 6″ x 12″.

Arenaria, sandwort: *A. balearica*, Z. 6–9, 1″ x 12″; *A. montana*, Z. 5–7, 6″ x 12″.

Arrhenatherum elatius bulbosum 'Variegatum', bulbous oat grass, Z. 5–10, 8″ x 12″.

Artemisia ludoviciana, Z. 4–9, 24″–36″; *A. stelleriana* 'Silver Brocade', Z. 3–7, 10″ x 12″; *A. schmidtiana*, Z. 3–7, 15″ x 18″; *A. versicolor*, Z. 5–8, 10″ x 12″; 'Powis Castle', Z. 6–8, 20″ x 24″.

Arum italicum 'Pictum', Z. 6–9, 12″ x 6″.

Aruncus aethusifolius, dwarf goat's beard, Z. 6–7, 6″ x 12″.

Asarum, wild ginger: *A. europeanum*, Z. 4–7, 4″ x 12″; *A. canadense*, Z. 5–10, 8″ x 12″; *A. shuttleworthii*, Z. 5–8, 4″ x 6″; *A. splendens*, hardiness range undetermined, 7″ x 5″.

Athyrium filix-femina, lady fern, Z. 3–8, 24″ x 36″; *A. nipponicum* 'Pictum', Japanese painted fern, Z. 4–8, 14″ x 12″.

Aubrieta x *cultorum*, rock cress, Z. 3–8, 6″ x 15″.

Bergenia, pigsqueak, Z. 3–8, 12″ x 12″.

Brunnera macrophylla, Z. 3–7, 12″ x 18″.

Caladium, fancy-leafed hybrids, Z. 10, 18″ x 12″.

Calamintha nepeta, Z. 5–10, 18″ x 12″.

Carex, sedge: *C. elata* 'Aurea', Bowles' golden sedge, Z. 6–9, 18″ x 15″; *C. glauca*, Z. 5–9, 6″ x 12″; *C. morrowii* 'Aureovariegata', Z. 6–9, 12″ x 12″; *C. siderostica* 'Variegata', Z. 7–9, 10″ x 10″; *C. texensis*, Catlin sedge, Z. 7–10, 4″ x 6″. *C. glauca* is invasive.

Ceratostigma plumbaginoides, blue leadwort or plumbago, Z. 6–9, 8″ x 12″.

Chasmanthium latifolium, northern sea oats, Z. 5–9, 24″ x 24″; somewhat invasive by seeding.

Chrysanthemum pacificum, Z. 5–9, 12–16″ x 12–16″.

Chrysogonum virginianum, green and gold or pots of gold, Z. 5–9, 8″ x 12″.

Convallaria majalis, lily-of-the-valley, Z. 4–9, 6″ x 6″; invasive.

Corydalis cheilanthifolia, Z. 5–10, 12″ x 12″; *C. lutea*, Z. 5–7, 12″ x 12″.

Cyrtomium fortunei, Japanese holly fern, Z. 7–8, 12″ x 12″.

Delosperma, hardy ice plant: *D. cooperi*, Z. 6–8, 4″ x 12″; *D. nubigena*, Z. 5–9, 1″ x 10″.

Dennstaedtia punctilobula, hay-scented fern, Z. 3–8, 24″ x 24″.

Dicentra eximia, fringed bleeding heart, Z. 3–8, 12″ x 12″; *D. formosa* and its hybrid cultivars 'Luxuriant', 'Snowdrift', 'Sweetheart', and 'Zestful', Z. 4–7, 14″ x 12″.

Dryopteris erythrospora, autumn fern, Z. 5–9, 20″ x 20″; *D. filix-mas*, male fern, Z. 5–8, 18″ x 12″.

Duchesnea indica, false strawberry, Z. 5–8, 4″ x 12″.

Epimedium, barrenwort: *E. grandiflorum*, Z. 5–8, 12″ x 12″; *E. perralderianum* 'Frohnleiten', Z. 5–8, 12″ x 12″; *E. pinnatum*, Z. 4–9, 8″ x 12″; *E.* x 'Rubrum', Z. 3–8, 12″ x 12″; *E.* x 'Youngianum', Z. 5–8, 6″ x 10″.

Equisetum hyemale, horsetail or scouring rush, Z. 4–10, 18″–36″; extraordinarily invasive.

Erysimum 'Bowles' Mauve', Z. 7–9, 20″ x 24″; *E. semperflorens*, Z. 7–9, 15″ x 36″.

Eupatorium coelestinum, hardy ageratum, Z. 6–10, 24″ x 18″; invasive.

Festuca ovina glauca, blue sheep's fescue, Z. 4–8, 10″ x 10″.

Fragaria 'Pink Panda', *F. vesca*, Z. 6–8, 10″ x 10″.

Galium odoratum, sweet woodruff, Z. 4–8, 8″ x 12″.

Geranium, cranesbill, many species and cultivars, Z. 5–8, 6–15″ x 12–18″, depending on kind.

Hakonechloa macra 'Aureola', Z. 6–9, 18″ x 12″.

Helictotrichon sempervirens, blue oat grass, Z. 4–7, 18″ x 12″.

Helleborus foetidus, Z. 5–9, 18″ x 18″; *H. lividus*, Z. 6–8, 18″ x 18″; *H. niger*, Z. 3–8, 14″ x 14″; *H. orientalis*, Z. 4–9, 14″ x 14″.

Herniaria glabra, rupturewort, Z. 4–9, 2″ x 8″.

Heuchera, alumroot: *H. americana* and its cultivars 'Dale's Strain', 'Garnet', 'Montrose Ruby', and 'Palace Purple', Z. 4–9, 12″ x 20″; *H.* x *brizoides*, coral bells, Z. 3–8, 8″ x 12″.

Hosta, Z. 3–9, immensely variable in height, spread, and foliage.

Houttuynia cordata 'Chameleon', Z. 3–8, 12″ high and extremely invasive, particularly in moist soil.

Iberis sempervirens, perennial candytuft, Z. 3–20, 10″ x 12″.

Imperata cylindrica 'Rubra', Japanese blood grass, Z. 6–9, 16″ x 12″.

Lamiastrum galeobdolon, yellow archangel, Z. 4–9, 15″ x 12″; highly invasive, although the cultivar 'Hermann's Pride' is not.

Lamium maculatum and its cultivars 'Aureum', 'Beedham's White', 'White Nancy', and others, Z. 3–8, 12″ x 12″.

Lavandula angustifolia, lavender, Z. 6–9, 18″ x 12″.

Liriope muscari, lily turf, Z. 6–10, 12″ x 12″; *L. spicata*, Z. 4–9, 12″ in height and extremely invasive.

Lysimachia congestiflora, nosegay plant, Z. 7–9, 8″ x 12″; *L. japonica minutissima*, Z. 4–8, 1″ x 6″; *L. nummularia* 'Aurea', golden moneywort or golden creeping jenny, Z. 3–8, 1″ x 6″.

Marrubium cylleneum, Greek horehound. Z. 3–10, 12″ x 12″; *M. incanum*, Z. 3–10, 15″ x 12″; *M. rotundifolium*, Z. 5–10, 4″ x 12″.

Mazus reptans, Z. 4–8, 3″ x 10″.

Melissa officinalis 'All Gold', golden lemon balm, Z. 7–9, 18″ x 12″.

Mertensia virginica, Virginia bluebells, Z. 3–9, 12–18″ x 12″.

Oenothera speciosa, showy evening primrose, Z. 7–10, 12″ x 18″; highly invasive.

Ophiopogon, mondo grass, Z. 7–9: *O. japonicus*, ranges in height from 3″ to 18″ and spreads thickly; *O. planiscapus* 'Arabicus', black mondo grass, 10″ x 10″.

Origanum laevigatum 'Hopley's Purple', Z. 7–9, 6″ x 12″; *O. libanoticum*, Z. 7–9, 8″ x 12″; *O. vulgare* 'Aureum', Z. 3–10, 6″ x 12″.

Orostachys erubescens, Z. 5–9, 3″ x 8″; *O. furuseii*, Z. 5–9, 4″ x 8″.

Pachysandra procumbens, Allegheny spurge, Z. 5–9, 6″ x 10″; *P. terminalis*, Japanese spurge, Z. 4–9, 8″ x 8″.

Pennisetum alopecuroides 'Hameln', dwarf fountain grass, Z. 5–9, 18″ x 18″.

Petasites japonicus, Z. 4–9, 36″ x 24″; extremely invasive.

Phalaris arundinacea 'Fleece's Form' and 'Picta', gardener's garters or ribbon grass, Z. 4–9, 24″ x 24″. Invasive.

Polystichum acrostichoides, Christmas fern, Z. 3–9, 12″ x 12″.

Potentilla tabernaemontani (syn. *P. verna*), Z. 4–8, 4″ x 8″; *P. tridentata*, Z. 2–8, 4″ x 10″.

Pulmonaria saccharata, lungwort, Z. 3–8, 12″ x 12″.
Pycnanthemum flexuosum (syn. *P. tenuifolium*), mountain mint, Z. 7–10, 16″ x 16″.
Ranunculus ficaria, lesser celandine, Z. 3–8, 5″ x 12″.
Sagina subulata, pearlwort, Z. 5–7, 1″ x 8″.
Saponaria ocymoides, rock soapwort, Z. 2–10, 6″ x 12″.
Saxifraga stolonifera, strawberry begonia, mother of thousands, strawberry geranium, Z. 6–10, 6″ x 10″.
Stachys byzantina, lamb's ears, Z. 4–8, 15″ x 12″.
Stylophorum diphyllum, celandine poppy, Z. 4–9, 15″ x 10″.
Symplocarpus foetidus, skunk cabbage, Z. 3–9, 15–30″ x 24″.
Thelyphus kunthii, Florida shield fern, Z. 7b–9, 24–36″ x 24–36″.
Tiarella, foamflower, Z. 3–9, 8″ x 10″.
Tradescantia pallida 'Purple Heart', Z. 7–10, 12″ x 18″.
Vancouveria hexandra, American barrenwort, Z. 5–7, 12″ x 12″.
Verbena canadensis, Z. 6–10, 8″ x 14″.
Veronica, speedwell: *V. alpina* 'Alba', Z. 3–8, 8″ x 10″; *V. incana*, Z. 3–9, 12″ x 10″; *V. prostrata* (syn. *rupestris*), Z. 5–8, 3″ x 8″.
Vinca minor, periwinkle, Z. 4–9, 8″ x 12″.
Waldsteinia ternata, Z. 4–9, 3″ x 12″.

APPENDIX B:
Selected Woody Groundcovers

Arctostaphylos uva-ursi, Z. 2–6, 6–12″ x 24–36″.
Calluna vulgaris, many cultivars, Z. 4–7, ranging from 4″ to 24″ in height, 2′ to 3′ in spread.
Cotoneaster apiculatus, Z. 4–7, 2′ x 3′; *C. adpressus*, Z. 4–7, 1′ x 4′; *C. dammeri*, Z. 5–8, 16″ x 6′; *C. microphyllus*, Z. 5–8, 20″ x 20″.
Daphne cneorum 'Eximia', Z. 4–7, 6–12″ x 24″.
Deutzia gracilis 'Nikko' Z. 4–7, 2′ x 4′, Z. 4–8
Erica carnea, heath, many cultivars, Z. 4–7, 6–24″ x 18″ x 36″.
Euonymus fortunei, Z. 4–8, 6″ x 36″ as a trailer, to 10′ as a climber.
Forsythia x *bronxensis*, Z. 5–7, 20″ x 20″.
Genista lydia, Z. 6–9, 24″ x 30″; *G. pilosa* 'Vancouver Gold', Z. 5–8, 12″ x 36″; *G. tinctoria*, Z. 4–7, 24–36″ x 24–36″.
Hedera helix, Z. 4–9 (although some cultivars are tender); 8″ high as a spreading groundcover to 90′ as a vine; *H. colchica*, Z. 6–9, to 30′.
Hypericum, St. Johnswort: *H. buckleyi*, Z. 5–8, 12″ x 18″; *H. calycinum*, Z. 5–7, 12″ x 18″; *H. olympicum*, Z. 6–7, 8″ x 12″.
Juniperus conferta, Z. 5–6/9, 12–18″ x 6–9′; *J. horizontalis*, 12–24″ x 4–8′.
Lagerstroemia indica, crape myrtle, dwarf forms, Z. 7–9, 12–24″ x 12–24″.
Leiophyllum buxifollium var. *prostratum*, Z. 5–7, 12″ x 18″.
Microbiota decussata, Z. 3–8, 12″ x 4′.
Nandina domestica, Z. 6–9: 'Atropurpurea Nana', 18″ x 18″; 'Harbour Dwarf', 24″ x 36″; 'San Gabriel', 18″ x 18″.
Parthenocissus quinquefolia, Virginia creeper, Z. 3–9, to 30′ or higher; *P. tricuspidata*, Boston ivy, Z. 4–8, to 50′ or higher.
Pieris japonica, Z. 5–8; 'Pygmaea', 24″ x 24″.
Rosa 'Snow Carpet', Z. 6–9, 6″ x 36″.
Rubus calycinoides, Z. 7–8, 1″ x 24″; *R. nepalensis*, Z. 7–8, 2″ x 24″.
Salix yezoalpina, Z. 5–7, 8″ x 36″.
Santolina chamaecyparissus, Z. 5–9, 12–24″ x 24–36″; *S. rosmarinafolia* (syn. *S. virens*), Z. 7–8, 12–18″ x 24–30″.
Sarcococca hookerana var. *humilis*, Z. 5–8, 18″ x 30″.
Skimmia japonica 'Rubella', Z. 7–8, 24–36″ x 24–36″.
Vaccinium crassifolium 'Wells Delight', creeping blueberry, Z. 7–8, 6″ x 18″.

APPENDIX C:
Selected Woody Perennial Vines

Actinidia arguta, kiwi, Z. 3–8, to 25' or more; *A. deliciosa* (syn. *A. chinensis*), Z. 8–9, to 15'; *A. kolomitka*, Z. 4–8, to 15' or higher.

Akebia quinata, Z. 4–8, to 40'; *A. trifoliata*, Z. 5–8, to 30' or higher.

Ampelopsis arborea, Z. 7–9, to 15' or higher; *A. brevipendulata* 'Elegans', Z. 4–8, 10'.

Aristolochia macrophylla (syn. *A. durior*), dutchman's pipe, Z. 4–8, 20–30'.

Bignonia capreolata, crossvine, Z. 6–9, (Z. 5 with protection), 30' or higher.

Campsis grandiflora, trumpet vine, Z. 7–9, 20' or higher; *C. radicans*, Z. 4–9, to 40' at least.

Clematis armandii, milder regions of Zone 7 and southward, 20' or higher; *C. montana*, Z. 5–7, 10' to 25'; *C. terniflora* (syn. *C. maximowicziana*, *C. paniculata*), Z. 5–9, to 30'; large-flowered hybrid cultivars, Z. 3–9, 6–18'.

Gelsemium sempervirens and *G. rankinii*, Carolina jasmine or jessamine, Z. 7–9, 15' to 20'.

Hydrangea petiolaris (syn. *H. anomala* subsp. *petiolaris*), climbing hydrangea, Z. 4–7, to 60' slowly.

Jasminum officinale, jasmine, milder regions of Zone 7 and southward, 15' or higher; *J. polyantha*, Z. 8–9, 15' or higher.

Lonicera flava, Z. 5–8, to 12'; *L. japonica*, Z. 4–9, to 30'; *L. sempervirens*, Z. 5–9, to 12'.

Parthenocissus quinquefolia, Virginia creeper, Z. 3–9, to 30' or higher; *P. tricuspidata*, Boston ivy, 4–8, to 50'.

Schizophragma hydrangeoides, Z. 5–7, to 18'.

Wisteria floribunda, Japanese wisteria, Z. 4–9, to 30' or higher.

ℬibliography

Armitage, Allan M. *Herbaceous Perennial Plants: A Treatise on their Identification, Culture, and Garden Attributes.* Athens, GA: Varsity Press, 1989.

Blanchan, Neltje. *The American Flower Garden.* New York: Doubleday, Page & Co., 1909.

———. *Nature's Garden.* Toronto: William Briggs, 1900.

Cathy, Henry Marc. "Groundcovers Can Cure Headaches Such as Problem Sites, Bare Spots." *Landscape for Living: 1972 Yearbook of Agriculture.* Washington, DC: United States Department of Agriculture.

Clausen, Ruth Rogers, and Nicolas H. Ekstrom. *Perennials for American Gardens.* New York: Random House, 1989.

Darwin, Charles. *The Movement and Habits of Climbing Plants.* London: 1888.

Davies, Dilys. *Alliums: The Ornamental Onions.* Portland, OR: Timber Press, 1992.

Dirr, Michael A. *Manual of Woody Landscape Plants: Their Identification, Ornamental Characteristics, Culture, Propagation, and Uses.* Fourth edition. Champaign, IL: Stipes Publishing Company, 1990.

Downing, Andrew Jackson. *The Fruits and Fruit-Trees of America.* Second edition, revised. New York: John Wiley and Son, and Orange Judd & Company, 1869.

DuPuy, William Atherton. *Our Plant Friends and Foes.* New York: Dover Books, 1969. Reprint of original edition, 1941.

Fairchild, David. *The World Was My Garden: Travels of a Plant Explorer.* New York: Charles Scribner's Sons, 1938.

Fish, Margery. *Ground Cover Plants.* London: Collingsbridge, 1964.

Gerard, John. *The Herball, or General History of Plants.* Second edition, 1633. Reprint. New York: Dover Books, 1975.

Greenlee, John. *The Encyclopedia of Ornamental Grasses.* Emmaus, PA: Rodale Press, 1992.

Lawrence, Elizabeth. *A Rock Garden in the South.* Edited by Nancy Goodwin, with Allen Lacy. Durham, NC: Duke University Press, 1990.

———. *A Southern Garden: A Handbook for the Middle South.* Chapel Hill, NC: The University of North Carolina Press, 1942.

Parkinson, John. *Paradisi in Sole: Paradisus Terrestris.* 1629. Facsimile ed. London: Methuen, 1904.

Raulston, J. C., editor. *North Carolina Grown.* Raleigh: North Carolina State University Arboretum, 1992.

Schmid, George. *The Genus Hosta.* Portland, OR: Timber Press, 1991.

Scott, Frank J. *The Art of Beautifying Suburban Home Grounds.* New York: D. Appleton & Co., 1870.

Seidenberg, Charlotte. *The New Orleans Garden.* New Orleans: Silmont & Count, 1990.

Sitwell, Sir George. *On the Making of Gardens.* 1909. Reprint. London: Gerald Duckworth & Co., 1951.

Spongberg, Stephen A. *A Reunion of Trees.* Cambridge, MA: Harvard University Press, 1990.

Thaxter, Celia. *An Island Garden.* Boston: Houghton Mifflin, 1988. Facsimile of original edition, 1894.

Waugh, Frank A. Preface to Leonard H. Johnson. *Foundation Planting.* New York: A. T. DeLaMare, 1927.

Index

Boldface page numbers refer to plants mentioned in the photograph captions. Where a boldface number follows a person's name, the photograph shows a scene from that person's garden.